The Illustrated Encyclopedia of
FOSSILS

GIOVANNI PINNA

The Illustrated Encyclopedia of
FOSSILS

Translated by Jay Hyams

Facts On File
New York • Oxford

The author wishes to thank Giorgio Teruzzi
and Nicoletta Toniutti for their assistance.

The Illustrated Encyclopedia of Fossils

Edited by Mariolina Sguazzini

Copyright © 1985 by Istituto Geografico De Agostini, S.p.A., Novara

English translation © 1990 Facts On File

The photographs in this book were taken for it by Gianalberto Cigolini, with the following exceptions:
IGDA Archives p. 46 (left, center); G. Dagli Orti pp. 11 (top), 17 (3), 18 (5), 61 (top), 62 (top), 101 (top right), 102 (2, 6, 7), 108 (2), 109 (1), 112, 147 (top left & right), 168 (middle right), 170 (bottom), 172 (bottom row), 175 (bottom left), 182, 183; IGDA/Bevilacqua pp. 9 (top), 14 (7), 17 (1), 19 (4), 21, 26, 27 (2), 28 (bottom), 52, 55 (1, 3, 5), 59 (10), 60 (right), 61 (bottom), 62 (right), 67 (bottom left), 72, 73, 74 (middle), 75, 77, 78, 88 (middle left), 91 (6), 92 (bottom), 97 (top left, bottom center), 98 (1), 99 (2), 100 (1), 101 (bottom right), 102 (5), 104 (top), 106 (2), 108 (7), 111 (bottom), 127 (4), 143, 145, 146, 160, 168 (middle left, bottom right), 170 (top right), 172 (middle), 181 (middle, bottom); IGDA/Cooper p. 219; IGDA/Gratziu p. 55 (2, 4); Natural History Museum, London pp. 222 (3, 5), 224, 225, 226; G. Nimatallah pp. 10 (6, 7), 17 (2), 19 (1), 24 (top), 42, 46 (right), 47 (6), 173 (6), 192 (bottom left & right), 194 (6); G. Pinna pp. 9 (bottom), 10 (4, 5), 17 (5), 18 (3, 4), 28 (top & middle), 60 (left), 63 (top), 88 (bottom), 91 (4), 93 (top), 102 (1), 103, 106 (5, 6, 7), 107 (4, 5, 7), 108 (1, 4), 114 (b, c), 164 (d), 165 (b, d, e), 173 (4, 5, 7), 189 (middle & right), 192 (top), 199 (top), 210 (3, 5), 206 (2, 3, 4, 6), 209 (top right, bottom), 212 (top left, bottom left & right) 213, 214, 215, 216, 217, 220. The photographs using scanning electron microscopes (pp. 11 bottom, 38, 53, 54) were taken in the laboratory of CNR Alpi Centrali, Milan, Italy.

Facts On File, Inc.   Facts On File Limited
460 Park Avenue South   Collins Street
New York NY 10016   Oxford OX4 1XJ
USA   United Kingdom

Library of Congress Cataloging-in-Publication Data

Pinna, Giovanni.
    [Enciclopedia illustrata dei fossili. English]
    Illustrated encyclopedia of fossils / Giovanni Pinna.
        p.   cm.
    Translation of: Enciclopedia illustrata dei fossili.
    Includes bibliographical references.
    ISBN 0-8160-2149-X (alk. paper)
    1. Fossils.   I. Title.
QE711.2.P5413   1990
560—dc20   90-3217

A British CIP catalogue record for this book is available from the British Library.

Facts On File books are available at special discounts when purchased in bulk quantities for businesses, associations, institutions or sales promotions. Please call our Special Sales Department in New York at 212/683-2244 (dial 800/322-8755 except in NY, AK or HI) or in Oxford at 865/728399.

Printed in Hong Kong

10 9 8 7 6 5 4 3 2 1

PREFACE

The study of fossils is essential for understanding the mysteries of life and for reconstructing the history of the earth's surface, which is in a state of perpetual and constant change. Indeed, early in this century the German geologist Alfred Wegener based his famous theory of continental drift (later revived, updated and amplified in the theory of seafloor spreading) on insights drawn from his study of paleontology. The presence of marine fossils on dry land intrigued even the ancients and led Aristotle to believe that the oceans had not covered the same land areas throughout the earth's history—and prompted Tertullian to say, "All the earth was once covered by sea, and seashells can be found on the mountains."

Such intuitions, however, were virtually ignored for many centuries, people preferring to believe that the above-water areas of the earth had always been the same and considering fossils, at most, as freaks of nature (*lusus naturae*). An alternate theory explained that seashells were present on areas of dry land as a result of the Great Flood.

Around the end of the Middle Ages, various people began to oppose the dominant opinions. Boccaccio gave credit to these revolutionary ideas and, in his prose romance *Filocolo* (ca. 1340), spoke of fossil seashells. Leonardo da Vinci also questioned the standard view of fossils. In 1517, the Italian physician and poet Girolamo Fracastoro, describing fossil seashells found in the course of excavations in quarries near Verona, identified them as remains of marine animals that had once lived in the very place where they were found.

It was during the 16th century that the first fossil collectors appeared, as well as scholars who began to make tentative classifications. Interest in fossils grew over the centuries, and in addition to private collections, paleontological departments were established in museums of natural history. Meanwhile, the classification of fossils proceeded at an equal pace, and around the end of the 18th century, thanks to the work of the Frenchman Alexandre Brongniart, the Englishman William Smith and the Italian Gian Battista Brocchi, stratigraphic geology made such substantial progress that layers of sedimentary rocks could be dated according to paleontological criteria.

Thus one can say that the modern science of paleontology is only two centuries old. In that brief period the earth's surface has been studied by scholars who have enriched the world's museums with their discoveries and also further identified affinities and relationships among the various groups of fossils, greatly contributing to the basis of the study of evolution.

The reader will find that the fossils on display in this book are arranged according to the same criteria by which fossils are organized in a museum. The major aim of this concise but complete illustrated encyclopedia is to teach the reader how to "read" the marks indelibly left in stone by ancient lives. This world of stone comes to life through a text that runs parallel to the illustrations, underlining the importance fossils have had in the study of the evolution of the living world and in the reconstruction of landscapes of the past.

—The Editor

CONTENTS

185 THE CHORDATES

FOSSILS AND PALEONTOLOGY

Today, the word fossil has a precise meaning: It indicates the remains of organisms found inside the rocks that form the outermost portion of the earth's crust. Such organisms are sometimes petrified, sometimes transformed into rare and beautiful minerals, sometimes compressed into the rock and barely visible. But they are always ancient, having lived in a period of time before the present age.

This definition of the term fossil is quite modern, having been introduced only recently. The Romans used the word, which is derived from the verb *fodere*, meaning "to dig," in a general sort of way to indicate anything dug up from the earth, and until the 18th century the word was used to indicate both minerals, which were called *fossilia nativa*, and true fossils, which were called *fossilia petrificata*.

Even the concept of a fossil is not very old. Only during the past 200 years, perhaps a little earlier, has the true nature of fossils been ascertained and universally recognized. The true fossil can be defined as the remains of any plant or animal that lived in an age before this one, or as any trace that such an organism has left in the layers of the earth's rocks, or even any impressions left by an organism's activity, such as the tracks, footprints or trails left by its movements.

The branch of science devoted to the study of fossils is paleontology, from a Greek word meaning literally "the study of ancient organisms." This name was coined early in the 19th century, almost simultaneously, by two famous paleontologists, H.M. Ducrotay de Blainville and G.I. Fischer von Waldheim. Since they are the remains of ancient organisms, fossils are precious witnesses of the earth's past. They are scientific objects that permit us to reconstruct the biological, geological and geographical history of our planet.

Fossils are preserved within sedimentary rocks due to a series of complex physical and chemical phenomena known as the process of fossilization.

The Process of Fossilization

This process begins immediately after an organism's death, and many factors may be involved.

The first act of fossilization is often a form of movement known as postmortem transport. This phenomenon very often carries organisms far from the area in which they lived, sometimes to an area with a very different environment. In the sea, the action of currents can move the lightweight shell of a mollusk several hundred kilometers from its original area, while heavier organisms may be carried only a short distance. Clearly, postmortem transport is variable.

When analyzing a group of fossils it is always important to distinguish between those that originated in the place where they were found (autochthonous) and those that, over time, have been moved from their original environment (allochthonous).

Opposite: During the process of fossilization, only the impression of the outer shell of this ammonite of the genus Dactylioceras *was preserved, while the calcareous shell was completely dissolved. Early Jurassic of Holzmaden, Germany.*

If we examine sessile (attached) organisms—such as corals, that live attached to the sea bottom—we find that in almost all cases fossils are found in deposits located in what was once their original habitat. This is not true for those organisms that lived in the open sea, such as the nektonic (free-swimming) ammonites, which lived below the water's surface and, upon death, most have undergone at the very least a vertical transport, slowly falling to the sea floor and thus leaving their original habitat. This is also the case with the birds and flying reptiles of the Mesozoic era (about 230 million to 65 million years ago), the skeletons of which have been found preserved in marine environments simply because the birds died while flying over a wide expanse of water.

After death begins the process of decomposition that acts with varying speed on the different parts of the organism's body. The destructive agents that cause this decomposition can be divided into three types: biological, mechanical and chemical.

Above: *This group of Tertiary fossil mollusks of various sizes was formed through accumulation, with no selection.*

Left: *The history of paleontology is studded with enormous errors of interpretation. As a joke, the students of the German Bartholomew Beringers (1667–1740) carved stones and buried them in the sediments in which he was digging. When he dug them up, he thought them true fossils.*

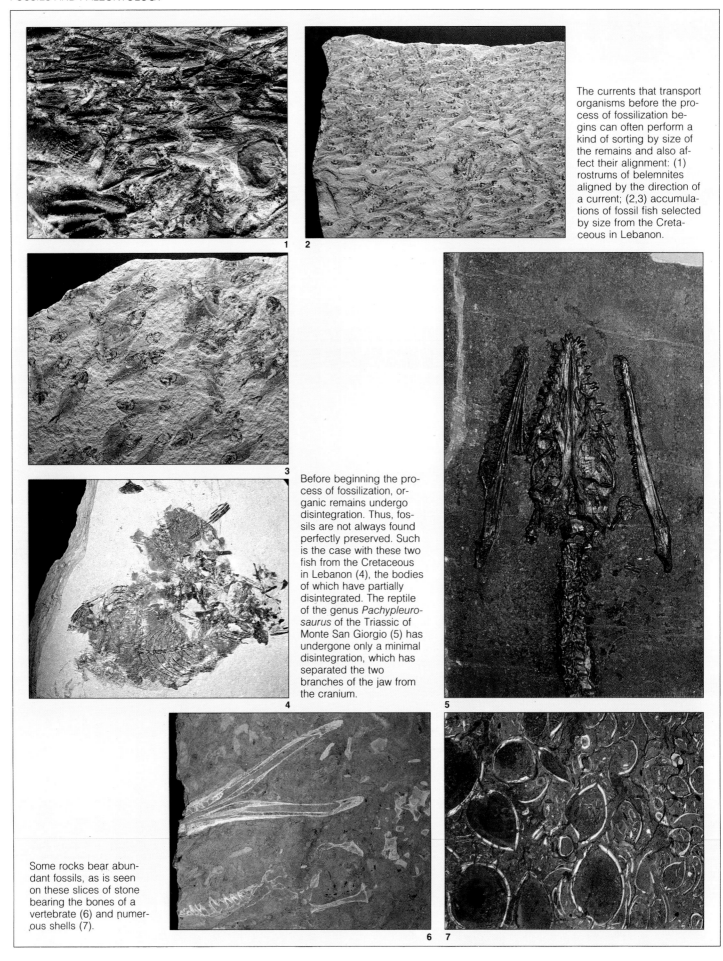

The currents that transport organisms before the process of fossilization begins can often perform a kind of sorting by size of the remains and also affect their alignment: (1) rostrums of belemnites aligned by the direction of a current; (2,3) accumulations of fossil fish selected by size from the Cretaceous in Lebanon.

Before beginning the process of fossilization, organic remains undergo disintegration. Thus, fossils are not always found perfectly preserved. Such is the case with these two fish from the Cretaceous in Lebanon (4), the bodies of which have partially disintegrated. The reptile of the genus *Pachypleurosaurus* of the Triassic of Monte San Giorgio (5) has undergone only a minimal disintegration, which has separated the two branches of the jaw from the cranium.

Some rocks bear abundant fossils, as is seen on these slices of stone bearing the bones of a vertebrate (6) and numerous shells (7).

Below top: Silurian calcareous fragment from Dudley, England, with various fossil organisms. Holdings rich in fossils like this one have allowed geologists to reconstruct the fauna of prehistoric periods.
Below center: In the fossil record wood preserves all the details of its structure. Such is the case with this silicified trunk from the Sudan, probably from the Pliocene.

Below bottom: Muscular tissue from a fossil crustacean (Ostenocaris cypriformis) from the Jurassic of Osteno in Italy. Muscular fibers have been preserved thanks to the replacement molecule-by-molecule of the organic material by calcium phosphate.

Among the destructive agents that most frequently act on the soft parts of the body—those most quickly lost—are bacteria. Because bacteria are present almost everywhere that oxygen is, even in the highest layers of sediment, the soft parts of a body will be preserved only if abundant sedimentation in an oxygen-free environment immediately covers the dead organism before these soft parts are destroyed. In addition, other organisms, such as sponges and scavengers of all kinds, contribute to the destruction of organic remains. It follows that the sooner the organic remains avoid these destructive factors, the greater the possibility that the remains will eventually be preserved in a fossil state.

The same can be said for the mechanical destruction wrought by currents, wave action and wind, agents that apply abrasion to the organism and quite often destroy it completely. Biological and mechanical agents are so powerful that most fossils are found incomplete, broken and often scattered across a vast area.

Chemical action plays an important role in the eventual destruction, and preservation, of organic remains. This process of destruction can go on even when the organism has already been transformed into a fossil. Chemical dissolution acts on the "hard parts" of the animal, which are usually made of calcium carbonate, calcium phosphate, silica, or such organic substances as chitin and keratin, which often form very resistant structures—the shells of mollusks, the skeletal structures of coelenterates, the bones and teeth of vertebrates, and the chitinous exoskeletons of arthropods.

The resistance of such hard parts varies even within the same taxonomic group and often depends on the shell's level of calcification when the organism died. Furthermore, various parts of an organism may become fossilized while others do not. This results from the fact that various structures react differently to dissolution. Thus the teeth of mammals are more often preserved than the bones, which are more susceptible to destruction.

Finally, much depends on the type of sediment into which the organism is deposited. The same species of mollusk will be preserved much differently, for example, in clay rather than sandstone. In general, coarser kinds of sediment, such as sand or pebbly conglomerates, allow for greater passage and filtration of water and thus are not conducive to well preserved remains—fossils are rare in such rocks. Clays, marl and other less permeable sediments offer more protection and can thus be rich in fossils.

Thus, the nature of the sediment is of great importance for the preservation of the organism. The sea, where the sedimentation is abundant, constant, and usually composed of fine-grained elements, is much more advantageous than an area on dry land, where both the scarcity of sedimentation and the more violent action of destructive agents, like the wind, tend to permit only partial preservation of an organism. There are, of course, exceptions to this rule: in the sea, rocky areas near coasts are poorly suited to fossilization because of the destructive action of waves and the roughness or lack of sediment. On land, certain areas offer good conditions for fossilization,

Pyritized fossils:
(1) Brachiopod of the genus *Paraspirifer* from the Devonian in North America.
(2) Cross section of an ammonite from the Jurassic in Germany, showing completely its internal structure divided by septa.
(3,4) Ammonites of the genus *Psiloceras* from the Jurassic of Somerset, England.
(5,6) Ammonites from the Jurassic, England.

among them lakes, swamps, and loess deposits where the sedimentation is undisturbed and abundant.

There is another way dry land has an effect on the preservation of organisms: Under certain conditions, heaps of fossils are formed that, on the one hand, make research easier and on the other create for the scholar serious difficulties when trying to reconstruct prehistoric environments, as such heaps can include organisms from widely different environments.

Because the solutions permeating sediments are rich in mineral salts, they act on organisms deposited in the rocky matrix, or background materials in two ways: They may dissolve the organic remains or they may impregnate the organism with mineral substances, rendering it more resistant (stable) to chemical change or decomposition and assuring its preservation. This second process is called permineralization.

In simple impregnation, the substitution of the organic material by the inorganic is total; in this way the area left empty by the loss of organic material is filled by the mineral substances and made stronger.

More interesting is the process of *metasomatism* in which existing minerals are replaced by new minerals, molecule for molecule. In this case, the chemical composition of the hard parts is changed while their appearance remains unchanged and, in fact, is preserved even in the smallest detail. The process has occurred in a great many cases; one can cite fossil wood in which the concentric annual rings are well preserved; the shells of minute aquatic organisms, with their tiny cavities intact; and the shells of mollusks in which the various layers of which they are constructed have been well preserved.

The mineral substances most often involved in the process of permineralization are calcium carbonate and silica, followed by calcium phosphate, pyrite, lead or zinc phosphate, and many sulfates. Calcareous and siliceous fossils are very common: Entire forests have been preserved due to the transformation of the trees into blocks of opal or chalcedony, the trees in some cases with roots attached. More rare are instances of replacement by elements in their pure state, such as silver, creating natural jewels.

Carbonization is a process of fossilization usually involving plants. During the decomposition of the organic matter under anaerobic water or sediment, the hydrogen, oxygen, and nitrogen are driven off, leaving a carbon residue that may retain many of the features of the original organism. This process resulted in the formation of the world's great deposits of coal during the Carboniferous period, beginning at least 340 million years ago. During this period, large areas of the earth—in particular today's China, India, Australia, Africa, North America and parts of Europe—were covered with vast swamps containing luxuriant forests, which grew in a warm-humid climate typical of tropical and semitropical zones. The remains of these ancient forests constitute the base of today's vast coal deposits.

The formation of these enormous deposits of plant matter is a subject of debate. Some hold that the deposits were formed in the same place the forests had stood, a belief supported by the finding of deposits of carbonized plants with their roots still anchored in the ground. Others believe that the deposits are the result of a movement of dead plants into lagoons or coastal bays. This theory is supported by the fact that within the levels of coal can be found plants that must have lived in drier areas. In all probability, both theories are accurate, in the sense that the deposits of coal were formed both of plants originally indigenous to the area and of plants swept in from surrounding zones.

The process of carbonization itself is a result of the action of certain bacteria that attack plant remains, eliminating both oxygen and nitrogen while indirectly enriching them with carbon. This enrichment increases over time, beginning at the moment a plant begins carbonization, and thus some fossil remains can be classified according to age based on the percent of carbon they contain.

Another interesting process of fossilization is incrustation. This process is limited to rather recent fossils and is a result of calcium-rich water flowing over organic remains and covering them with a thin mineral film. When the organic material dissolves it leaves as the only trace of its existence a negative

This sea urchin from the Late Cretaceous in Egypt (above) and sponge of the genus Plocoscyphia *from the Cretaceous in France (left) were fossilized in marcasite.*

Silicification, one of the most common processes of replacement, involves organisms of all kinds. Shown here are mollusks transformed into quartz (1) and chalcedony (2); an echinoderm (3), slices of a tree trunk (7) and a coral (5) completely silicificated; a brachiopod enclosed in a nodule of silica (6).

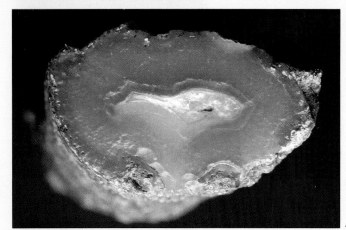

Fossils transformed into silica are always very hard, making it easy to free them from the matrix holding them, particularly if that matrix itself is not silica. Siliceous fossils held in calcareous rock can be freed by dissolving the calcite with hydrochloric acid, which does not damage silica.

The preservation of organic remains can involve replacement with various minerals. Shown here are a plant mineralized in talc (1); a belemnite fossilized in vivianite (2); an echinoderm transformed into azurite (3); an insect (4) and a coral (5) fossilized in bitumen; and several small gastropods fossilized in sulphur (6).

The nature of the mineral substances that replace organic remains depends most of all on the environment in which the organisms are deposited after death, on the substances present in the environment, and on the type of mineral salts permeating the rocks in which the organic remains are buried.

The fossilization process of carbonization has led to the preservation of fossil plants. Deposits of coal hold abundant remains of the plants that formed the forests of the Carboniferous period. Carbonized fossil plants, however, can come from other geological periods. From top to bottom: Archaeopodocarpus from the Permian in Germany; a branch of pteridospermale, twigs of Mariopteris, and twigs of Woodwardites from the Carboniferous in Germany.

imprint on this mineral layer. Travertine, a rock used by the ancient Romans for decorative purposes, is famous for its plant remains preserved in this way.

Another rarer process of fossilization is distillation. In this process, the more volatile elements of an organism (liquids and gases) are distilled, leaving a thin film of carbon on a rock as the only testimony of the original form of the organism. Fossils formed through this process are usually imperfect, so much so that graptolites, a primitive marine organism most frequently preserved this way, were not fully understood until examples, which had turned into pyrite through the additional process of mineralization, were discovered.

As a result of special conditions or truly unusual factors, certain organisms have been preserved in a most unusual way, with not only the usually preserved, hard parts, but also traces of the soft parts—those that in most cases disappear without leaving even the slightest trace.

One deposit in which conditions were so favorable as to permit the preservation of delicate structures is the famous one at Solnhofen in Bavaria. The skeleton of the earliest bird, Archaeopteryx, was discovered there and was recognized as a bird because its exceptional preservation included its feathers. In the same deposit were found impressions of the wing membrane of flying reptiles, tentacles of jellyfish, insects complete with thin and delicate wing membranes, and squid-like belemnites complete with their tentacles.

This extensive preservation was made possible at Solnhofen both by very fine sediment that quickly covered the dead organisms, protecting them from the effects of destructive agents, and the absence or scarcity of such destructive agents themselves. There was no strong mechanical alteration at Solnhofen, largely because there were no strong currents: The area was a closed basin, very tranquil, with stagnant water that did not circulate much, and was probably poorly suited for life.

Similar deposits have been found in the Burgess Shale formation in British Columbia, believed to be from the Cambrian period, and that of Holzmaden, in Germany, from the Jurassic, both of which contain truly exceptional remains—delicate organisms perfectly preserved due most of all to the absence of destructive agents, both biological and mechanical, in their ancient environments. Holzmaden had a marine environment with water that was almost stagnant, a kind of lagoon, lacking oxygen and thus not favorable to bacterial life, an area of sea closed off and free of waves and currents.

Additional examples of the preservation of particularly delicate organisms can be found in amber deposits. As amber, a resin exuded by coniferous trees, moved along the trunks it covered insects and arachnids that lived in prehistoric forests, thus protecting them from the action of external agents and preserving them intact. The most famous amber deposits are those from the Oligocene epoch, found in the Baltic region and Rumania, and those from the Miocene found in Santo Domingo, Sicily, and the Apennines in Italy.

The last process of fossilization, natural mummification, is quite rare and only a few examples are known. This process involves complete preservation, even of the most delicate parts

(1) A leaf preserved in Quaternary travertine of Tivoli through the process of incrustation. (2) A graptolite (Monograptus) of the Silurian in England, preserved by way of the process of distillation. (3) Some deposits preserve even the most delicate parts of fossil organisms. Such is the case in the Jurassic limestone of Solnhofen from which comes this *Isophlebia aspasia*. (4) The Cambrian deposits of the Burgess Shale in British Columbia, Canada, are famous for the preservation of fossils. Shown here is a fossil from that deposit, a crustacean of the subclass Phyllocarida, *Canadaspis perfecta*. (5) An ant perfectly preserved in Oligocene amber from the Baltic region.

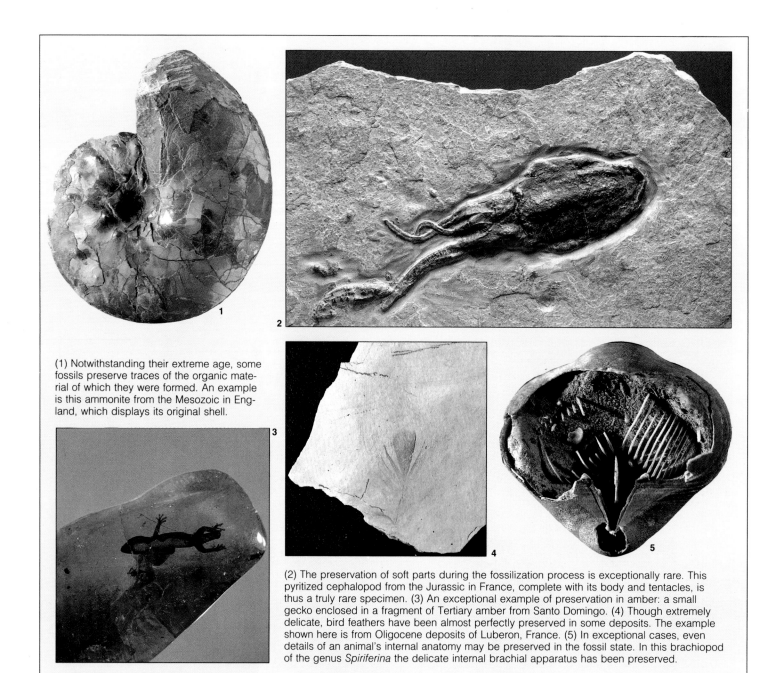

(1) Notwithstanding their extreme age, some fossils preserve traces of the organic material of which they were formed. An example is this ammonite from the Mesozoic in England, which displays its original shell.

(2) The preservation of soft parts during the fossilization process is exceptionally rare. This pyritized cephalopod from the Jurassic in France, complete with its body and tentacles, is thus a truly rare specimen. (3) An exceptional example of preservation in amber: a small gecko enclosed in a fragment of Tertiary amber from Santo Domingo. (4) Though extremely delicate, bird feathers have been almost perfectly preserved in some deposits. The example shown here is from Oligocene deposits of Luberon, France. (5) In exceptional cases, even details of an animal's internal anatomy may be preserved in the fossil state. In this brachiopod of the genus *Spiriferina* the delicate internal brachial apparatus has been preserved.

of an organism. Two examples of the Anatosaurus, a dinosaur of the Cretaceous period, were found complete with their wrinkled skin pressed against the bones of their skeletons as if they had undergone a powerful dehydration at death. This is believed to be the result of the animals being buried in sand that isolated them from the action of circulating water and that, because of its mineral content, led to the almost perfect preservation of the skin.

As has been seen, water permeating the sediment often leads to the destruction of organic remains, including the impregnation of the remains with mineral substances. If the sediment is already in an advanced state of consolidation, the dissolution of the organic matter leaves an empty cavity that is filled with other substances; thus is created an external model or mold that reflects perfectly the outside form of the organism.

An internal mold results when a shell of an organism becomes filled with sediment and then dissolves, leaving on the mold an impression of the surface of the inside of the shell.

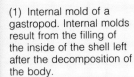

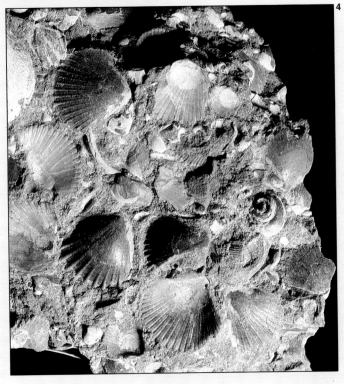

(4) This fragment of Miocene rock from the Apennines around Bologna bears fossil clams in various forms: Some have their original shell, others are internal molds, and yet others are external molds, impressions of the exterior shape of the shell pressed in the sediment.

(1) Internal mold of a gastropod. Internal molds result from the filling of the inside of the shell left after the decomposition of the body.

(2) Some fossil organisms show traces of traumas suffered in life. Such traces are often useful for understanding the behavior of the animal or its relationships with other organisms. The shell of this brachiopod of the genus *Spirifer* was fractured while the animal was still. alive.

(3) The weight of sediment sometimes produces great distortions in fossils. Of these two specimens of Pygites from the Jurassic in the Alps, the one on the left has been compressed, while that on the right is preserved in its normal shape.

The Stratigraphic and Chronologic Importance of Fossils

In the preceding pages we have reviewed the various processes that affect organic remains before and during their transformation into fossils, and we have noted that there is a close relationship between such organic remains and the sediment in which they are preserved. In most cases, we can say that the sediment and the fossil contained in it were formed at the same time; that is, the deposit was formed at the same time and in the same environmental conditions.

Even so, several external factors often disturb the environment-time relationship that links the fossil to the sediment in which it is found. Following death, an organism can, in fact, be transported far from its original habitat into one where the environmental conditions are very different; and geological phenomena can move a fossil after its formation and relocate it.

The study of the relationship between a fossil and its sediment is fascinating. With extinct organisms that are different from any organism now living, only the study of the surrounding sediment can provide clues to the habitat in which the organism lived. This is possible by carefully observing what occurs in present-day habitats and then applying the information concerning the relationship between habitat and sediment that exists in our time to the most ancient sediments.

A classic example of the attempt to reconstruct a prehistoric environment is that involving the first vertebrates. Fragments of these were found in layers from the Ordovician period (from about 590 to 435 million years ago), fragments that correspond to a group of marine vertebrates without jaws or paired fins, related to today's lampreys. The sandstone that held these fragments is typical of sublittoral (shoreline) habitats, but this fact alone is not sufficient to prove that these were marine animals since they do not appear in any other Ordovician marine area. It is possible that these vertebrates lived in fresh water and were transported into the sea later, as fragments. However, since no continental sediments from this period have ever been found containing remains of vertebrates, the question cannot be resolved with what we now know.

Thus the first step in a serious paleontological analysis is defining the relationship between the fossil and its sediment. Doing so first requires clarification of the true meaning of sedimentation and sediment. Sedimentation is the process of the accumulation of particles originating from the break up of preexisting rock. This process can occur in a continental environment, with the formation, for example, of dunes, or in a marine environment. Each case involves the accumulation of particles of varying size and nature; all together, these particles are called sediment.

Sediments are usually divided into two basic types: clastic, or mechanical, sediments, which are the result of the transportation of particles and sedimentation caused by various means, among them water or wind; and chemical sediments, formed by the precipitation of minerals from sea water. Just as organic remains undergo particular chemical-physical pro-

cesses as part of the process of fossilization, so sediments, when deposited, must undergo a change, called by geologists diagenesis, to become sedimentary rock.

Sedimentation began with the beginning of the earth, and the sediments deposited over time constitute the topmost layer of the earth's crust. These sediments form successive strata, or layers, of various thickness, which have a direct correlation with geological time periods. In the fossils contained in these strata is recorded much of the history of the earth. Paleontologists and geologists call the arrangement of the strata of sedimentary rocks stratification, and stratigraphy is the branch of science devoted to its study.

Stratigraphic layers offer the possibility of analyzing the succession of life and the occurrence of geologic events, based of course on the supposition that the various layers can be accurately dated. The basic rule in the study of stratification is that any layer is older than the layer above it and younger than the one below it. Beginning with this principle, the fossils found in the layers are thus used most of all to establish stratigraphic correlations and to date the layers. Such correlations and dating are the two major aims of stratigraphy, which seeks to determine which sediments were deposited in a certain geographical area during a certain period of time, and to correlate these sediments with those deposited in the same period in other areas.

Fossils are extraordinarily useful for this purpose. According to the associations of flora and fauna that they contain, the layers have been divided into various time units, recognizable even in rocks with different characteristics. This is done following so-called index fossils, specific animals or plants that had broad geographical distribution but existed for relatively short periods of time. Ammonites, for example, are excellent guide fossils. Their evolution was such that each species of ammonite lived for a relatively short time but had such a broad geographical distribution that they can be found today in stratigraphic rock layers often separated by great distances. Thus finding in different layers in different localities the same ammonite, one can say that those layers were deposited during the same period of time.

The study of fossils permits, among other things, the attribution of a relative date to rocks, permitting something extremely interesting for paleontologists—the establishment of whether a layer is older or younger than the layers above or below it. This is based on the theory that the fossils included in the sediments of different ages represent the evolution of the organisms that occurred in the course of geological time. As always, there are certain difficulties in the practical application of this dating system, the first of them being the possible presence in rock complexes of different fossils, which are impossible to compare, the result of deposits made from differing environments.

During the course of more than 150 years of study, and thanks to guide fossils and their widespread geographical distribution, a satisfactory system of dating the different layers of the earth's rock has been established. It has become possible to subdivide the history of the earth, using these fossils, into

Ammonites are excellent index fossils. Their widespread distribution and the brief lives of the species make them useful for correlating rocks of the same age located at great distances. This rock from the English deposits of Lyme Regis bears numerous specimens of Arnioceras, an ammonite typical of the Early Jurassic.

time periods not based solely on the type of rock found in the different layers.

Such a subdivision of the layers of rock—that is, a chronostratigraphic subdivision—has an absolute value, since each period corresponds to a certain period of time that, naturally, endured everywhere and under all conditions. A subdivision of the layers based on their composition is very different and has, in fact, only a local value since every kind of rock is tied, as has been pointed out, to a precise kind of deposition. A lithostratigraphic subdivision thus faithfully reflects what has happened only in a local area.

Based on the evidence of the evolution of flora and fauna, the rock record of the history of the earth has been subdivided into time-rock units characterized by fossil flora and fauna that are found only within those units. The first subdivision of earth's history is based on two eons, the Cryptozoic (Precambrian), or period of "hidden life," and the Phanerozoic, or period of "visible life." The first includes only three eras, the Azoic, Archeozoic and Proterozoic, the last two in which there was little or very primitive life. The second eon includes the Paleozoic, Mesozoic, and Cenozoic eras, in which the organisms developed and differentiated. Each era is then subdivided into ever shorter periods of time, called—from longer to shorter—period, epoch and age.

Each of these subdivisions, which are based on a time-rock unit, has been given a name derived either from the name of the place where the rocks formed in that time period were first recognized (or are most abundant) or from the name of the ancient population that inhibited the zone. Thus, the Jurassic is named for the Swiss-French Jura Mountains, composed of rocks of that period, and the Silurian is named for the ancient Silures, a people that lived in England.

Paleontology, unfortunately, is of no use in trying to determine the duration or exact date—the age in an absolute number of years—of various chronologic subdivisions. The problem of determining the exact age of rocks has always been fascinating and has only recently been resolved by radiometric methods, those that make use of radioactive isotopes. The method is simple enough: From the moment of its consolidation in a mass crystallization of igneous rock, every radioactive element gives off a series of radiations at a constant velocity during its slow and regular transformation into a stable isotope. By knowing the rate of transformation of a given isotope, and estimating the relative proportions of the remaining radioactive material, one can arrive at the age of the rock in question or, more precisely, at the age of its crystallization.

Uranium, for example, changes in the course of time into various elements, ultimately becoming an isotope of lead, which represents the final, stable phase of the process. Uranium's half-life is 4,560 million years (meaning 4,560 million years are necessary for half of a quantity of uranium to transform into lead). This property of uranium lets us date very ancient rocks. Using uranium, it has been estimated that the earth's oldest rocks are more than 3.8 billion years old.

By using other radioactive isotopes, such as isotopes of potassium, rubidium and strontium, it has been possible to date many igneous (molten) rocks and thus also the fossil-bearing rocks found in contact with them. The final result is that the dates often cited for a particular geologic period or for a certain event are not abstract dates but correspond to a rather precise reality.

As has been seen, the strata are the product of the environment that existed during the time and in the place of their formation. Environmental changes, which change the kind of sediment, its grain size and its quantity, have led to differing rock formations in differing locales.

In reality, nowhere in the world is there a series of strata that represents in continuity all the periods of the earth's history. To obtain this ideal series and thus to understand all the biological events that have taken place during the geological eras, it is necessary to make correlations among the different strata or, even better, among different areas where they exist. Such correlations seek to resolve two great geological questions: the reconstruction of a continuous chronological succession, despite any gaps in a particular strata; and the identification of rocks of the same age deposited in different places and environmental conditions.

The work required to reconstruct a continuous chronological succession is not easy. Erosion, active in almost all the earth's environments, has often carried away sediments, and tectonic phenomena, such as the movement of the earth's crust, have folded, fractured and often moved entire strata in such a way that one can no longer say with certainty if they are today located in the exact spot where they were originally deposited.

Among the various gaps in the rock record that paleontologists must face, one of the most frequent is that called an unconformity. During the process of sedimentation, for example in a marine environment, undersea currents may remove layers of sediment where fossils have been deposited. The fossils in these layers may be destroyed or, in other cases, may be redeposited with sediments of a different age. The difficulties encountered by the presence of such gaps—which can also be difficult to identify—are understandable. The paleontologist must always be alert to avoid identifying as coeval (of the same age) fossils that, due to one or another geological process, just happen to be found together while in fact they lived in different times. Such interruptions in the strata are very common.

Even where interruptions do not exist and one finds instead layers of strata deposited continuously, without any disturbance, there is still the possibility that fossils of different ages were joined through a mechanism called non-deposition, another cause of difficulty for the paleontologist. The process of sedimentation, as is known, is very variable in intensity, and in certain moments can in fact be entirely absent. During such a stasis in sedimentary activity no new material will be deposited, but during the same period there will be no similar disruption or organic activity. That means that the organisms that lived during a period characterized by the absence of sedimentation will all be deposited together and become mixed with the remains of the organisms that lived before them, thus generating a heap of fossils of different ages very difficult to disentangle.

Other sedimentary phenomenon have contributed to complications in the analysis of rock strata. The partial immersion

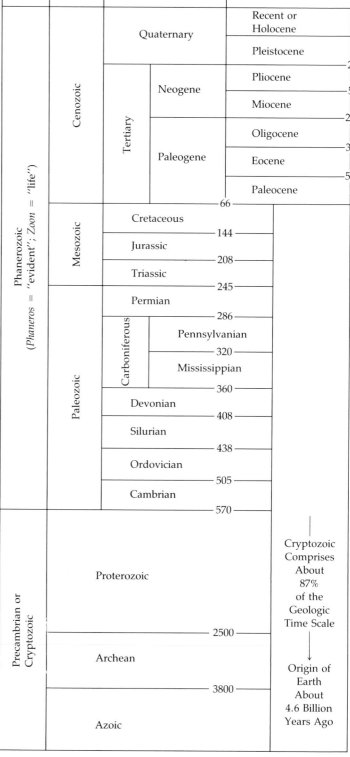

of an area of rock strata can lead to the destruction through erosion of large sections of the strata and of the fossils in them. There are also changes of facies, that is, lithological variations that result from changes in the environment, which can be observed in the same stratum going laterally.

The problems involved in correlating one stratum to another are many and complex. Even so, paleontologists, assembling an intricate mosaic of tiny bits of information, have successfully created a reasonably complete picture of what has happened during the course of geological history. They have been able to determine the relationship among rocks of the same age and to establish that a certain marine area was deposited at the same time that, on a continent, a certain desert or lagoon area was deposited. They have thus, for example, established that while the ammonites and the belemnites lived in the seas, on solid ground life was dominated by dinosaurs; that while the amphibians were becoming the rulers of the dry land, in the sea modern fish, the teleosts, had not yet appeared; and that during the period when the first coral reefs appeared in the sea, on land lived the earliest land animal, a kind of primitive scorpion.

The Paleoecologic Importance of Fossils

Paleoecology is simply the reconstruction of the environments of the past, in terms of geographic, physical and biologic characteristics. The ecologist who studies the modern world has before him or her a complete panorama, with a variety of organisms and environments to examine; the paleoecologist, on the other hand, is confronted with only the most fragmentary evidence, the remains of the animals and the plants found in rock strata.

Through the examination of fossils, the paleoecologist tries to determine what kind of environment existed in a certain place in a certain time, and to determine the relationships that organisms of that period had among themselves and with the environment. Paleoecology thus involves not only the reconstruction of a prehistoric shoreline based on the discovery of certain fossil remains but also the study of trace fossil to establish, for example, relationships between prey and predator, or to bring to light ancient cases of parasitism and symbiosis.

In addition to fossils, the paleoecologist has at his or her disposal another element of extreme importance that helps make reconstructions of the past more precise—the sediment that encases the fossil, which generally reflects the type of environment in which the fossil was deposited.

Every contemporary environment, and thus every environment of the past, is composed of complex physical, chemical and biological factors that characterize and delimit it and that have a determinant effect on the distribution of organisms. Among such physical factors are the medium (for example, air or water), temperature, light, depth and so on. Chemical factors include the salinity of the water or the amount of dissolved oxygen or carbon dioxide present. Biological factors are predation, competition with other organisms, and so on.

Four fundamental principles, common to both ecology and paleoecology, regulate the relationships between organisms and the environment: adaptation to the environment, adaptation to a way of life, factors that characterize the environment, and the dependence of species on each other.

First, each organism is adapted to a particular environment that may vary notably in size. Thus, for example, while the ammonites populated the seas extensively, with a broad tolerance of salinity or temperature, other mollusks lived only in more restricted and clearly defined environments. The size of the area an organism can occupy depends on that organism's ability to survive these environmental variations.

Second, each species is adapted to a particular way of life. This means that the species can react to the demands of the environment by changing itself in ways that make survival possible. Thus, for example, those vertebrates that adapted to life in the deep sea, which required fast swimming to be a successful predator, have bodies hydrodynamically shaped for such swimming. Other groups of animals react to the same environmental conditions by assuming similar forms.

The third fundamental principle of ecology is based on limiting factors, which regulate the distribution of organisms. For example, certain coral can survive only if the water temperature of their habitat remains steady at around 20 degrees celsius (68 degrees Fahrenheit).

The fourth principle is that of the dependence of each species within an environment on the other species that coexist with it. Thus, the presence in a certain geographical area of a certain type of predator excludes the presence of other predators but favors the existence of other organisms that live off carrion left by those predators. This leads to a chain of relationships so finely drawn that the slightest disturbance can have disastrous consequences, including the disappearance of entire groups of plants or animals.

Analysis of sediment is the first step for the paleoecologist in trying to reconstruct an environment. Various kinds of factors must be taken into consideration, including the kind of rock, its mineralogical makeup and its physical structure, and also any sedimentary structures that might be present. Clearly, certain kinds of rock can be formed only in a certain type of environment: Thus a conglomerate (coarse-grained) rock indicates a fluvial environment but could never be attributed to sedimentation from the deep sea bottom; the presence of evaporites such as rock salt or gypsum indicate that the original environment was an enclosed basin with strong evaporation; a rock must be the product of a restricted basin with little oxygen; and so on. The stratification of a rock, the thickness of the strata and the presence of massive strata are factors that will all aid in the identification of a certain kind of environment.

In many arenaceous (sandy-textured) rocks one can observe the presence of a characteristic alignment of the granules inclined with respect to the surface of the stratum. If repeated, this alignment indicates a "crossed stratification" and also the direction of the currents in existence at the time of the deposition. Another sedimentary structure is "ripple marks," parallel undulations on the surface of the sea bottom that are

Below: The shape and anatomic structure of extinct organisms can give information on their way of life. The ichthyosaurs of the Mesozoic, with their elongated bodies and limbs transformed into fins, were doubtless organisms adapted to life in the open seas.

Center: Fossil corals are excellent ecological indicators. Their presence in a given period in a given area indicates the onetime existence in that place of a warm sea.

Bottom: Ripple marks are parallel undulations on the sea floor resulting from undersea currents or the influence of wave action on the sea bottom. Their presence thus indicates an environment of that type.

formed through the action of currents on the sea bed. There are also glacial striations in continental environments, formed by the movement of enormous masses of rock-bearing ice across bedrock, and cracks, caused by the drying of muds, which clearly indicate the climatic situation at the moment of their formation.

When analyzing sediment with the intent of making a paleoecological reconstruction one must remember that the relationship between sediment and the organisms it contains is sometimes very close, a fact that may be useful for research but that can also be destructive. Thus, for example, although numerous kinds of sediment—such as siliceous rocks formed by the skeletons of ancient marine planktons (radiolarians), coral reefs, strata of coal—are the result of accumulated organic remains, often the organisms themselves have acted as destroyers, canceling those traces and those structures that, as we have seen, would have proved important in the determination of the characteristics of the deposit. To give but a single example, burrowing worms, through their digging, work such destruction on the inside of sediments as to completely destroy the original stratification.

In the paleoecological reconstruction of any environment, one must above all keep in mind, as we have seen, that not all the fossils present in a given rock can be used for the reconstruction because many of them may have been transported there, perhaps from much different environments. Before doing anything else, one must make that determination.

The difference between ecology and paleoecology is clearly marked. While ecology examines the total of living flora and fauna in a determined environment, sometimes called an eco-

Groups of different organisms found together in the fossil record can furnish useful information for understanding the relationships that existed among the organisms during the ancient geological time. These three pictures show a Jurassic belemnite (1), a pettinide of the Quaternary in Sicily (3), and a Jurassic brachiopod (2) encrusted by Serpula worms.

system, paleoecology must content itself with a complex of dead organic remains—fossils. A group of fossils present in a given locality and in a certain stratum of rock is called a *thanatocoenosis*.

There is a profound difference between a biocoenosis and a thanatocoenosis, both of which are fossil assemblages. While in the first the scholar is in the presence of organisms with certain characteristics, all of which come from a single environment, in the thanatocoenosis can be found organisms gathered from different original habitats by postmortem transport.

Let's examine what happens upon the death of the various organisms that compose a biocoenosis. Part of the organism remains at the site (the fossil elements defined as autochthonous) and part resists fossilization because of the absence of structures that can be preserved. A third part is transported away from the original environment, carried by various mechanical agents like currents, wind and wave movements to make up the allochthonous component of the thanatocoenosis.

In a fossil assemblage, the problem therefore exists in distinguishing between the autochthonous elements, on which will

be based the definition of the environment, and the allochthonous elements. Obviously, sessile organisms—those that live permanently attached to a base, such as certain brachiopods and clams—are likely to fossilize in the same place in which they lived. The same is true of infauna that live immersed in mud, while the organisms that move freely are more likely to be transported and thus become allochthonous elements in a new environment. To determine with certainty which are the autochthonous elements on which to base paleoecologic deductions it is necessary to know first how the various organisms of the past lived—knowledge not easy to come by, particularly for those groups of animals no longer alive.

Other elements can aid the paleontologist in this difficult process: The presence of fossils aligned on a stratum all in the same direction, for example, is an indication of transportation (allochthonous) elements for it presupposes movement due to currents or other mechanical means. Such means further influence the distribution of the organisms, depositing the remains according to size, weight and form; cases of heaps composed of shells of the same species are not rare. Only after the autochthonous elements of an assemblage have been identified

Some fossils are good climatic indicators. Certain mollusks of the Quaternary have aided in the identification of the climatic oscillations that characterized that period. Below: Mya truncata. Bottom: Cyprina islandica. Both species indicate cold-water environments.

can one begin the work of reconstructing an environment, following the clues that the organisms themselves furnish.

Many fossils are similar, if not identical, to living organisms. With these, it is easier to determine the habits and thus the environment in which they lived, for these will not differ greatly from those of their living descendants. Cenozoic seas were home to many mollusks, bivalves and gastropods similar to those that populate today's oceans and seas, and these early organisms certainly had the same habits as today's.

With fossils that clearly resemble living organisms it is relatively easy to establish their original environment and, finding them in a certain sediment, to deduce from their presence the type of environment that existed at the moment of their death. Fossils representative of a certain habitat are called by paleontologists "facies fossils," because by themselves, they indicate specific environmental characteristics. Thus coral, crocodile or freshwater fish fossils would all be facies fossils that clearly indicate a particular type of environment, while ammonites, which were widespread and can thus indicate no precise environment, would not.

It is not always so easy to establish the kind of environment in which organisms of the past lived, most of all for those groups that have disappeared from the face of the earth. It has happened that certain organisms have changed their habits with time, changing from one environment to another. This is the case of *Aysheaia pedunculata,* the most ancient known of the onychophorans, found in marine rocks of the Cambrian period (about 570 million years ago) in British Columbia. This ancient onychophoran lived in the sea, but its modern descendants live on dry land in the humid undergrowth of tropical regions.

Let us return to more ecologically simple fossils. Using these environmental indicators, as they are often called by paleontologists, it is often possible to achieve very accurate reconstructions of ancient environments. It is possible to determine the depth of ancient seas or the climatic conditions existing in various geological eras. Certain fossils can be considered true geological thermometers since they give us good indications of the climatic conditions and the temperatures that existed at the moment and place of their deaths.

Certain marine mollusks found in the more recent Quaternary rocks are very useful in this regard. These low temperature mollusks and high temperature mollusks alternate in the sedimentary strata of this geological period and give a sure indication of the climatic oscillations—the well known glaciations that repeatedly covered and uncovered the earth's surface—that occurred in successive stages during the most recent part of the history of the earth. These cold species and warm species, as they are called by paleontologists, entered the Mediterranean Sea during the glacial and interglacial periods, moving to the north and south, through Gibraltar, at the end of each climatic change.

Paleoclimatology has reconstructed the climates for the most distant periods. Thus, the coral reefs from the Triassic, widespread throughout the Alpine belt, are testimony to a warm, tropical climate. The deposits of natural carbon from the Carboniferous have revealed that in that distant time the climatic

(1) Determining the way of life of fossil organisms of which there are no living representatives is difficult. It requires much study, comparative analysis with other organisms, and research in the relations with organisms of which the habitat and way of life are known. In this way it has been possible to reconstruct the habitat and way of life of many species of trilobites, a group that disappeared about 230 million years ago. This photograph shows three specimens of *Basidechenella rowi* of the Devonian in New York.

(2) Analysis of impressions left in sediments can be very useful in reconstructing the way of life of extinct organisms. The example shown, called Arthrophycus and found in Silurian sediments at the Oases of Cufra in Libya, has been interpreted as a track left by the movement of arthropods or worms.

Below: *Fossil footprints of a carnivorous bipedal dinosaur, found in Jurassic sediments in Gadoufaoua' in Niger.*
Center: *Footprints of a bird left in a Miocene sediment from Spain.*

Right: *Coprolite of Iena, from the Quaternary in Sicily. The analysis of coprolites, fossilized excrement, helps to establish the kinds of food eaten by animals of the past and, in many cases, to determine what parasites infested the animals.*

conditions must have been very similar to those found today in certain equatorial regions. Naturally, such reconstructions of climate become very difficult when one is confronted by organisms that cannot be compared to contemporary life. In such cases the paleontologist may go astray into the field of fantasy. But even such organisms, unknown to us today, can furnish interesting ecological information.

The trilobites, a group of marine arthropods that became extinct at the end of the Paleozoic, provide an example. Looking at them one notices that certain anatomical details are indications of life in a particular environment. Certain trilobites have no eyes and most probably lived in sediment; others had light exoskeletons adorned with strong spines that probably favored life in upper sea waters.

Finally, even when a fossil organism offers not the slightest clue leading to a paleoecological reconstruction, the battle is not completely lost. Other organisms may be associated with it or have formed close relationships of symbiosis or parasitism that will lead us, by analogy, to discover the habitat of the mysterious organism.

Aside from sediments and fossil organisms themselves, the paleontologist uses other elements that are effective in the reconstruction of prehistoric environments. These are the impressions left by organisms while moving or, in general, all the traces of their biological activity. These traces and impressions, preserved like all other organic remains, are very useful for understanding the life of the past. The discovery of impressions left by amphibians or reptiles in Paleozoic rocks has shown the way in which these ancient animals, known only by their skeletons, moved, while impressions left by the fearsome dinosaurs have permitted us to determine the environment in which these enormous reptiles lived. Sedimentary rocks are literally full of these traces of biological activity, and a practiced eye can spot on the surface of strata many elements that are indispensable to the reconstruction of the environment in which the strata themselves were deposited. We can, with a certain experience and from these useful indications, draw on the relationships that existed among the various organisms in a certain area.

Such traces and impressions are not always easy to decode. While it may be reasonably easy to attribute an impression to a reptile or an amphibian, it is very difficult to establish to which kind of invertebrate belongs a certain marine impression or certain borings left in a rock. Footprints, traces, remains of tunnels left by burrowing organisms, fossilized excrement, the holes made in shells by parasites—all are interesting elements for the reconstruction of the biological story of earth.

The Paleogeographical Importance of Fossils

As we have seen in the preceding pages, the organisms of the past had, like today's organisms, specific geographical distributions, dependent in most cases on environmental parameters—such as the salinity, depth and temperature of water—

that are called limiting factors. All animals and plants have a limited distribution, are tied to a particular environment throughout their lives. Observation of the animals living on rocky or sandy stretches of the same coastline immediately reveals the existence of great diversity, while if we put together the animals and plants from two ecologically similar stretches of the same coastline, the differences disappear. Ecological limiting factors are the principal cause of these differences and these similarities.

If instead we observe the species present in two similar environments separated by a great distance, for example in two different continents, we see immediately that these do not present the same similarity that they might be assumed to have, since they come from similar environments. The two groups of animals display differences although they live in identical environments. The existence of these differences among the flora and fauna that populate the various regions of the earth is due to what we can call geographical factors, that is, the presence of barriers that keep organisms from achieving total distribution.

In reality, the distinction between ecological and geographical factors is not all that marked, since factors we describe as geographical are in fact also ecological, and a geographical barrier is at the same time an ecological barrier, preventing certain organisms from crossing from one region to another.

The Atlantic Ocean is an example. Because of its width, it constitutes a geographical barrier as a result of which the fauna on the coast of North America is different from that on the coast of Europe. Yet this geographical barrier is also an ecological barrier, since it is so wide, and thus an ecological factor that keeps certain organisms from crossing it. Other geographical barriers, for terrestrial organisms, include mountain ranges, deserts, rivers and swampy areas; impassable barriers for marine organisms include dry land and unfavorable temperatures.

Another factor that plays an important role in the distribution of organisms is time, in the sense that during the course of the geologic time the distribution of the areas of dry land and the seas change dramatically, thus influencing changes in the flora and fauna of the various regions. The mammals found today in South America are an excellent example of how geological changes over time affect the distribution of organisms. South America's mammals are, in fact, the result of a mixture of those groups that: established themselves in that area during the Early Cenozoic; during the following geological periods managed to overcome the barrier caused by the submersion of the Isthmus of Panama; and those that arrived from the North American continent at the end of the Cenozoic, when the connection between the two continental masses had been reformed.

Throughout the various geological eras, geographical distribution has had a major influence on evolution. It has been demonstrated, in fact, that with the passage of time the differences between geographically separated groups become greater. Indeed, the longer two regions are separate, the greater will be the diversity of the flora and fauna that inhabit them. This leads to divisions in the distribution of organisms, facilitating the process of differentiation known as speciation, which, in substance, leads to the ongoing formation of new and diverse groups.

Although they have only extremely fragmentary information, paleontologists have successfully demonstrated that in the past, as today, there were a variety of animal and plant kingdoms. In some cases, they have even been able to define the extensions of these and describe their characteristics. Thus, for example, the ammonites of the Jurassic can be divided into three large provinces, Boreal, Mediterranean and Arab-Madagascaran. In each of these areas the ammonites underwent a different evolution, complicated by contacts of interdependence occurring through migrations of groups of ammonites from one area to another.

We thus arrive at the branch of science called paleogeography, which reconstructs the geographic realities of the earth during the various geological ages. This branch of geology makes use of all the other earth sciences, from sedimentology to paleoecology to stratigraphy to paleobiogeography. The last-named is one of the fundamental bases of paleogeography. During the course of the geological eras, the geography of the earth has continuously changed, and since every change altered the previous geography, no direct comparison can be made of these changes. The paleontologist must thus depend on the only sure information available, information that comes, of course, from fossils and their distribution.

Determination of the geographical evolution of any particular region is thus based for the most part on fossil remains. As has already been noted, the Isthmus of Panama has been subject during the course of the geological eras to elevations and submersions that have led to the joining and separating of North and South America. These movements have been deduced through study of the fossil marine mollusks and sedimentary rocks on the Atlantic and Pacific shores of the isthmus. During the periods of elevation, the fossils on the two shores were different; during the submersions of the isthmus they began to show similarities, a sure sign of the joining of the two oceans.

Throughout the history of the earth, the continental landmasses have undergone profound changes in their position. According to the famous theory of continental drift proposed by German meteorologist Alfred Wegener in 1912, all the continents originally broke away from one single mass. The proof Wegener gave included paleontological evidence—the presence of very similar terrestrial flora and fauna in continents now separated by great distances—and the geology of matching coastlines.

Wegener's theory was not accepted until the 1960s, when it became accepted as a result of the new study of changes in the earth's geomagnetic field (paleomagnetism) and the elaboration of the theory of plate tectonics, or movements of the earth's crustal plates, which has enabled scientists to reconstruct the arrangement of the land and seas over the various geological eras. Using this paleogeographic base, dozens of scientists the world over are now working on environmental and biological reconstructions of the earth's varied past.

THE CLASSIFICATION OF ORGANISMS

The science of biological classification, also known as systematics, studies the hierarchy of organisms and groups plants and animals in categories known as taxa (singular, taxon). The aim of systematics is to organize the vast number of known plants and animals into categories that permit the formation of a common basis of knowledge of the organisms and that constitute a beginning for more complex studies, such as those of evolution, ecology and biogeography. In fact, it would be impossible to carry out an evolutionary study of a group of animals if one could not first identify the organisms that belong to the group, if any subgroups had not been identified, or if the characteristics that led to the formation of the group had not been clarified.

Since fossils are the remains of animals and plants that once actually lived, the paleontologist, when classifying them, must treat them exactly as though they were still alive, using as a source for classification all the information offered by the abundant world of living animals. The paleontologist must bear in mind the individual variability of organisms, the variability within groups, and all the possible particular aspects of organisms that are not readily observable in fossils but that can be easily spotted among living organisms.

The fundamental unit of classification is the species, which consists of a group of interbreeding or potentially interbreeding individuals that are reproductively isolated from other similar groups. This definition of species takes us far from paleontology since a species, so defined, cannot be identified using the kind of fossil materials paleontologists have at their disposal. The paleontological definition of species thus becomes more complex, both because there is no way to verify species following the given definition and because with paleontology the dimension of time is of great importance, a dimension that has little influence on the study of living beings.

While the biologist's vision of the living world is only partial, limited to a single time plane (the present), that of the paleontologist is broad, since the paleontologist sees every group of animals or plants in different intervals of its history, using a global vision in the sense of time and evolution. While the biological species is definable only in the sense of space, the paleontological species (called a chronospecies) can be defined also in the sense of time. While the biological species changes only in space, the paleontological is variable in both space and time.

It is therefore very difficult to limit species in the field of paleontology as the paleontologist faces groups in continuous and gradual change over time, and this permits only a purely arbitrary establishment of systematic subdivisions within the evolutionary line.

The units of classification above the species are based on demonstrable biological characteristics, but are somewhat the result of subjective interpretations or custom. Species are grouped in "genera," which are grouped in "families," the families in "orders," the orders in "classes," the classes in "phyla." Aside from these major categories there are, for example, superfamilies, subfamilies, superorders, suborders and so on.

The science of systematics uses precise rules that are followed by all researchers, thus avoiding the extreme confusion inevitable if each used his or her own system. These rules have been assembled in an International Code of Zoological No-

Bison skull found in Quaternary alluvial deposits of the Po River, between the cities of Pavia and Stradella.

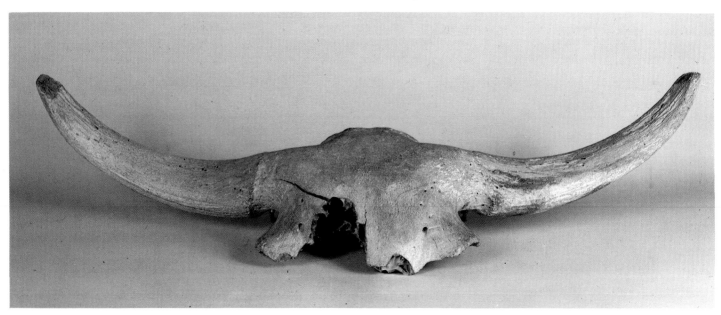

A recent case of synonymy. These two almost identical crustaceans—one (left) found in Early Jurassic deposits at Osteno and the other (right) found in Late Jurassic deposits at La Voulte—were placed in two different classes, the class Thylacocephala and the class Conchyliocarida. The two classes are identical, and the correct one is the first, since it was instituted a few months before the other.

menclature used by all who work in systematics. Its articles lay out the rules to follow for correctly naming organisms, for describing them and for publishing findings.

Every organism, animal or plant, is labeled by a Latinized double name, the first word of which is the genus and the second the species. The genus name (and the names of larger divisions: families, orders, classes, phyla) is capitalized, the species name is lowercased even if it is a proper name (like the name of a scientist). For example, the scientific name of the European bison is *Bison bonasus*. Following the scientific double name comes that of the person who first described the species and the year in which the description was first published, which aids researchers in looking up the data. Thus the name of the European bison becomes *Bison bonasus* (Linnaeus, 1758). The parentheses around the name of the "author" and the date indicate that the author attributed the species to a genus different from that in which it is today classified.

species	*Bonasus*
genus	*Bison*
family	*Bovidae*
order	*Artiodactyla*
class	*Mammalia*
subphylum	*Vertebrata*
phylum	*Chordata*

Linnaeus classified the species *bonasus* in the genus *Bos*, and not in *Bison*, which was introduced later following further systematic studies.

For an example of the complete classification of the European bison, see the box at lower left, which indicates that the European bison is a mammalian vertebrate, an artiodactyl of the bovine family. If we then look at the American bison, whose scientific name is *Bison bison* (Linnaeus, 1758), we see that the European and American bisons belong to the same genus.

Certain other rules apply to the writing of scientific names, and since we will be using them later they are worth remembering.

When in the course of classification it is possible to define the genus but not the species of a certain organism, one can write the generic name followed by the letters "sp." or "sp. ind.," which mean "species" and "species indeterminate." When the attribution of a species is uncertain, one can precede the specific name with a question mark or with the letters "cf.," "compare," thus indicating that one is limited to a simple comparison with a known species without making a precise attribution.

Returning to the example of the bison, if a somewhat inexpert zoologist captured a bison but found himself unable to define it, he might describe it as simply *Bison* sp., that is, a bison that cannot be further identified. If instead he wrote *Bison* cf. *bison* he would indicate that he was not sure he had captured an American bison but that the animal in his possession bore striking resemblance to that particular animal.

THE OLDEST FOSSILS

The history of life on this planet is known with some degree of clarity for a period that, in respect to the long history of the earth, is very brief. In truth, only beginning with the Cambrian period, about 570 million years ago, is the amount of fossil remains adequate to permit a detailed study of the flora and fauna and a reconstruction of the biological history of this world. The organisms found in rocks of that period demonstrate that the animal and algae kingdoms had by then already achieved a very advanced stage of development.

The kingdom of animals, already greatly differentiated, included all the principal groups of invertebrates that exist today (with the exception of the bryozoans), and with structures so complex as to suggest an origin and evolutionary history much older than 600 million years. Among the organisms present were protozoa, sponges, coelenterates, brachiopods, many groups of "worms," arthropods, mollusks and echinoderms, groups that were already differentiated into smaller systematic units.

The common characteristic of all the groups, plants and animals of the Cambrian is that their representatives are found only in rocks of marine origin, making it clear therefore that life during that period was limited to the seas.

If, however, we attempt to search back in time to before the Cambrian, our information becomes less complete. Reconstructing the development of life during the periods before the Paleozoic era (about 570 million years ago), remains a difficult problem because of the scarce number of fossil remains found in the rocks that would contain such fossils, rocks that cover a period of time of no less than 3.5 million years, so the period of time running from the formation of the earth's crust to the beginning of the Paleozoic era.

Only during recent years have detailed studies of very ancient rocks led to an increase in our knowledge of the earliest developments of life on earth. This information is based on a very few remains, and those, of marine animals.

Therefore, life began in the sea. The most primitive organisms moved in sea water. Analysis of fossils from periods before the Cambrian assumes a particular interest since with these organisms we find ourselves immersed in a period that has almost no similarities with life today. With Precambrian fossils we face a primitive sea populated by beings completely different from those we know today, a sea that cannot be compared with the realities of our world.

Before taking a look at these ancient organisms, we should make a few observations on the period of time in which they lived. The name Precambrian is used for the period of time, which lasted 3.9 billion years, that stretches from the consolidation of the earth's crust to the Cambrian. This long period of time is divided into three eras: the Azoic, the most ancient, the Archean and the Proterozoic, the most recent. (Precambrian time is also called the Early Precambrian, or Archeozoic, and the Late Precambrian, or Proterozoic.)

Fossils are rare in the ancient Archean rocks, a fact that must be attributed to two factors, one geological, the other biological. The Archean rocks are essentially igneous, formed of molten material, and metamorphic, strongly folded and fractured. This is because they are derived on the one hand from the consolidation of magma, and thus without fossils, and on the other from the transformation of rocks originally sedimentary, which then, following various geological phenomena, lost their paleontological contents. The biological factor is much more vague. As we know, in most cases only the hard parts of organisms, such as shells and skeletal remains, are preserved in the fossil state. It is thus believed, and this is only a hypothesis, that the organisms that lived in those distant times had no structures capable of preservation and were for the most part soft-bodied organisms.

There is another interesting consideration: The study of the Cambrian and Precambrian strata has brought to light the presence of a stratigraphic gap between the strongly folded Precambrian layers and the subhorizontal Cambrian strata, which are positioned almost normally. In all probability, this gap corresponds to a surface of erosion. It seems that the upper Proterozoic strata—the less ancient and thus, perhaps, less affected by geological upheavals and therefore the richest in fossils—disappeared, leaving a gap of which we know nothing and which in all probability corresponds to one of the most interesting chapters in the geological and biological history of our planet.

The oldest known Archean rocks are in Africa, on the border between the Republic of South Africa and Swaziland. They are composed of a series of strata many hundred of meters thick called by geologists the Swaziland Succession. The central part of this succession, known as the Fig Tree Formation, appears in eastern Transvaal. This formation consists essentially of black or greenish flint intercalated (layered) in iron-bearing rocks, schist and jasper.

These rocks are believed to be more than three billion years old, and the fossils found in them are among the oldest organisms known on earth. (Fossils remains that are almost three and a half billion years old have been found in Australia as well.) These are microfossils, very well preserved despite their great age—elongated bacteria, denominated Eobacterium, and spherical cells called Archaeosphaeroides. The existence of these organisms in a water environment, most probably a sea, more than three billion years ago proves that at that time the first stage of evolution, which is the passage from chemical evolution to organic evolution, had already been passed.

The second step in evolution was the acquisition by organisms of the capacity to photosynthesize. This ability seems to be demonstrated by other ancient fossils from Canada, from a formation of iron-bearing rocks known as the Gunflint Formation. These rocks, too, contain black flints of marine origin that have, however, an age of about two and a half billion years. The rock at Gunflint contains a relatively high number of fossils with far more complex forms than those of the Fig Tree Formation. Among the forms present in these rocks are filamentous organisms, stellate forms, forms similar to today's hydras, and globular forms—all organisms whose classification is very uncertain, although they are probably bacteria and blue-green algae.

The third step in the history of evolution seems to have been the ability of cells to organize their cellular structure. The amazing proof of this development was found in a series of

Below left: *Jacutophyton, a stromatolite of the Precambrian of Mauritania.*
Below right: *A sectioned specimen of* Ozarkcollenia laminata, *a blue-green algae of the Precambrian in Montana.*

calcareous and arenaceous rocks in Australia known as the Bitter Springs Formation. Here we found eukaryotic cells of a green algae, characterized by well-distinguished nuclei. The extraordinary fact is that paleontologists found in these 820-million-year-old rocks fossil cells in the act of cellular subdivision.

All of these interesting finds have pushed aside what was known up until recently about Archean rocks. The *Corycium enigmaticum,* a kind of Carbonaceous fossil 1.15 billion years old, found in Finland and attributed to an algae (probably erroneously), was once thought to be the oldest known fossil, but has lost its primary status.

During the Archean, life was already developed and abundant, although the forms were primitive and no more advanced than algae and bacteria.

The situation is vastly changed for the Proterozoic. Rocks from this period are decidedly less metamorphosed and less dislocated than the earlier rocks and preserve a much more abundant marine flora and fauna, with specimens that can be identified with a certain sureness. Among the rocks of the Proterozoic there is noteworthy development of sedimentary formations, most of all deposits of detritus.

Far and away the most interesting biological change of the Proterozoic is the notable development of marine plants. From the scarce remains attributed to algae and bacteria, one arrives at a well-defined flora in which several systematic groups are already identifiable and will become even more fully developed in later periods. These include, in particular, Cyanophyta, blue-green algae forming filaments that often have a hard sheath. Some of these algae, which are today relatively abundant, particularly in fresh water, had the ability to form calcium carbonate, amassing large incrustations.

The Cyanophyta are well known in Precambrian rocks, are found in relatively large banks, and show a characteristic concentric structure. Often, they form true reefs in which almost nothing of the original structure of the organisms remains, since the concentric structures found in the fossil state are only traces of the activity of the algae and not the true algae. Precambrian incrustations of Cyanophyta, called stromatolites, have been found in many rocks of the Proterozoic age.

In spite of the difficulties encountered in the study of organic remains as old as those from the Proterozoic—from 850 to 600 million years ago—today we have a relatively good idea of what animal life was like during Precambrian times, and we know it was relatively varied.

Sponges are fairly widespread in Precambrian rocks, which proves that these animals must not have been rare in the seas of that time. Almost all of those that are known are formed of spicules, the elements that make up the internal skeletons of the animals. These have been found in rocks of the Grand Canyon in Arizona and in Britain. In the latter area in particular are found spicules with three rods, comparable to those present in today's calcareous and glass sponges; these spicules have been given the name *Eospicula cayeuxi.* The only remains of sponges in which complete bodies are preserved are in Precambrian rocks. These appear to be asconoid sponges similar to today's Leucosolenia.

Coelenterates, primitive multicellular animals found in rocks from near the end of the Proterozoic, were reasonably abundant in those ancient seas. Ironically, the animals in these rocks are known only in the medusoid stage, which is similar to jellyfish, forms with soft bodies lacking any hard parts. In effect, what is found of these jellyfish-like fossils is not the true body but the impression of the bell- or umbrella-like form—left in the sediment in which the body of the animal was deposited.

Although they have left only impressions, these ancient jellyfish have been the subject of detailed studies, permitting the identification of several types different from today's jellyfish and resulting in the creation of the class Protomedusae. Examples of Protomedusae have been found in Precambrian rocks in North America; the best examples come from the Grand Canyon and are known by the name *Brooksella canyonensis.*

During Precambrian time, other coelenterates such as colony-building corals, those that live fixed to the sea bottom and

The most diverse and abundant Precambrian fauna known comes from Australia. Known as the Ediacara fauna, it dates back 600 million to 700 million years and includes organisms of all types: traces of worms (1); segmented worms (probably polychaetes), such as *Dickinsonia costata* (2) and *Spriggina floundersi* (5); coelenterates without calcareous skeletons, such as *Charniodiscus oppositus* (3); and medusae (4).

have hard, calcareous skeletons, had not yet appeared, and the first coralline constructions appear only during the Silurian period (or about 435 million years ago).

One of the most interesting and controversial paleontological discoveries concerning the Proterozoic was made in 1932 by the American paleontologist Carroll Fenton. On the surface of a calcareous rock in Montana he discovered a dozen ovoid structures that he attributed to the brachiopod Lingulella, which is present as early as the Early Cambrian (or about 570 million years ago).

Unfortunately, the fossils Fenton had found were not well preserved; they were internal molds with no trace of the original shell. While some authors support the organic nature of these remains, and others hold them to be brachiopods but assert that the rocks from which they came are from the later Paleozoic, there is a 50% possibility that these are true inarticulate brachiopods from the Precambrian, making them the oldest known representatives of this animal group.

When we deal with more highly evolved forms of life, the uncertainty that reigns in the identification of Precambrian animals increases. Many impressions and other structures first assigned to groups of invertebrates located somewhat higher on the evolutionary scale have later been revealed as inorganic. Such was the case, for example, with the Chuaria tubiformis; first held to be a type of mollusk, it was later recognized as a sedimentary structure.

Even more sensational was the case of the genus Beltina from rocks in Montana. These were thin fragments, distorted and compressed, of a kind of shell that seemed to be without surface ornamentation. These fragments were attributed first to

an arthropod of the group of Merostomata, then it was considered a calcareous algae, and finally it is believed to be a sedimentary structure.

Another "arthropod" once the subject of much discussion is the genus Protadelaidea of southern Australia, a genus based on quartzitic fragments with very regular ornamentation. A true arthropod, however, is the Xenusion auerswaldae, which is about 8.5 cm (3.4 in.) long, with a segmented body on which each segment has two appendages. There are doubts concerning its provenance in Precambrian rocks, and many scholars believe it is from a more recent epoch. If its more ancient origin proves true, Xenusion would indicate the presence during the Precambrian of the first onychophorans.

Again, although it may seem unlikely, the most certain traces of life from Proterozoic rocks come from animals with soft bodies. Like the jellyfish, which are completely without hard parts, even worms have left notable traces of their existence. Worms of various kinds and jellyfish, or coelenterates, of the class Anthozoa have been found together in fossil groups from the Proterozoic in Australia and, most recently, in Russia. Worms do not comprise a systematic group, but under the name are found many different groups. It is not yet possible to provide a classification for the Precambrian forms, nor can they be divided into clear groups.

An Australian fauna, the most abundant of Precambrian fossils yet discovered, is called the Ediacara Fauna. This group includes many well preserved organisms, although always in the form of reverse imprints (impressions or molds), and traces of movement by organisms on the sea floor that are between 600 and 700 million years old.

This specimen of Giryanella of the Early Cambrian in California is very similar to Cyanophyta algae of the Precambrian.

PLANTS

The branch of paleontology devoted to the study of fossil plants is known as paleobotany. The study of these organisms has revealed the history of the evolution of plants over the course of geological time and has led to the reconstruction of the succession of the various flora, beginning in the distant Precambrian.

We will try to follow here, at least along the broadest lines, the evolution of plants from the time in which they lived—along with all other organisms—only in the sea, to the point when they began to inhabit dry land, in that way forming many greatly diverse groups leading to the plants of today.

Reconstructing the evolutionary history of plants is a difficult task so it will be necessary to sidestep the classification of plants and focus our attention on those groups that, more than the others, have left traces of their existence in the form of abundant fossil remains, and also on those that present particular interest for the reconstruction of the story of life on earth. Thus we will deal here only with the bacteria and the blue-green algae, the phytophytes, pteridophytes and spermatophytes.

In the previous chapter, we saw that in Precambrian rocks are frequently found remains of bacteria and of blue-green algae, or Cyanophyta. These remains have documented the first stages of the evolution of primitive organic life, the evolution from prokaryotic to eukaryotic organisms, but not the origin of the groups of the most complex plants.

Bacteria

Bacteria are very simple microscopic protists (one-cell organisms) formed of a single cell without color and without chlorophyll. Bacteria occupy a special place in paleontology because it is likely that they represent the first stage of recognizable organized life. These are very vigorous organisms, capable of surviving in the most prohibitive environments and thus suitable for representing the first stage of plant life.

The great vitality of bacteria, indispensable at the beginning of the long and complicated history of plants, was dramatically demonstrated when living bacteria were discovered in oilfields at depths of over a thousand feet. These bacteria had survived millions of years in unfavorable environmental conditions. The strength of bacteria was also demonstrated when bacteria were found within saline formations in some German deposits; these bacteria were capable of living in solutions derived from the dissolution of the salt.

Bacteria are common in the fossil state. They have been identified in many deposits, and many rock formations are the result of the action of these microscopic but indestructible organisms. Deposits of sedimentary iron and carbonaceous rocks were formed in the course of geologic time as a result of the action of bacteria, which resulted in the precipitation of iron oxide and calcium carbonate.

Cyanophyta

The Cyanophyta are discussed at length in the previous chapter. Here it is worth noting their ability, already mentioned, to

Silicified wood is very common in the fossil record. Its preservation usually permits identification of the kind of tree, and the replacement by silica makes the specimens particularly fascinating. The examples above come from Triassic rocks in Arizona, where an entire petrified forest has been found.

Opposite: *Leaves of oak and alder in the filliti Quaternary of Val Vigezzo in Italy's Piedmont region.*

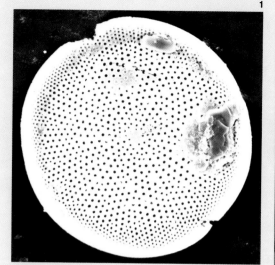

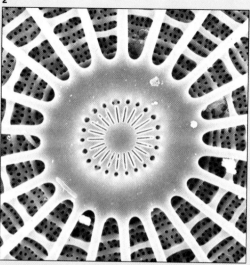

(1,2) Algae have had a primary role in the formation of rocks during the history of the earth. Shown here are a complete specimen of a diatom and a detail. Diatoms are algae with a siliceous test (hard covering), and the accumulation of the shells has given rise in certain places to sedimentary deposits called diatomaceous earth.

(3–6) Shown are examples of coccolithophorids, microscopic algae formed of calcareous disks called coccoliths. Accumulation of the skeletons of these algae has formed calcareous rocks, including the chalk of the white cliffs of Dover.

Below: *Limestone with Diplopora from the Triassic in the Italian Dolomites. These are calcareous algae of the group of the Dasycladaceae that have contributed to the formation of ancient calcareous reefs.*
Center: Fascicularia tubipora, *an algae from the Jurassic in England.*

build, like other algae and other plant organisms, those calcareous laminated structures called stromatolites, which were widespread during Precambrian time and which are today found only in a few areas, including the western coast of Australia.

Algae

The organisms grouped under the very general name algae are subdivided by botanical systematics into numerous groups, but in a strictly paleontological sense only one characteristic aspect of this group of plants must be cited: the ability of certain algae to deposit calcareous sediments in considerable quantity.

The tissue of many algae, both those that are microscopic and those of larger size, produce calcium carbonate or silica and are thus capable of forming structures preserved in the fossil state in the form of vast accumulations. These exclusively marine and aquatic plants are found in sediments from all the geologic eras.

Diatoms

In certain areas of North Africa, Europe and Italy are deposits of a chalky, lightweight, friable rock. This rock is used industrially in the manufacture of bleach, abrasives and dynamite and other explosives. Observing a fragment of this sediment under a microscope one sees that it is composed of the accumulation of skeletal remains in the form of tiny siliceous shells. These are diatoms, fossil algae that appeared during the Jurassic around 180 million years ago, and became extremely widespread, particularly during the Tertiary (from 65 million years ago onward) and in our own time.

These small siliceous algae, found today in fresh and salt water, are able to absorb silica from water and construct an opal shell. The accumulation in certain zones of these microscopic shells has led to fine-grained, whitish rocky formations known as diatomaceous earth.

Coccolithophorids

The coccolithophorids are also microscopic algae that have the ability to construct a shell by assimilating the necessary minerals from the water. Coccolithophorids appeared during the Early Jurassic period (about 195 million years ago) and have a calcareous shell composed of numerous disks, known as coccoliths, which are often found separately in sediments. Coccolithophorids, in various forms, are important in stratigraphic correlation, since they are excellent and abundant guide fossils. These algae, like the diatoms, can produce sediments. Some calcareous rocks, such as the chalk of the Paris basin, are composed of the accumulation of an enormous number of microscopic coccolithophorids.

Dinoflagellates

Among the microscopic algae of importance from the paleontological point of view must be numbered the dinoflagellates. These have a chitinous shell with overlapping plates that is well preserved in the fossil state and that, because of its varied form, has furnished numerous guide fossils for various geo-

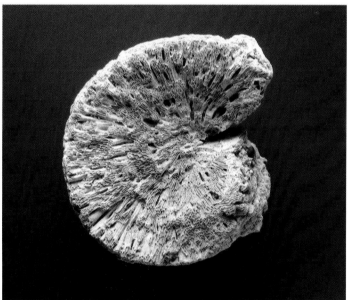

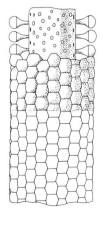

Reconstruction of a Dasycladaceae algae (detail).

Fragments of bark of Cordaitales (Cordaianthus), Equisetaceae (Calamites) and Lycopsida (Sigillaria, Lepidodendron and Syringodendron) of the Carboniferous:

(1) *Sigillaria boblayi*
(2) *Sigillaria exagona*
(3) *Lepidodendron* sp.
(4) *Lepidodendron* sp.
(5) *Lepidodendron aculeatum*
(6) *Sigillaria elongata*
(7) *Sigillaria* sp.
(8) *Lepidodendron rimosum*
(9) *Calamites* sp.
(10) *Cordaianthus undulatus*
(11) *Knorria imbricata*
(12) *Syringodendron* sp.

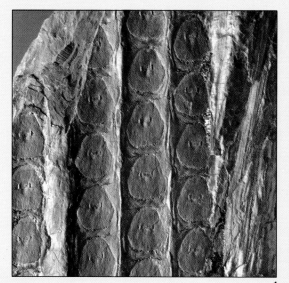
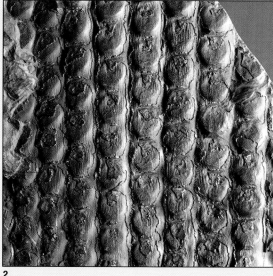

1 2

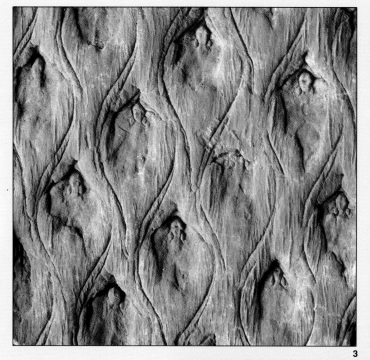

3 4

The bark of Lycopsidas is ornamented with strange designs. These correspond to scars left by the falling of the leaves (microphylls) that completely covered the trunk. The classification of these plants is based on the shape of the scars.

5 6

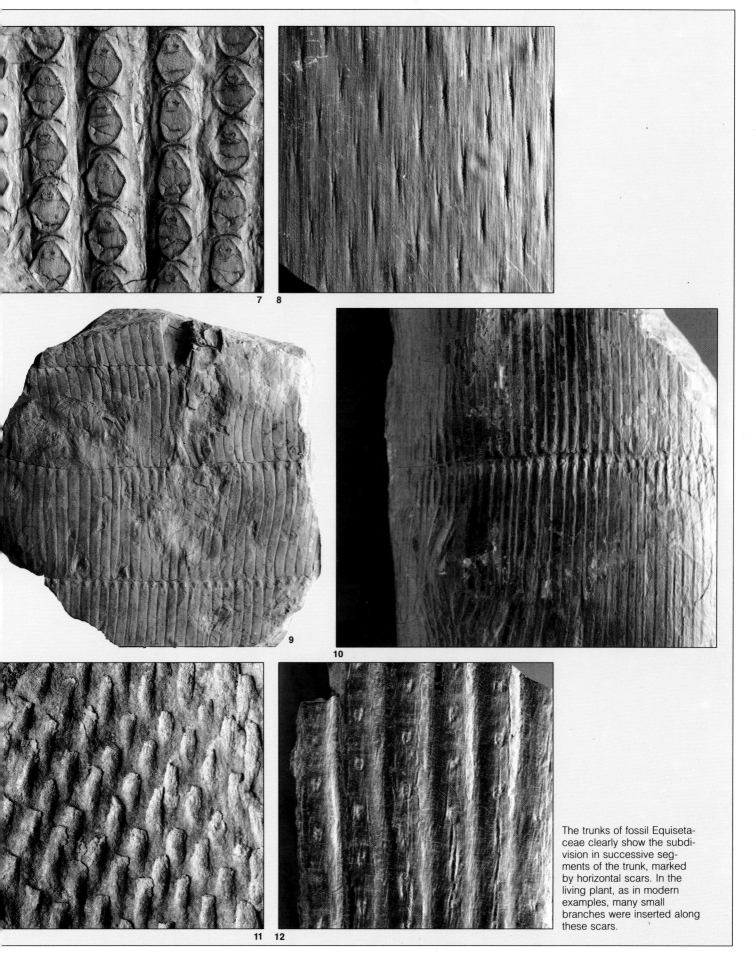

7 8

9

10

The trunks of fossil Equisetaceae clearly show the subdivision in successive seg-
ments of the trunk, marked
by horizontal scars. In the
living plant, as in modern
examples, many small
branches were inserted along
these scars.

11 12

logical periods, beginning with the Ordovician (about 590 million years ago). Like the diatoms, the dinoflagellates are important planktonic organisms.

Macroscopic Algae

The larger algae can be grouped in several large subdivisions that we will call here, following the classic method, green algae or Chlorophyta, brown algae or Phaeophyta, and red algae or Rhodophyta. Of these algae, considered by many to belong to separate groups, only those capable of precipitating mineral substances, most of all calcium carbonate, and forming structures capable of surviving over time, are known in the fossil state. These algae have had an important role as builders and have, along with coral, formed reefs in almost all the geological periods, reefs that sometimes rival the impressive constructions of corals. Among these builders the Codiaceae and Dasycladaceae groups, both green algae, are of paleontological importance. Both appeared during the Silurian period, more than 400 million years ago.

The Codiaceae are plants formed of branching tubes divided in tiny stems in rows and crossed by small holes. The Dasycla-

daceae, perhaps more important in the fossil state, are formed by a branching stem that has the ability of creating an internal skeleton by precipitating calcium carbonate from water. The branches that grow off the stem pass through holes in the calcareous covering, and in fact the number, density and alignment of these holes are used to classify the various forms. These branches, sometimes joined along the entire stem, sometimes grouped at the end of the plant, are topped with a rounded reproductive structure. Among the best-known fossil forms are Diplopora and the Gyroporella, which contributed to the building of calcareous constructions during the Triassic (230 to 195 million years ago) in the Alpine region.

The red algae, too, include builders, the first examples of which appeared during the Silurian period (435 million years ago). Among these algae are the Solenoporacea and the Corallinacea, which appear in globular masses that under the microscope reveal radial lines of cells.

All the calcareous algae discussed here were not, during the ancient geological eras, more evolved than the modern forms; as early as the Silurian, the calcareous algae had in fact reached the stage of evolution that they are at today. Unfortunately, these algae do not furnish any information concerning a plant world problem of great interest—the problem of the conquest of dry land by plants. From the Precambrian to the Silurian, in fact, only marine plants, bacteria, Cyanophyta and algae were present. Only toward the end of that period and around the beginning of the next, the Devonian (395 million years ago), did plants begin to appear on land.

Pteridophytes

Fossils of the first terrestrial plants appear in Australian rocks from the Upper Silurian to the Lower Devonian. These are vascular cryptogamic structures (reproducing by spores) attributed to the group of the Psilophytales and the Lycopsida (Lycophyta). Among the latter is classified the oldest known terrestrial tree, *Baragwanathia longifolia*, formed of a single stem two or three cm. (.8 to 1.2 in.) in diameter, dichotomously divided and covered by simple, oblong, pointy leaves from 4 to 7 cm. (1.6 to 2.8 in.) long. Although the Baragwanathia, a Lycopsida, is the oldest known terrestrial plant, the Psilophytales are believed to be the first plants to inhabit dry land. During the Devonian these constituted the beginnings of vegetation outside water.

The Psilophytales were plants without true roots or leaves, but they already had well defined woody trunks. Among these first land plants was the genus *Rhynia*, probably adapted for life in swamps, formed of a horizontal stem that grew resting on the ground and from which rose, to a height of about 20 cm. (8 in.), a few aerial stalks without leaves, divided dichotomously and terminated with broad sporangia. Very similar was the genus *Psilophyton*, which had vertical, leafless stalks, curved at the ends and covered with thornlike hairs.

The Psilophytales became very widespread during the Devonian. At the end of that period they became fewer in number and survived to the present with only two taxa, the genera *Psilotum* and *Tmesipteris*, which some botanists consider representatives of a separate group with even older beginnings.

Above: *Section of a Solenoporacea alga.*

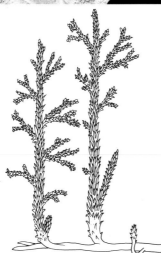

Right: *Reconstruction of a Silurian Psilophytale of the genus Asteroxylon.*

During the Devonian, Psilophytales populated the continent of Laurasia, which included Asia, Europe, Greenland and North America. This continent was known for its ancient, red sandy areas in which were deposited by wind during the Devonian, at a thickness of many hundreds of meters, reddish eolian sands, indications of a more or less desert climate. These ancient deserts were studded with lakes and oases that permitted the development of plant life and certain interesting animals.

During the middle of the Devonian, new plant forms began to appear on the Laurasian continent, and these established themselves alongside the primitive Psilophytales. Rocks of this period bear precursors of those groups that became widespread during the Late Devonian and, even more so, during the Carboniferous (beginning about 345 million years ago). Rocks of the Middle Devonian thus hold the first Equisetaceae, the first treelike Lycopsida with the genus *Protolepidodendron*, and even the first ferns (or Phyllicopsida) with the genus *Cladoxylon*. Lycopsida, Equisetaceae and Phyllicopsida were the plant groups that had the dominant roles in the constitution of continental flora during the middle part of the Paleozoic era.

The Lycopsida are today represented by small herbaceous forms, such as Lycopodium and Selaginella, but during the Devonian and Carboniferous they included treelike forms that reached 30 meters (99 ft.) in height and formed great forests on the borders of swamps. The Lycopsidas were then made up of a high trunk that ended with many branches in the Lepidodendra and few branches in the Sigillaria. The base of the trunk, a kind of root system known as the stigmaria, was formed of four horizontal arms laid out in a cross pattern, each divided in two in the soil and covered by temporary roots. The entire trunk of the plant had simple, long, narrow leaves, which in falling left scars on the surface of the trunk in characteristic patterns that are used today to classify fossil forms.

The Equisetaceae today includes only one genus, the *Equisetum*. These are the small plants commonly called horsetails, and they generally live in moist habitats. The stem is jointed with small scalelike leaves in whorls around each joint; the stem ends in a thick "bud" formed by stroboli that contain only one kind of spore. During the Paleozoic, the Equisetaceae included treelike forms, some of which reached large sizes.

The Phyllicopsida, present today with many different species, constituted a large part of the Carboniferous flora. These plants were then very large and are known as tree ferns.

An occurrence of great importance to the history of plants took place during the Devonian with the appearance of leaves or, put more correctly, of macrophyll, that is, of large-size leaves veined with vascular tubes.

The Lycopsida, Equisetaceae and Psilopsida did not have leaves as we know them today. They had instead small microphylls, which were without any direct circulation to the interior of the trunk and were sustained by a thin nervature. These microphylls are in reality only small scalelike appendages of the trunk that did not permit an efficient exchange of water, so these plants had to live in humid areas, sometimes with their roots immersed in the water of a swamp or pond.

When the first true leaves appeared, with internal circulation (i.e., vascular tissue) and surfaces suited for transpiration, the process by which water vapor is expelled, plants began a greater move from the aquatic environment. This happened with the Phyllicopsida, which have large, complex leaves with a complicated system of supporting canals and a complex tissue structure. Compared to previous plant forms, in which the trunk was the most important part, beginning with the ferns the trunk became a simple organ made to sustain the leaves, which became in turn the essential part of the organization of the plant.

Spermatophytes

During the Late Devonian, terrestrial flora was dominated by Pteridophyta, including the last Psilopsida, the Lycopsida, the Equisetaceae and the first Phyllicopsida. During this period of time, higher plants appeared as well, characterized by the presence of seeds and flowers. These were the first spermatophytes, in particular the gymnosperms, which although not very abundant during the Paleozoic assumed widespread distribution during the first two periods of the Mesozoic era, the Triassic and the Jurassic (from about 245 to 144 million years ago).

During the Late Devonian the gymnosperms were represented by two groups: the Pteridospermales, plants similar to ferns, with flowers and with seeds that had no protective coverings; and the Cordaitales, treelike gymnosperms of large size somewhat similar to conifers.

All these plants—the Pteridophytes and the first Spermatophytes—constituted by the end of the Devonian a flora that

(1) *Lycopodites elegans*, Lycopod of the Carboniferous in Bohemia
(2) *Sphenopteris elegans*, Pteridospermale of the Carboniferous in Germany
(3) *Pecopteris* sp., Pteridospermale of the Carboniferous in the United States
(4) *Neuropteris gigantea*, Pteridospermale of the Carboniferous in Germany
(5) *Sphenopteris* sp., from the Carboniferous in Germany
(6) *Sphenopteris distans*, from the Carboniferous in Germany

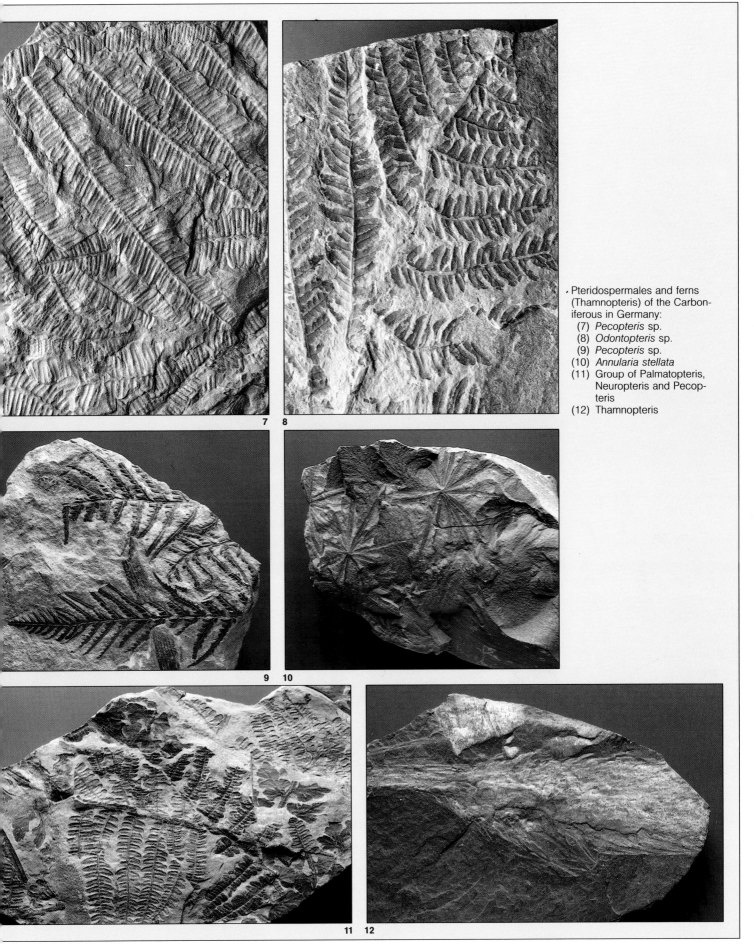

Pteridospermales and ferns (Thamnopteris) of the Carboniferous in Germany:
(7) *Pecopteris* sp.
(8) *Odontopteris* sp.
(9) *Pecopteris* sp.
(10) *Annularia stellata*
(11) Group of Palmatopteris, Neuropteris and Pecopteris
(12) Thamnopteris

Below, left to right: *Reconstructions of* Lepidodendron, Sigillaria, Ginkgo biloba *and* Cordaites.

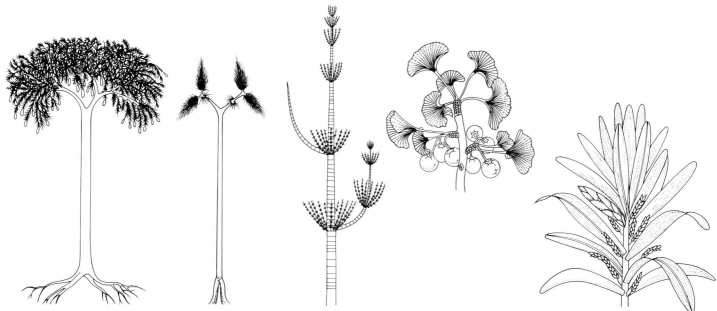

was very uniform and widespread, across all the areas of dry land, from the Laurasian continent to Australia and the Antarctic.

During the next period, the Carboniferous, the characteristics of plants did not change in any substantial way, with the exception of a greater spreading of the forests. The Carboniferous was marked by a warm, humid, tropical climate (in the Northern Hemisphere) and by the enormous spreading of large forests made up of Pteridophytes and Spermatophytes. These large forests were spread across almost all the northern continents of that time, from Europe to China, from Siberia to North America; their accumulation of plants gave rise to the deposits of coal that for many years now have constituted the primary source of energy throughout the world.

The vast and luxuriant forests of the Carboniferous period were extremely humid and were located on the borders of lakes,

swamps and the sea. This environment permitted the development of an exceptional fauna. It was during this period, as we will see, that amphibians reached their high point of expansion, the first reptiles appeared and the insects diversified into many different groups.

Like during the Late Devonian, during the Carboniferous the Pteridophytes constituted the forests in low-lying areas, the forests on swampy ground. The Psilopsids had disappeared, while the Lycopsids enjoyed great profusion, including enormous treelike forms. Among these was the genus *Lepidodendron*, with its straight, cylindrical trunk divided at the top in two branches, each bearing an umbrella-like clump of

Bottom, left: *A magnoliaceae of the Eocene.*
Center: Ptilophyllum grandifolium, *a cicadeae of the Early Jurassic.*
Right: Nelumbium, *a ninphytaceae of the Late Cretaceous.*

(1) *Glyptolepis keuperiana,* a primitive conifer of the Late Triassic, Raibl.
(2) Frond of a cycadeae of the genus *Podozamites* together with a fish of the genus *Leptolepis,* in lacustrine Jurassic sediment from Australia.
(3) *Anomopteris distans,* from the Late Triassic, Germany.
(4) *Voltzia* sp., a primitive conifer similar to the araucaria, Triassic, from Italy.
(5) Leaf of *Glossopteris browniana,* Permian, from Australia.
(6) Trunk of a cycadeae, Cretaceous, from the Apennines.

Fossil plants from the Early Jurassic of Osteno, in northern Italy: (1) *Pachypteris rhomboidalis;* (2) *Otozamites* sp.; (3) Undetermined fern; (4) *Zamites* sp.; (5) *Pagiophyllum* sp.

branches with sporangia as long as 30 cm. (12 in.), and the genus *Sigillaria*, a tree that could reach 40 meters (132 ft.) in height with trunks more than a meter and one half (5 ft.) in diameter topped by long, narrow microphylls that were rigid and almost cylindrical.

Also abundant were the Equisetaceae, with the Calamitales, among which the genus *Calamites* is perhaps the best known. This plant reached 20 to 30 meters (66 to 99 ft.) in height and was constituted of a reedy and articulated trunk and thick foliage. In this plant the trunk began at a root that ran parallel to the ground and gave off a series of vertical branches.

In the higher, less humid areas, the forests of the Carboniferous period were composed primarily of gynmosperms, in particular by Pteridospermales and Cordaitales, with species that reached 40 meters (132 ft.) in height; by the Ginkgoales, a group that experienced great expansion during the Mesozoic and is today limited to a single living species, the *Ginkgo biloba;*

and by the first Cycadeoidales, tropical plants similar to palms, with a cylindrical trunk topped by elongated leaves. This diffusion of plant forms lasted until the end of the Carboniferous period.

With the beginning of the Permian, 280 million years ago, the earth underwent important geographic and climatic changes. The Laurasian continent was covered by deserts, but was invaded in certain areas by the sea, lakes and salt marshes, which left large deposits of rock salt, gypsum and potash. On the eastern border of this continent, the Ural Basin was becoming a lagoon, thus making way for the joining of North America and the continent of Angara (constituted of Siberia, Mongolia and part of central-southern Asia). This union was completed toward the end of the Permian period. In the Southern Hemisphere the continent known as Gondwana had formed of parts that would later break apart to become South America, Africa, Madagascar, India, Australia and Antarctica. By the end of the

Permian, 245 million years ago, all the present continents had joined to form the supercontinent of Pangaea.

In the Northern Hemisphere, a dry, at times desert, climate replaced the warm, humid one of the Carboniferous period. The Pteridospermales, Cordaitales and Cycadeoidales became the dominant elements of the flora.

In the Southern Hemisphere the evolution of plants took another step with the appearance of the first conifers with the genus *Walchia*, similar to the modern Araucarias. On the continent of Gondwana during this period appeared a flora completely different, characterized by species unknown in northern lands. These were forests of Glossopteris, a Pteridospermale with simple, oval fronds, Equisetaceae as well as Cordaitales.

A new change in terrestrial vegetation took place at the beginning of the Mesozoic era, during the Triassic, which began about 230 million years ago. The reign of the gymnosperms began, the Lycopsida and Equisetaceae tree forms disappeared and the Pteridospermales were drastically reduced. At the same time the Northern Hemisphere experienced a great diffusion of the Cycadeoidales, with the genera *Otozamites* and *Zamites*, the Ginkgoales and the conifers, with the first Araucarias, the Cupressaceae, the Taxodiaceae. In the Southern Hemisphere the Glossopteris disappeared.

From this period through all of the Triassic and the following Jurassic, for about 95 million years, there were no important changes in terrestrial flora. During the Jurassic the known flora is composed principally of Cycadeoidales and conifers, among which appeared the first sequoias, the genera *Araucaria* and *Widdringtonia*, both genera still in existence. As for the Pteridophytes, they were by then reduced to the herbaceous forms we know today. Some new groups of plants did appear during this period; these were the bennettilaeans, gymnosperms that have since become extinct. These plants had feathery leaves and a cylindrical trunk whose principal characteristic was the presence of a bisexual flower that anticipated the flowers of future angiosperms. In the largest examples, this flower grew to a size of 12 cm. (4.8 in.) in diameter and was often located on the trunk between the scales left by falling leaves.

The appearance of angiosperms—flowering plants—without a doubt the most revolutionary occurrence in the evolution of plant life, took place during the Mesozoic era, in the Cretaceous period, about 130 million years ago. From the Mesozoic forest made up of conifers, Cycadeoidales, bennettilaeans and Ginkgoales the transformation was made in this period to forests of angiosperms, already quite similar to modern-day vegetation. The development of angiosperms happened suddenly at the beginning of the Cretaceous, although it is possible that the first representatives appeared even earlier, during the Jurassic, if not even the Triassic.

The angiosperms are without question the most highly evolved of plants. They became, beginning in the Cretaceous, the dominant plant group because of their greater ability to expand and their ability to adapt to their surroundings, because of their specialized leaves and the extreme differentiation of their reproductive structures. The oldest known angiosperms are from the Early Cretaceous and were found in Greenland, where plants that survive today, including a type of poplar, existed together with forms that later disappeared.

The appearance of the angiosperms and the subsequent changes in terrestrial vegetation had an enormous impact. New groups of animals adapted to the new vegetation (one need think only of insects); others became extinct. One can say that the birth of the angiosperms marked the arrival of the modern age, from the point of view both of plants and of animals.

During the course of the Cretaceous these plants became increasingly abundant and differentiated. Even during the early part of the period there appeared plant genera that exist today, such as the magnolia, the eucalyptus, the willow and the larch. During the second half of the period many new families made their appearance, most of which are still alive. Among the monocotyledons appeared the Gramineae and the palms; among the dicotyledons, the fig, the vine, the birch, the oak, the Leguminosae and the chestnut.

From this point onward, which is to say from the beginning of the Tertiary about 65 million years ago, terrestrial vegetation did not undergo other significant evolutionary changes. Small variations were the consequence of minor geographic and climatic variations. During the Paleocene, the first epoch of the Tertiary period, these plants were practically identical to that of today: the angiosperms then constituted 90% of the flora, with genera equal to or very similar to our own.

PLATE I

Carboniferous plants from the deposits of Mazon Creek, Illinois:
(1) Pecopteris; (2) Pecopteris; (3) Neuropteris; (4) Pecopteris; (5) Neuropteris; (6) Oligocarpia; (7) Asterotheca; (8) Odontopteris; (9) Odontopteris; (10) Alethopteris; (11) Calamites; (12) Neuropteris; (13) Cyclopteris; (14) Annularia.

PLATE II

Miocene plants from the deposits of Kumi in Eubea:
(1) Myrica; (2) Sequoia; (3) Quercus; (4) Glyptostrobus; (5) Quercus; (6) Quercus; (7) Ulmus; (8) Cinnamomum; (9) Myrica; (10) Ulmus; (11) Celtis.

PLATE I

PLATE II

INVERTEBRATES

Protozoa

There is one category of fossils that is particularly little known to the public—microscopic fossils, which are, with a few exceptions, difficult to see with the naked eye and difficult to collect, but very abundant in many ancient sedimentary rocks. Because of their minuscule size, these fossils require methods of research, collection, preparation and study much different from the methods used for other categories of fossil. There is therefore a special branch of paleontology dedicated to their study—micropaleontology, the science that studies fossil remains so small that a microscope is necessary to observe them.

According to this definition, it should be clear that micropaleontology studies many different kinds of organism. In sedimentary rocks can be found the tiny algae we discussed in the preceding chapter, plant spores, minuscule crustaceans, microscopic remains of large and complex organisms, such as spicules of sponges, sclerites of Holothuroidea (sea cucumbers), fragments of bryozoans, jaws of annelids (scolecodonts), and, naturally, protozoa (or single-celled organisms).

Micropaleontology embraces a vast field made even more complicated by the techniques involved, which vary according to the kind of research to be undertaken, the nature of the rock or the fossil organisms embedded in the rock.

Protozoa are found in all types of sedimentary rock and are spread throughout the world. The methods used to gather fossil protozoa vary according to whether the rock in question is unconsolidated, such as sand or clay, or only slightly consolidated, such as marl or friable limestone marl, or highly consolidated rock that is very hard, such as limestone, dolomite or sandstone. If the rock is unconsolidated, it is possible to extract specimens by washing the rock in a sieve under a jet of water. This breaks up the sediment, leaving a residue from which, once dried, the fossils can be extracted using long needles. The fossils can then be examined under a microscope. Rocks with little cohesion must be broken up before the wash by crushing them and boiling them in oxygenated water. When that has been done, they are washed as with the unconsolidated rock. Using these two techniques one obtains, at the end of the process, microfossils freed from the matrix that held them, and it is thus possible, after inserting them in a special container, to study them under the microscope.

In the case of a hard rock that is impossible to break up, the method of study and research for microfossils is very different. Extremely thin slices of the rock (called thin sections) are applied to a microscope's slide; transparent, they allow the viewer to study the fossils. In this case, however, the microfossil is not completely separated from the rock but is only sectioned. To study the microfossil thoroughly, it is therefore necessary to prepare from the same piece, or from identical specimens, many sections on different planes. Only in this way can one reconstruct the external form and the internal structure of the shell of the tiny animal.

In recent years, the scanning electron microscope has come into use. This provides perfect three-dimensional views of mi-

Opposite: Astrangia lineata, a colonial Hexacorallia, Miocene, Virginia.

crofossils, showing even the tiniest details in the structure of the shells of these animals, as can be seen in the images used to illustrate this chapter.

Protozoa are mostly water-dwelling animals, widespread in the seas and in fresh water, where they often live free, sometimes fixed to the bottom, sometimes as parasites, isolated or joined in colonies. Their body is made of a single cell capable of carrying out all the functions of life, from reproduction to movement to nutrition to defense. Because of their simplicity, protozoa represent the most primitive form of animals, of which they are held to be without doubt the oldest representative, the animal that first populated the waters of the earth.

Because of the simple structure of protozoa, made of fragile protoplasm, most of these organisms are destroyed before reaching the stage of fossilization. Thus the only protozoa we know in the fossil state are those with a solid shell of mineral material for their defense, which have been at least partially preserved. Among these are radiolarians with a siliceous shell; the foraminifers with a chitinous, calcareous or arenaceous shell; and the tintinnids with calcareous shells.

Radiolarians

The radiolarians are protozoa that live abundantly today, as they lived in the past, in pelagic (open sea) marine environments. They are constituted of a cell enclosed in a spherical, ovoid or lenticular siliceous shell, intensely perforated, on which are inserted spines or long aculei. The importance of these organisms, known since the Cambrian, 570 million years ago, rests most of all in their having formed, during the course of

Below: A radiolarian, photographed and enlarged 250 times with a scanning electron microscope.

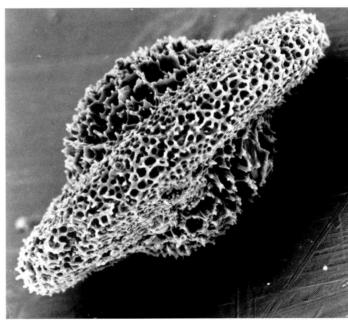

Microfossils photographed with a scanning electron microscope.
Below left and center: *Foraminifers of the group of the Lagenidi (×400).*
Below right and bottom: *Foraminifers of the group of the Globigerina (×700).*

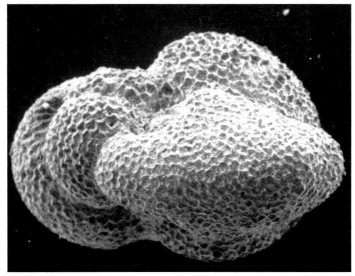

geological time, accumulations of stratified siliceous rocks (radiolarites) caused by the consolidation of "radiolarian ooze." Radiolarites are formed today at great depths on the bottom of the Pacific Ocean through the accumulation of shells of radiolarians. Beautiful red, green and yellow radiolarites from the Jurassic (between 208 and 144 million years ago) can be found in the Prealpine region of Lombardy, in France and in the Apennines. Observation by microscope of thin sections of deposits from these areas often reveals the remains of radiolarians.

Foraminiferids

The foraminiferans, certainly the most common among all the fossil protozoa, have a very simple structure. They consist of a cell with one or more nuclei with long, branching extensions of the cell, called pseudopods. The cell is enclosed in a variously shaped shell that sometimes has a very complicated structure. The shell of foraminiferans can be chitinous, calcareous or agglutinated when it is made of sediment particles glued together. The shell may have no perforations and possess only a single large opening or may be perforated, in which case in addition to the large opening the entire surface is covered by tiny holes from which the cell's pseudopods extend.

The form of the shell is extremely variable. In some, called monothalamic foraminiferan, the shell is composed of a single chamber and is globular, lenticular, elongated, stellate, or spiral. With polythalamic foraminiferan, the shell is composed of numerous chambers in a linear series, double or triple, sometimes spiral or even concentric.

Foraminiferans are adapted to various marine environments, from the pelagic to the littoral. A single family, the Allogromidae, unknown in the fossil state because its members do not have shells or have chitinous shells that do not preserve well, lives in fresh water.

Foraminiferans are important to paleontology for two principal reasons. First of all, a large number of them are extremely sensitive to environmental conditions, in particular to salinity, temperature, depth and type of sea bottom. For this reason, each species is tied to a particular environment. These fossils can supply much useful information, when compared with species alive today, on the environments of the rock formations in which they are found.

The second factor that makes the study of this group of animals important is the presence, during the entire Phanerozoic eon, from the Cambrian to today, of numerous different species, each known to have lived only for a certain period. These species are useful as guide fossils for giving relative dates to the rocks in which they are found.

Leaving aside the numerous families that are composed for the most part of organisms with sizes that vary from .001 to 1 mm. (.0004 to .04 in.), we will consider here only those groups with large-size representatives, true giants that can reach diameters of several centimeters and thus, like macrofossils, are easy to find. These are known as macroforaminiferans.

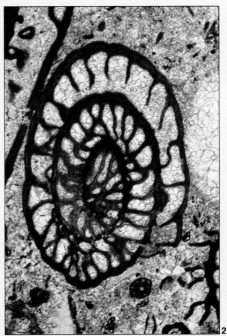

(1) Limestone with foraminifers of the group of the alveoline, Middle Eocene of Kras.
(2) Section of foraminifer (fusilinid) in Carboniferous limestone. Visible is the complex structure with septa of the shell.

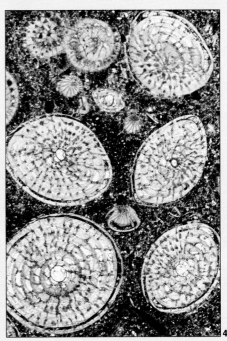

(3) *Neoschwagerina craticulifera*, a fusulinid of the Late Permian in Japan.
(4) Thin section of nummulitic limestone with numerous foraminifers with the internal structure visible.
(5) Foraminifers of the genera *Discocyclina* and *Nummulites* in Eocene limestone from Burgenstock, Switzerland.

Below: Tricites *sp. from the Pennsylvanian of Kansas. This is a
foraminifer of the group of the fusulinids.*
Center left: *Reconstruction of a fusulinid.*
Center right: *Reconstruction of a nummulite.*
Bottom: Nummulites *sp., from the Eocene, Egypt.*

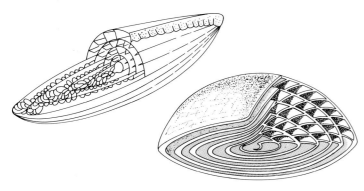

Among these the fusulina are the most ancient. They appeared during the Carboniferous about 345 million years ago, developed during the Permian and became extinct at the end of that period after having lived for about 115 million years. Among all foraminiferans, the fusulina are the largest, with the most complexity in the structure of their shells. These were not perforated and were spherical, more or less elongated, and were constructed of an external wall that wound around an axis and was partitioned at regular intervals, forming inside a large number of elongated chambers. Each partition corresponds to a visible furrow on the external surface.

Fusulina are found most often in calcareous rocks, often together with algae, and are believed to have lived in warm seas, not at great depths and in clear water. Numerous examples are found in the United States in rocks of the Upper Carboniferous, in the Midwest and Southwest, and in the great masses of white calcerous rocks from the Permian, originally marine, in the Valle del Sosio near Palermo, Italy.

Better known and more widespread are the nummulites. The representatives of this family are the only foraminiferans accorded a place of honor in human history. Ancient Egyptian priests found these small lenticular shells in great abundance around the pyramids of Giza and were convinced they were petrified lentils, remains of meals eaten by the slaves employed in the construction of the pyramids. However, the pyramids were in fact, made with blocks of calcareous rock, rich with fossils from the Eocene. These fossils, characterized by their lenticular shell, were given the Latin name *nummulite*, which means "small coin."

Nummulites are a group rich with species that lived in great abundance during the Paleocene and the Eocene, between 65 and 40 million years ago. The shell, which in the largest examples reaches a size of several centimeters in diameter, is composed of an external wall formed of two calcareous layers that wind spirally around an axis, progressively increasing the size. The interior of the shell is divided into numerous chambers, formed by the rhythmic inflections of the lower layer of the wall, that communicate through a small opening. Nummulites were benthic (sea bottom-dwellers) and probably lived at depths between 50 and 150 meters (165-495 ft.) on calcareous or sandy bottoms. Nummulites are found in many places where there are sedimentary rocks from the Early Tertiary.

The tintinnids are tiny protozoa with a calcareous shell, called a lorica, that is bell-shaped and has a collar. They are found most of all in rocks of the Late Jurassic (the Titonic), for which they constitute guide fossils.

Poriferans

Among the flagellate protozoa, small organisms equipped with whiplike flagella that help them move, some species live in colonies. Numerous individuals, sometimes all alike and independent, sometimes with different functions—respiration, vegetation, nutrition—are grouped within the colony. Such organizations point to the existence, among protozoa, of a tendency toward the formation of multicellular animals with differentiated cellular tissues. When and how this step was taken during the course of geologic time is a problem not yet resolved in the history of animals.

However, there exist today, as in the oldest fossil-bearing strata of the earth's crust from the Precambrian, certain animals that can be considered, from many points of view, intermediate between protozoa and multicellular organisms. These animals are the porifera, better known under the generic name of sponges, which represent an organization of cells more advanced with respect to colonies of protozoa and which are, in all probability, derived from primitive flagellates, since in the larval state they have simple cells, each of which has a long flagellum.

The organization of sponges is so particular that they are sometimes separated into the subkingdom Parazoa to distinguish them from the subkingdom of the Protozoa, or the single-celled organisms, and from the subkingdom of the Metazoa, or the more advanced multicelled animals.

Porifera do not have cells organized into tissues, as do the Metazoa, but their bodies are composed of three well-differentiated kinds of cells: flattened epithelia cells that cover the external surface; flagellum-bearing cells, called collar cells or choanocytes, that line the inner cavity and the internal canals of the body; and movable cells, called amoebocytes, that form the gelatinous material between the canals. They can move throughout the body and live in isolation, if only for a few days. The characteristics that make these animals resemble protozoa include, aside from the partial individuality of the cells, the ability to regenerate an entire individual from a fragment or, even more, the ability of several individuals to join and form a colony.

Porifera are marine animals with bodies that lack any well defined shape, but contemporary examples can be divided into three types of body structure that certain scholars consider to represent successive stages in Porifera evolution. This process took place many millions of years before any fossil remains could be preserved, so that this evolution cannot be documented by paleontology.

The simplest type of Porifera is the asconoid, a soft sac that lives fixed by its lower part to a solid substrate on the sea floor; it is covered by tiny pores, called ostia, through which water flows to the inner cavity, the spongocoel, which is lined with choanocytes. The whipping action of the flagella of the choanocytes creates a current of water that flows into the spongocoel through the pores and out through an upper opening, known as the osculum.

The second type, called the syconoid, is organized basically the same way, but the wall of the spongocoel has a certain degree of regular folding, thus forming niches lined with choanocytes that increase the vibrating surface.

The most evolved form of porifera, called the leuconoid, contains a system of incurrent canals that direct water from the outside toward chambers lined with choanocytes, and other canals that direct water toward a much smaller spongocoel, from which it is expelled through the osculum.

This soft material of sponges (porifera) is easily destroyed and only rarely preserved in the fossil state. It is supported by

Phylum	Class	Order	Geologic Time Range
Porifera	Demospongea	Keratosida	Carboniferous–Recent
		Haplosclerida	Cambrian–Recent
		Poecilosclerida	Cambrian–Recent
		Hadromerida	Cambrian–Recent
		Epipolasida	Cambrian–Recent
		Choristida	Carboniferous–Recent
		Carnosida	Cambrian–Recent
		Lithistida	Cambrian–Recent
	Hyalospongea	Lyssakida	Cambrian–Recent
		Dictyida	Ordovician–Recent
		Lychniskida	Triassic–Recent
		Heteractinida	Cambrian–Carboniferous
	Calcispongea	Solenida	Cambrian–Recent
		Lebetida	Jurassic–Recent
		Pharetronida	Permian–Recent
		Thalamida	Carboniferous–Cretaceous

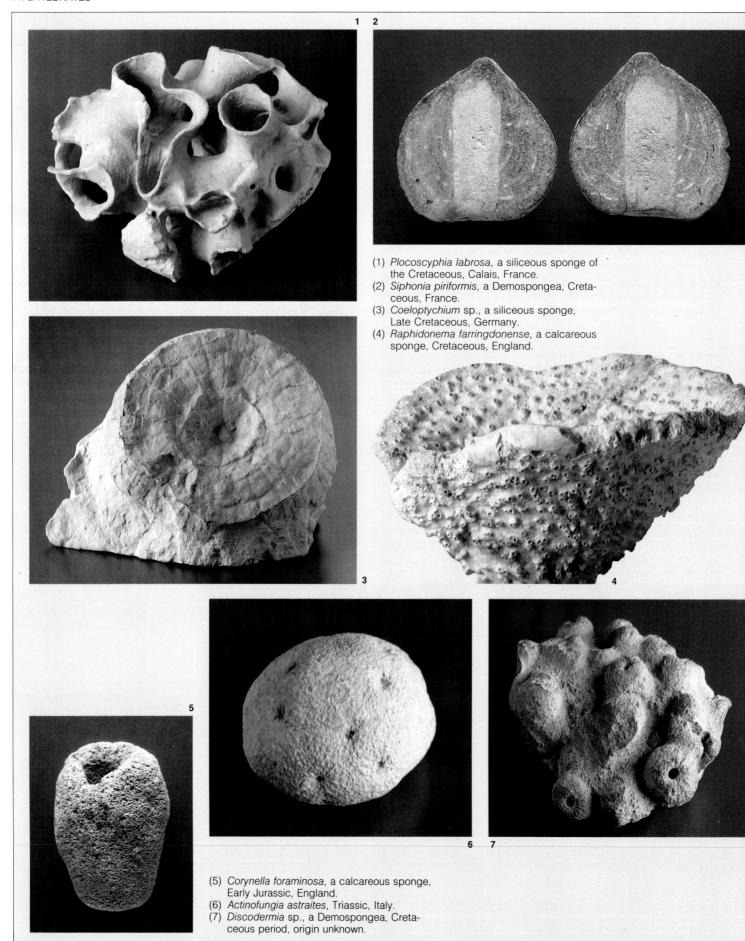

(1) *Plocoscyphia labrosa,* a siliceous sponge of the Cretaceous, Calais, France.
(2) *Siphonia piriformis,* a Demospongea, Cretaceous, France.
(3) *Coeloptychium* sp., a siliceous sponge, Late Cretaceous, Germany.
(4) *Raphidonema farringdonense,* a calcareous sponge, Cretaceous, England.

(5) *Corynella foraminosa,* a calcareous sponge, Early Jurassic, England.
(6) *Actinofungia astraites,* Triassic, Italy.
(7) *Discodermia* sp., a Demospongea, Cretaceous period, origin unknown.

(8) *Siphonia* sp., Cretaceous period, origin unknown.
(9) *Astaeospongia meniscus*, siliceous sponge, Silurian, United States.
(10) *Synolynthia* sp., probably a calcareous sponge, Cretaceous, England.

8

9

10

an internal framework of calcareous or siliceous spicules, called megascleres, joined to form a reticulate structure sometimes visible to the naked eye. Other spicules are spread throughout the body; much smaller and visible only under a microscope, they are called microscleres. These are used, with the choanocytes, in the taxonomic classification of sponges. Since they are not connected to each other, the spicules disperse on the death of the sponge. The classification of fossil sponges is therefore based on the composition and geometry of the megascleres and the type of framework they form.

Because of the tiny size of spicules, which are sometimes dispersed in sediments in such abundance as to form siliceous rocks called spongolites, they are studied using the techniques of micropaleontology, performed with microscopes. These studies have revealed the existence of different kinds of spicules, sometimes siliceous (opal crystalized in chalcedony), with a small central canal that is always visible in the fossil; sometimes of calcite, in which the small canal is only rarely preserved; and sometimes of spongin, a proteinaceous substance.

The simplest type of spicule is the monaxon, a long needle formed of a single rod; more complex are the triaxon or esattine spicules, formed of three perpendicular rods; the tetraxon spicules with four rods; and the triattine with three rods that meet on the same plane and are characteristic of calcareous sponges.

The importance of sponges in paleontology is primarily the result of their use as indicators of ancient environments. Their forms, in fact, vary according to the character of currents, the turbidity of the water and its depth, so that species typical of a particular environment indicate, when found in the fossil form, the conditions present during their lives.

Porifera are known in the fossil state from some of the oldest fossil-bearing rocks. In Precambrian rocks, usually with few if any fossils, traces of these animals have been found that date back to many millions of years before the great explosion of life that took place at the beginning of the Paleozoic era (about 570 million years ago).

From the Precambrian there are siliceous spicules of *Tyrkanispongia*, 1.5 billion years old, found in eastern Siberia. These are considered the oldest known representatives of the group. Spicules of sponges have also been found in Precambrian rocks in the Grand Canyon in Arizona, a true mine of ancient fossils. Fossils of uncertain origin but similar to the calcareous sponges of today have also been found in Precambrian rocks discovered in central Africa, while in Britain calcareous spicules attributed to a very ancient sponge called Eospicula have been located.

From the beginning of the Paleozoic era to today, the evolutionary history of the sponges does not hold much interest for scientists. These animals, in fact, have remained almost unchanged through the course of geologic history for the last 600 million years. As early as the Cambrian period, the phylum Porifera numbered representatives of the three classes into which sponges are today divided: Demospongiae, to which belong the common bath sponges; the Hexactinellida, or glass sponges; and the Calcarea, or calcareous sponges.

Below left: *A sponge preserved completely in a Jurassic deposit, Solnhofen, Germany.*
Below right: Protospongia rhenana, *a siliceous sponge of the Early Devonian, Bundenbach, Germany.*

Class Demospongia

The majority of living sponges belong to this class. However, most of these sponges disintegrate so fast and so completely after death that it is easy to understand why they are extremely rare in the fossil record. They are identified most often by spicules found in sediment or by the effects they produce on other organisms. The discovery in very ancient deposits of the tetraxon and monaxon spicules characteristic of this class demonstrates their enormous diffusion, most of all during the Triassic and Jurassic from 245 to 144 million years ago.

Among the Demospongiae is the genus *Cliona*, widely distributed in marine Tertiary deposits of the world. This is a boring sponge, known in the fossil record only through the pits it produces in the shells of various mollusks.

The Litistidi is an abundant group, easily recognized by the presence of modified or swollen spicules in Mesozoic sediments united in a solid network; it includes sponges known from the Cambrian to the present day. Examples of this group have been found perfectly fossilized with the complete body visible.

Class Hexactinellida

The Hexactinellida sponges are siliceous and their skeleton is composed of hyalline (glassy) spicules. In most cases, the spicules are joined to form a light, transparent latticework, or "glass sponge," the name by which they are commonly known.

The body, shaped like a cup or basket at the end of a long peduncle, is extremely fragile and rarely found intact in sediments. On the other hand, it is not unusual to find the typical spicules, which are abundant in many rocks from the Cambrian to the present.

Modern-day representatives of this class usually live in tropical seas at a depth between 200 and 500 meters (660-1,650 ft.), but there are also deep sea forms dredged up from 4,000 meters (13,200 ft.) and, on rare occasions, even from 6,000 meters (19,800 ft.) deep. Many glass sponges from the Cretaceous period have been found in sediments from shallow seas and even sometimes in what were once offshore, or littoral, environments.

Class Calcarea

These sponges have highly variable forms supported by calcareous spicules (usually triattine) and live most often in relatively shallow seas. Their spicules are widespread in rocks of all ages, but complete examples of them are common as well, including that of the genus *Raphidonema*, which had a characteristic cup shape and lived from the Triassic to the Cretaceous period, or from 245 to 144 million years ago.

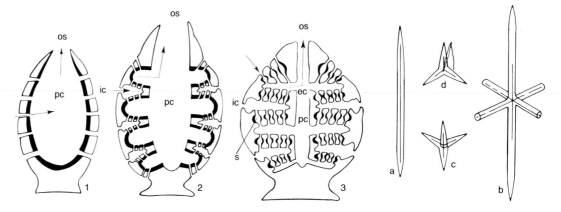

Right: *Schematic drawings of the three kinds of internal organization of sponges: (1) ascon, (2) sycon and (3) leucon—with (ic) incurrent canals; (ec) excurrent canals; (s) spongocoel; (pc) pseudogastric cavity; (os) osculum.*
Far right: *Spicules of sponges: (a) monoaxon; (b) triaxon or esattina; (c) tetraxon; (d) triattina.*

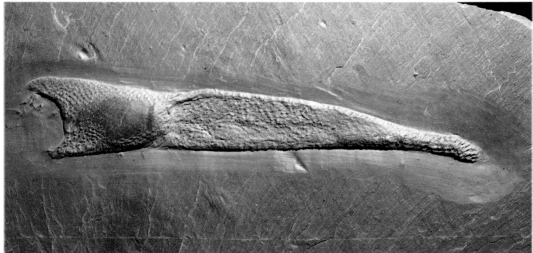

Receptaculitids

Very little is known about the Receptaculites, a group of fossil forms that lived in the seas of the Paleozoic era, from the Ordovician to the Carboniferous (between 590 and 345 million years ago). These organisms left ovaloid or globular calcareous colonies made of small hexagonal plates that form regular surface designs. These animals, believed to have an affinity with the sponges, have yet to be even classified.

Right: Receptaculites *sp., a strange Paleozoic organism considered to have affinity with the sponges; Devonian, Germany.*

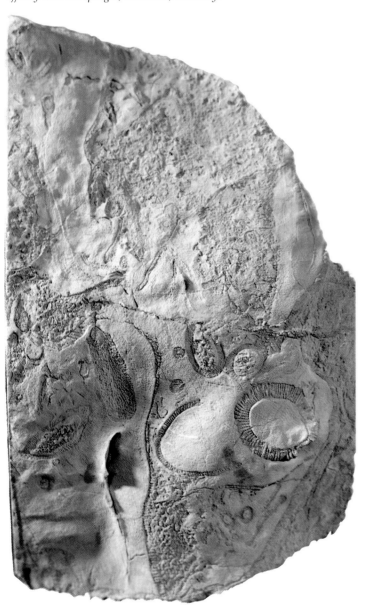

Archaeocyaths

In sedimentary rocks in southern Sardinia, Normandy, the Sierra Morena, North America, the Sahara, Morocco, China, Siberia and Australia—rocks that were formed in the Cambrian seas of 570 million years ago—have been found certain fossils whose classification has been for many years the subject of ongoing discussion.

These organisms occasionally have been attributed to the coelenterates because of the presence of vertical radial septa (partitions); to the sponges because of their porous walls and the presence of a central cavity; to the protozoa; and to calcareous algae. These are members of the phylum Archaeocyatha, which is today considered to have been a separate phylum,

Left: *The effect of weathering on this Cambrian limestone has exposed the presence of an archaeocyathid in which the walls divided by radial septa are visible.*
Right: *Schematic reconstruction of an archaeocyathid.*

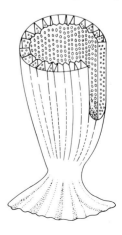

Below left and right: *Two fragments of limestone bearing archaeocyathids; Middle Cambrian, Italy.*

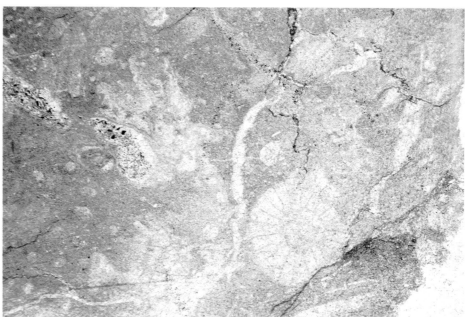

Phylum	Class	Age
Archaeocyatha	Regular	Early and Middle Cambrian
	Irregular	Early–Late Cambrian

distinct from the coelenterates and the Porifera, that became extinct at the end of the Cambrian, with no descendants.

The Archaeocyatha are conical organisms with a height that varies between 2.5 cm. and 10 cm. (.9-4.0 in.), formed of two porous concentric walls joined by vertical, radial septa and by horizontal surfaces that divide the area inside the walls into small, nearly cubical chambers. In the center is a large cavity similar to that found in sponges.

The archaeocyathids lived attached to the sea bottom, probably in shallow coastal waters, fixing themselves in place with projections that formed on the apex of the cone. These animals were of great importance during the Cambrian as builders of reefs, a role filled, when the archaeocyathids became extinct, by the corals (coelenterates).

Coelenterates (Cnidaria)

The multicelled metazoans developed during the middle Archean. Their presence during that geological era has been documented, but the number of known fossils is still not large. Thus paleontology can prove their existence in that distant time but cannot reconstruct the first phases of their evolution. This is due, on the one hand, to geological events that removed the traces and, on the other, to the lack of hard parts in the delicate bodies of these organisms, which only rarely have been transformed into fossils.

The coelenterates are at a more advanced stage than the Porifera (which we can consider the simplest metazoans). Their bodies include the presence of a primitive digestive cavity, the further differentiation of certain cells with particular functions, and the formation of a third layer to their body wall (the mesogloea), between the external (epidermis) and the internal (gastrodermis). They are thus considered the first animals with well defined tissues.

The coelenterates are well known due to their widespread distribution in all the world's seas. Nearly everyone has seen, at least once, a slender branch of red coral or a slimy jellyfish. Few people, however, realize that these organisms, so different from each other, are classified in the same taxonomic group. The fact is that the coelenterates are found in nature in two different forms, the polyp and the medusa, the first nonmotile (stationary), the other free-swimming.

The polyp has a cylindrical body with a sac-shaped gastric cavity that communicates with the exterior through a mouth opening located at one end, encircled by tentacles. It affixes itself on a hard substrate using a disk.

The medusa has a convex, umbrellalike upper body (exumbrella), fringed laterally with numerous tentacles. The lower, concave part of the body (subumbrella) extends to the manubrium, which leads to the mouth. The body of the medusa is composed of up to 96.5% water and is flatter than that of the polyp. The two forms described here are characteristic of sev-

Below left: *Life cycles of the principal groups of coelenterates.*
Below right: *Although very delicate, the impressions of medusae can be found in many deposits. This specimen is from Jurassic limestone, Solnhofen, Germany.*

Bottom left: Simplicibranchia bolcensis, *a medusa of the Scyphozoa; Eocene, Monte Bolca, Italy.*
Bottom right: Dactyloidites *sp., Cambrian, United States. This ancient stellate organism is attributed doubtfully to the coelenterates.*

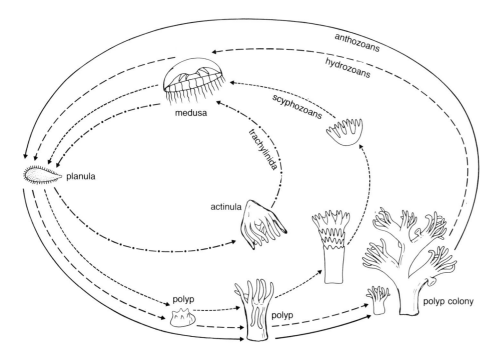

eral groups of coelenterates, and can form alternate generations within the same species.

While the medusoid stage is represented by individual organisms, in the polypoid stage polyps join to form colonies of numerous individuals, colonies that may have the ability, as with corals, to construct a calcareous external skeleton (exoskeleton), which supports and defends the animal.

The earliest coelenterates are believed to have been medusae and polyps without mineralized exoskeletons, because in the oldest fossil-bearing strata have been found impressions that many scholars attribute to the umbrellas of medusae or to colonies of polyps without these exoskeletons. Coelenterate colonies characterized by a resistant calcareous skeleton seem to be completely absent in those distant ages, beginning to appear only in the seas of the Silurian. Beginning in that period, in fact, about 438 million years ago, colonies of coelenterates with skeletons formed large, reef-like structures that played an important role in the origin of sedimentary rocks.

Although the oldest medusae are often most interesting to the paleontologist, the polyps, particularly their skeletons, provide an excellent source of evolutionary evidence in various forms and in a variety of periods. Extremely well preserved and common, they enable us to reach important paleogeographical and paleoecological conclusions.

We have already noted the great reef building ability of these organisms, and we have added that they are very useful for reconstructing environments of the past. In fact, beginning in the Silurian, they began to create strong coralline constructions that accurately indicate, based on what we know about their activity today, the environmental conditions of the seas in which they were formed.

The corals that build these structures are delicate organisms

that need precise environmental conditions, and without these conditions they have no hope of survival. The coral polyps need clear water at a temperature of at least 20 degrees Celsius (68 degrees Fahrenheit) and good light, which is seldom found at depths over 40 meters (132 ft.). The diffusion of coralline constructions is limited by these factors so that reef-building corals are found only in a band of the world between 27 degrees south and 30 degrees north latitude. However, they are not found where there are cold sea currents, such as on the western coast of Africa, which is touched by the Benguela Current, or on the west coast of South America, where the Peruvian, or Humboldt, Current passes.

The 40-meter depth limit might seem to prohibit the enormous growths observed in coralline constructions, except that the parts of such reefs lower than 40 meters are clearly composed of skeletons of once-living organisms. How, then, did the reef get to be so thick? It is clear that remains at greater depths indicate a progressive rise of the sea level, while remains above the highest limit of the sea indicate a lowering of sea level. Thus, in coralline constructions, progressive raising of sea level is matched at the same speed by growth on the upper part of the reef, permitting it to reach great thicknesses while also permitting the corals to maintain the same conditions.

Modern coral reefs can be divided into three basic types: fringing reefs, which are more or less continuous with the shoreline; barrier reefs, deposited parallel to the shore and separated from it by a broad lagoon; and atolls, which form in rings that enclose a central lagoon that may fill with sediment and itself become an island or extension of land.

The largest and most famous coral reef is the Great Barrier Reef off Australia's northeast shore. This enormous structure stretches parallel to the coastline for more than 2,000 km. (1,250 mi.) at a distance from the continent of about 100 km. (62.5 mi.).

Beginning in the Silurian, many coralline structures were built in almost all the marine areas of the world and are found today in the fossil state. They have been transformed into hard calcareous or dolomitic rock, inside of which it is almost always possible to find remains of the organisms that build them. Devonian coral reefs, built 380 or 390 million years ago, can be found in Italy, England, Germany and western North America. In the Triassic seas, which covered the northeastern part of the Italian peninsula 230 million years ago, the Dolomites were constructed slowly. This enormous coralline barrier, with abundant coral and calcareous algae remains, reached great vertical heights due to a progressive rise of the sea level during that entire period. There are also abundant reefs from the Jurassic in the Alps, in the Apennines, in Switzerland, and in many other European and non-European areas, at higher latitudes than contemporary reefs.

During the Tertiary period (from 65 to 1.8 million years ago), the reefs disappeared from central Europe (where today corals remain only in isolated forms), while in the Mediterranean area others were built during the Eocene and the Oligocene. With the passing of time, the reefs, following a general chilling of the climate, moved progressively south, reaching their present-day locations during the Quaternary.

As for the classification of the coelenterates, we must note that the abundance and great variety of these organisms as early as the Early Cambrian indicates for this phylum a long evolutionary story. As early as the Cambrian, in fact, they appear divided in several principal groups that correspond taxonomically to different classes. The phylum Coelenterata includes the subphyla Cnidaria, very rich with fossil representatives, while the phyla Ctenophora has far fewer fossil representatives (aside from a few uncertain remains).

The Cnidarians are in turn subdivided into four classes; some are known only in the fossil state, others are still widespread in the earth's oceans and seas.

Phylum	Subphylum	Class	Subclass	Order	Age
Coelenterata or Cnidaria	Cnidaria	Protomedusae		Brooksellida	Precambrian–Silurian
		Scyphozoa	Scyphomedusae Conulata		Cambrian–Recent Cambrian–Triassic
		Hydrozoa		Hydroida Milleporina Stylasterina Trachylinida Siphonophorida Spongiomorphida Stromatoporoidea	Cambrian–Recent Cretaceous–Recent Cretaceous–Recent Cambrian–Recent Ordovician–Recent Triassic–Jurassic Cambrian–Cretaceous
		Anthozoa	Ceriantipatharia Octocorallia Zoantharia		Miocene–Recent Silurian–Recent Ordovician–Recent
	Ctenophora				Recent

Anthozoans from Oligocene reefs from near Vicenza, Italy:
(1) *Thamnastraea* sp.
(2) *Phyllocoenia irradians*
(3) *Favia confertissima*
(4) *Oulophyllia irradians*
(5) *Placophylla* sp.

Class Protomedusae

In this class are grouped certain primitive medusae found in Cambrian rocks in British Columbia, in Ordovician rocks in Sweden and France, and in Precambrian rocks in North America. These are the oldest known fossil remains of coelenterates, grouped in the genus *Brooksella*, among which is an impression of the discoidal umbrella, without tentacles. The oldest of these impressions, found in rocks dated to the Proterozoic, are believed to be from 700 to 800 million years old.

Class Schyphozoa

Within this group the medusa form is more common than the polyp, which represents, when it exists, a transition stage. This class includes all of the largest jellyfish, which can sometimes reach 2 m. (6.6 ft.) in diameter. Members of this class are only rarely found in the fossil state, and since they lack hard body parts they are represented only by impressions left by the medusa's umbrella. These are grouped in the subclass Scyphomedusae and are found in various rocks from the Cambrian

Various medusoid species have been found in Carboniferous deposits at Mazon Creek, Illinois.
Below, from left to right: Essexella asherae, Octomedusa pieckorum, Reticulomedusa greenei.

period to today.

The subclass Conulata includes organisms known to us exclusively from fossils, which lived in the earth's seas from the middle Cambrian until the Early Jurassic period (about 195 million years ago), at which time they became extinct. Until a short while ago, these coelenterates were erroneously believed to be gastropods (mollusks) or worms. They had a pyramid-form chitinous external skeleton about 4 to 10 cm. (1.6-4 in.) long, inside of which the animal lived. Tentacles reached out of the shell through openings located around the base of the pyramid, which could be closed by way of mobile plates when the animal had withdrawn completely. During their young stages these organisms, which have no modern counterpart, are believed to have lived fixed to the sea floor by means of a disk applied to the end of the shell, while at the adult stage they became medusae, capable of free swimming.

Class Hydrozoa

The Hydrozoa are coelenterates that are found in medusae or polyp form, isolated or grouped in colonies. Because the first group are only rarely found in fossil form (of which only the impression of the umbrella remains), we will deal here only with the polyps. Due to the presence of a more or less calcified skeleton, they can be found much more frequently in sediments and have played a very important role in the genesis of coralline formations since the Paleozoic.

The typical Hydrozoa polyp consists of a base with which the organism attaches itself to a hard substrate (a surface on which something grows), a thin, erect stem, and a terminal expansion that bears the mouth and the tentacles. The colonies are formed by budding stems that spread and an excrescence that generates other stems. The stems in turn develop other terminal extensions, and the branching process is re-

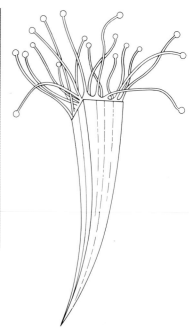

Above left: *A pyritized specimen of Conularia, a Scyphozoa of the subclass Conulata; Devonian Bundenbach, Germany.*
Above center: Conularia crustula, *Carboniferous of the United States.*
Above right: *Reconstruction of a Conularia.*

Below left: *Schematic reconstruction of an encrusted colony of Hydrozoa* (genus Millepora).
Below right: Stromatopora concentrica, *an encrusting Hydrozoa of the stromatoporoidea. Middle Devonian, Germany.*

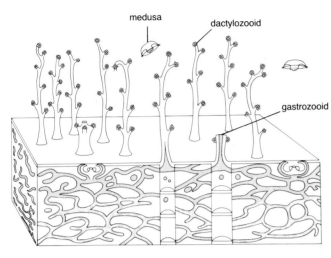

Right: *Section of Stromatoporoidea of the genus* Idiostroma; *Devonian, Iowa.*
Far right: Actinostroma verrucosa, *Stromatoporoidea of the Devonian.*

peated. These colonies are usually stiffened and protected by a skeleton, of chitinous tubes. In other groups, the polyps occupy cavities in a large calcareous mass.

In many Hydrozoa colonies one can spot a clear differentiation of function among the polyps. There are large polyps specialized in nutrition, small polyps that have defensive roles, and reproductive polyps.

Modern-day zoologists divide the Hydrozoa in five orders: the Hydroida, Milleporina, Stylasterina, Trachylinida and Siphonophorida, for each of which there are living examples and fossil remains. To these, paleontologists have added the Spongiomorphida and Stromatoporoidea, known exclusively as fossils. We will discuss here only those that are most abundant and found most frequently as fossils.

Representatives of the order Hydroida are known since the Cambrian period and include polyps, which live alone or in colonies and medusoid forms. The first live most of all in littoral (shoreline) environments in branching or encrusted colonies and are rare in fresh water. The medusoid forms are nekto-planktonic, that is, free-swimming or floating. A char-

acteristic genus is that of the Ellipsactinia, which have bodies formed of concentric ovoid nodules of successive scaly layers of porous calcareous tissue joined by irregular columns.

The class Milleporina contains organisms that build calcareous structures that are branching or encrusted, with the latter more abundant. Among these the genus *Millepora,* known from the Cretaceous, is today widespread in coral reefs, where it lives at less than 30 m. (99 ft.) of depth. It is formed of a simple calcareous outer layer, on the surface of which exist many holes that lead to the interior through vertical canals in which live polyps, differentiated into larger feeding polyps surrounded by numerous, smaller defensive polyps.

The class Stromatoporoidea includes many coelenterates that are extinct today. These are encrusting organisms with large calcareous skeletons, laminar or dendritic, formed of many concentric laminae. Each lamina, corresponding to a period of growth (generation) of the colony, was formed in turn by a certain number of smaller lamellae joined one to another by pillars, of a very irregular form, perpendicular to the surface. On the external surface of the colony appear many holes, cor-

*Outlines of the various phases of appearance of the septa in the calyx of Te-
tracorallia and Hexacorallia: (A) Tetracorallia: (cs) cardinal septa; (vs) ventral septa; (ls) lateral septa. (B) Hexacorallia: The septa with the same number of order appear simultaneously.*

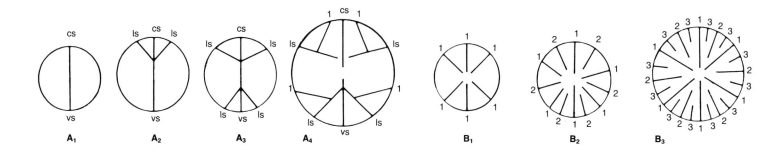

responding to internal tubes inhabited by polyps, and the "as-
trorhize," stellate pores, the function of which is not well
understood.

Known since the Cambrian, the Stromatoporoidea must have
lived in a habitat similar to that of the Milleporina, which replaced them when they became extinct in the Cretaceous. In
all probability they lived in warm water that was not very deep
and contributed to the formation of reefs in shallow-sea (neritic) zones, reefs that were widespread during the Silurian, Devonian and Jurassic.

Class Anthozoa

The Anthozoans constitute the dominant part of both fossil
and modern coral fauna. These are organisms that live fixed
to a hard, submerged base, isolated or united in colonies,
without medusoid forms. Their principal distinguishing characteristics are the central gastric cavity divided by radial partitions and the presence of a ring of tentacles surrounding the
mouth. The number of these tentacles varies in the different
groups: six or multiples of six in the Zoantharia, but eight in
the Octocorallia, in which they are sometimes branched.

The anthozoans are formidable builders. Their importance
is based on their ability to secrete a hard skeleton, sometimes
horny and thus not easily fossilized, but most often calcareous, which has been excellently preserved in the fossil record
and which, in accumulations of enormous size, with the remains of other organisms, leads to the formation of reefs. There
are, however, many ancient anthozoans without these skeletons, and of these little is known.

After a larval stage in which it is free to move, the young
polyp fixes itself and begins building a small cup (prototheca),
beginning with which it forms the calcareous walls and the
septa, by way of successive layers of calcification.

The outside of the skeleton is constructed of an external wall,
formed by the union of the ends of the thickened septa (false
wall), or by areas of calcification distinct from the septa (true
wall). In both cases a calcareous crust (epitheca), more or less
rugose (wrinkled), can envelop the wall. The cuplike cavity of
an anthozoan is thus divided in various segments by the radial
septa, which, when not joined at the center, leave an opening
occupied by a vertical column (columella).

This complex structure—described here in simplified terms—
is found in both the solitary forms (single corallites) with con-

ical cup and in the colonial forms (corallums) made of a union
of numerous cups.

The coralla exist in a wide range of appearances, always at-
tractive because of their beauty and variety. They create
branched forms, when the arms are free, and thick forms, in
which the various cups are joined by a common tissue (cenen-
chima). If this tissue is lost, the corallum may assume a
polygonal form, or some meandering form.

Anthozoans are known in the fossil record from as early as
the Ordovician and are divided in three subclasses: Cerianti-
patharia, Octocorallia and Zoantharia, all of which have living
representatives. Of these, only the last two groups are of paleontological value because of the abundance in which their
remains are found in the fossil record.

To the Octocorallia belong the Alcyonaria, colonial forms with
a skeleton made of a rod or calcareous spicule joined by a horny
substance. Most of the fossil remains of animals of this group
are thus scattered spicules found in sediments, since the horny
substance dissolves on the death of the organism and thus
does not always permit the preservation of the interior of the
animal. Among the best-known of this group is the red coral,
often used to make jewelry, which was already forming on sea
beds during the Cretaceous, more than 100 million years ago.

The Zoantharia include various species. Some are without a
skeleton, such as the well-known sea anemones, which are
therefore not preserved as fossils. Some have such tough calcareous skeletons that even today, after many millions of years,
we can admire their form and elegance. These are the madre-
pores, which today, as in the past, are important builders of
coral reefs.

The Zoantharia can be divided into Tetracorallia (also called
rugose corals) and Hexocorallia, according to the alignment of
the septa in the cup. The first group are exclusive to the Paleozoic and became extinct at the end of the Permian (about 230
million years ago); in the following period, the Triassic, the
hexocoralli (*Scleractinia*) took their place and have not changed
in any great way during the 200 million years of their existence
and, in fact, exist today.

In the rugose corals the specta usually appear in groups of
four. The first to appear is the counter septum; in the second
stage of growth two counterlateral septa appear alongside the
counter and support it. In the third stage another two septa
form in the area opposite the counter until, in the fourth stage,

Typical examples of Tetracorallia: (1) *Cystiphyllum* sp., Silurian, Dudley, England; (2) *Hexagonaria* sp., Devonian, Michigan; (3) *Zaphrentis* sp., Devonian, Bundenbach, Germany; (4) *Heliophyllum halli*, Devonian, Ontario, Canada; (5) *Acervularia* sp., Silurian, Dudley; (6,7) *Calceola sandalina* from above and from the side, Middle Devonian, Germany.

the counter narrows, forming a cardinal septum and a ventral septum, and other septa appear in groups of four, two between the alar and the cardinal on one side, and two outside the counterlateral. Thus is created a bilateral symmetry that becomes regularized in the adult stages.

In the hexocoralli the radial symmetry is achieved in the first stages of growth of the cup, after which the septa appear in groups of six at a time, within the sectors formed by the septa in the preceding stage.

This difference between Tetracorallia and Hexocorallia is difficult to observe with the naked eye. The distinction between the two groups is thus impossible to establish without the use of detailed methods, in particular the observation of polished or thin sections of the corallites. The external forms of the representatives of the two groups are so similar they are often confused.

A special order of the subclass Zoantharia is the Tubulata (tubulate corals), now extinct, coelenterates that are exclusively Paleozoic and that, because of their structure, are clearly different from other members of the group. Their skeleton is formed by cups in the shape of small tubes, crossed by horizontal tabulae, located near one another.

Colonial Hexacorallia and Tetracorallia with isolated polypierti:
(1) *Deltocyathys* sp., Pliocene from the Apennines in northern Italy.
(2) *Astrahelia palmata,* Miocene from the United States.
(3) *Aspidiscus cristatus,* Late Cretaceous, Algeria.

(4) *Caryophyllia* sp., Pliocene, Italy.
(5) *Thecosmilia trichotoma,* Late Jurassic, Germany.
(6) *Astrangia lineata,* Miocene, Virginia.
(7) Hexacorallia of the group of the genus Montlivaltia; Cretaceous, Madagascar.

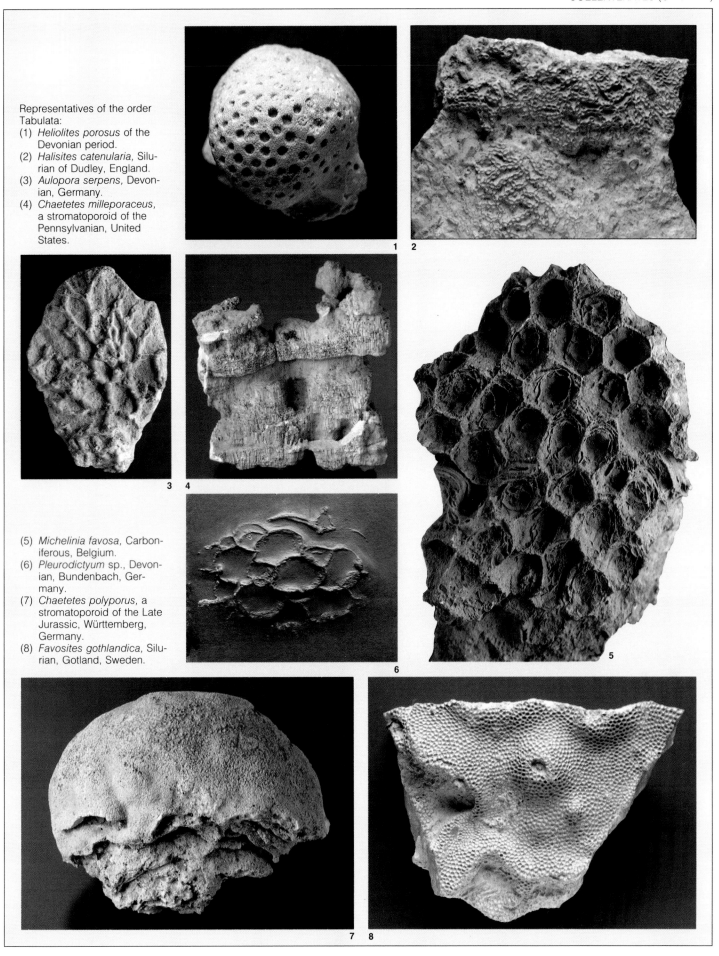

Representatives of the order Tabulata:
(1) *Heliolites porosus* of the Devonian period.
(2) *Halisites catenularia,* Silurian of Dudley, England.
(3) *Aulopora serpens,* Devonian, Germany.
(4) *Chaetetes milleporaceus,* a stromatoporoid of the Pennsylvanian, United States.

(5) *Michelinia favosa,* Carboniferous, Belgium.
(6) *Pleurodictyum* sp., Devonian, Bundenbach, Germany.
(7) *Chaetetes polyporus,* a stromatoporoid of the Late Jurassic, Württemberg, Germany.
(8) *Favosites gothlandica,* Silurian, Gotland, Sweden.

Encrustation of the cheilostome bryozoan Cellepora *sp. on the shell of a gastropod; Pliocene, England.*

Bryozoans

Following the steps taken by evolution toward ever more complex organisms, we come now to a group that is little known to those not involved professionally in zoology or in paleontology. These are the Bryozoa (bryozoans) or Ectoprocta, invertebrates whose evolutionary history is little known and who are classified in a phylum whose affinities with other groups of animals is not fully understood—with the exception of the brachiopods, which appear to be their relatives.

Bryozoans were once included among the zoophytes, which is to say they were considered intermediate organisms between plants and animals, because their external form is so similar to that of a plant. Later, the discovery that their forms were made up of many small individuals led certain authorities to place them nearer the coelenterates. It was then observed that each individual of the colony had a complete alimentary canal (a tube through which food is digested and absorbed into the body) which further complicated the problem of their classification. The debate was finally resolved by scientists with the recognition of important characteristics the bryozoans and the brachiopods had in common.

Bryozoans are very common in the fossil state, but because of their small size, collecting and studying them are difficult. Accurate classification can be achieved only with the use of a microscope, applying the methods used for microfossils. Even so, it is not rare for fragments of colonies to be visible to the naked eye.

Without going into extremely complex details, let's examine the structure of these organisms and the ways in which they are generally classified when found as fossils.

Bryozoans are colonial invertebrates that live today in seas at variable depths. Certain rare members are adapted to life in fresh water. Since their first appearance in the Ordovician, about 500 million years ago, the bryozoans have played an important part in Paleozoic and Mesozoic marine fauna. Although the appearance of various genera is reasonably constant, the form and size of colonies of bryozoans vary widely. These generally grow encrusted on shells, stones and other hard bodies, and can be delicate, lamellar, hemispherical, irregular, or branching. Bryozoan fossils are common in sedimentary rocks. Certain deposits in England and North America are particularly

Schematic drawing of the anatomy of a bryozoan:
(ao) anal opening;
(mo) mouth opening;
(hg) hermaphrodite gland;
(ng) nerve ganglia;
(l) lophophore;
(rm) retractor muscle;
(g) gut;
(z) zooecium.

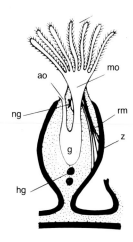

Phylum	Class	Order	Age
Bryozoa or *Ectoprocta*	*Phylactolaemata*		Cretaceous–Recent
	Gymnolaemata	*Ctenostomata* *Cyclostomata* *Trepostomata* *Cryptostomata* *Cheilostomata*	Ordovician–Recent Ordovician–Recent Ordovician–Triassic Ordovician–Permian Jurassic–Recent

Below: *Reconstruction of* Bowerbankia pustulosa, *a bryozoan of the order Ctenostomata.*

Below: Fistulipora carbonaria, *encrusting bryozoan of the order Cyclostomata. Carboniferous, Texas.*
Bottom left: Pseudohornera bifida, *a bryozoan of the Trepostomata. Ordovician, Estonia.*
Bottom right: *Group of* Pseudohornera bifida *and* Phylloporina furcata. *Ordovician, Estonia.*

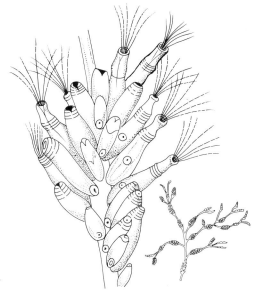

noteworthy, and these fragments of bryozoans sometimes completely cover the bedding surface of the rocks. In the United States bryozoan fossils are often found in Mississippian sedimentary rocks of the Midwest and Rocky Mountains.

A colony of bryozoans is formed by small zooecia with a chitinous or calcareous skeleton. The colony forms from the freely moving larvae of an individual that fixes itself to some solid object. Then, through a process called budding, new individuals begin as outgrowths, or "buds," from this one individual. The new organisms of the colony can take on varying appearances and sizes. Each individual, no longer than a millimeter, is called a zooid (like the polyps of coral) and is composed of a saclike body that has on its upper part a crown of tentacles (the lophophore) in the center of which is the mouth. The external wall of the sac secretes a chitinous or calcareous theca with an opening in which the animal lives (which is the only fossilizible part of the animal). The complete colony is thus composed of a great number of zooids, which live in small zooecia, most of which are shaped like polygonal tubes. On the exterior side of some zooecia are special "bodies," called

avicultures because of their resemblance to birds, that serve to protect the individuals from attacks from predators. Also on the exterior are sometimes long, vibrating cilia, which seem to serve the function of holding any harmful materials at a distance from the theca's orifices.

The group of the bryozoans was once held to include certain subphyla, including the Entoprocta, which has no fossil representatives, and the Ectoprocta. The difference between the two subphyla is found in the fact that in the first the anal opening lies within the lophophore, and in the second is located outside of it. Today the two groups are considered completely separate and independent phyla, the name Bryozoa is now used only for the phylum Ectoprocta.

Ectoprocta are very abundant in rocks of all ages and are subdivided into the class Phylactolaemata, whose representatives, the only bryozoans adapted to life in fresh water, include fossils known since the Cretaceous (about 140 million years ago), and the class Gymnolaemata, which includes organisms known since the Ordovician (about 505 million years ago), grouped into the following five orders.

Above: Chasmatoporella *sp., bryozoan of the order Trepostomata. Ordovician, Italy.*
Below: Fenestella bohemica, *bryozoan of the order Cryptostomata. Devonian, Germany.*
Bottom: Archimedes *sp., bryozoan of the order Cryptostomata. Mississippian, Kentucky.*

Order Ctenostomata

The order Ctenostomata includes species known from the Ordovician and some still living today. These are boring bryozoans, with horny or gelatinous zooecia that are not easily preserved, so they are known most of all through the remains of the excavations these organisms have made on stones, reefs and the shells of mollusks.

Order Cyclostomata

The order Cyclostomata includes colonies composed of tubular, calcareous zooecia that cement together along most of their length and have a large aperture with a hard protective closure. These ancient and abundant bryozoans are found for the first time in Ordovician strata, and from that time they were widely distributed during all the Paleozoic. They reached the height of their development during the Triassic, began to diminish during the Tertiary and today are found in much reduced numbers.

Order Trepostomata

The Trepostomata form colonies of elongated cylindrical or prismatic tubes, joined sometimes in compact forms, sometimes in delicate, branching forms. The oldest representatives are from the Ordovician, the period in which they had their maximum development and after which they began a slow decline that brought them near total extinction at the end of the Paleozoic, about 250 million years ago. It seems that they probably survived, although in much reduced numbers, during the Triassic.

Order Cryptostomata

The Cryptostomata built large colonies that took on the appearance of nets or leaves and were formed of elongated individuals with square or hexagonal cross sections. These are exclusively Paleozoic organisms, having lived from the Ordovician to the Permian, periods in which they were part of reef formations. Representatives of the family Fenestellida were the most common.

Order Cheilostomata

The representatives of the Cheilostomata are the most modern of the bryozoans since they appeared during the Middle Jurassic and are without doubt the most widespread in today's seas. They form branching or compact colonies made of oval or elliptical zooecia side by side and have small nonterminal apertures.

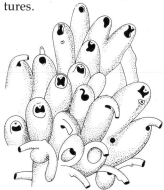

Reconstruction of Orthoporidra, typical representative of the order of the Cheilostomata.

Brachiopods

Many years ago, brachiopods were classified in the phylum Vermidi together with the bryozoans because the two groups possessed analogous general structures. Brachiopods, however, differ from bryozoans in several important ways: They do not form colonies; they are much larger; and they have a bivalve shell that is easily preserved. Since this shell is the only part of the organism that is preserved, the classification of brachiopods is based on variations in the characteristics of this shell.

The shells of brachiopods are bilaterally symmetrical, with the plane of symmetry perpendicular to the plane of contact of the two valves. Looking at the two valves, one can distinguish a large ventral (or lower) valve that has at its posterior end a curving or beaklike structure. The dorsal valve is slightly shorter but similar in appearance. All together, a brachiopod's shell, with its protruding beak, resembles an ancient oil lamp with the wick protruding, and for this reason brachiopods are commonly known as lampshells. (This resemblance is most striking in the genus *Terebratula*.)

The bivalve shell of the brachiopods should not be confused with the similar shell of the bivalve mollusks because of three principal characteristics that set them apart: The valves of brachiopods, unlike those of bivalves, are of different sizes; the beak is located only on the ventral valve; and there is in some a hole on this valve for the pedicle, the organ with which the animal attaches itself to the sea bottom.

Leaving aside a detailed description of the soft parts of these strange organisms, we should look briefly at the valves, which are lined on the inside with the membrane called the mantle. This also encloses a large central cavity called the mantle cavity, in which is found the animal's lophophore, formed of two ciliated ribbons surrounding the mouth. This organ, using its many vibrating cilia, produces a current of water that draws food and oxygen into the animal. The lophophore—and this is what interests us most—is sometimes supported by a calcareous apparatus, the form of which varies greatly. Called a brachial apparatus or brachidium, it is often preserved and is thus used in the classification of brachiopods. This apparatus does not exist in the more primitive types, however. In more evolved forms it has the appearance of two small symmetrical processes, called crura, which in some brachiopods is elongated and curved into the form of a spiral cone.

The shells of the brachiopods, upon which the paleontological classification is based, can be calcareous, calcareous-chitinous or chitinous. They come in a wide variety of forms: ovoid, globular, hemispherical, flattened, convex-concave or irregular. The shell is thin in those forms that live in deep water and thick in those that live near shore or live on reefs, and its surface is smooth or variously ornamented with ribs, grooves, or spines.

It is interesting to note that in those species ornamented with strong radial ribbing, the joining of the two valves can assume a zigzag pattern, thought to be useful in preventing outside particles above a certain size from entering the shell. In the

Group of Rhynchonellida in a Jurassic rock from England.

same way, some brachiopods have developed long spines along the edges of the valves that block entrance, much like a gate, and may serve the same defensive function.

In some brachiopods, the two valves of the shell are articulated by means of a tooth and socket arrangement that forms a hinge. The presence or absence of this fundamental apparatus is used as the basis for the primary subdivisions of the brachiopods, into the two classes of Inarticulata and Articulata. In the Inarticulata, the valves are held together by muscles alone. In the Articulata, the hinge is composed on the ventral valve, of two teeth aligned symmetrically on each side beneath the beak, and on the dorsal valve, of two small fossae, or sockets, into which the teeth fit. In both Articulata and Inarticulata brachiopods the movements of the two valves are controlled by adductor muscles that close the valves and di-

Nomenclature of a brachiopod; (A) internal anatomy; (B) dorsal view; (C) side view: (ant.) anterior margin; (post.) posterior margin; (mc) mantle cavity; (f) foramen; (l) lophophore; (hl) hinge line; (m) mantle; (p) pedicle; (u) umbo; (s) sinus; (vs) visceral sac; (dv) dorsal valve; (vv) ventral valve.

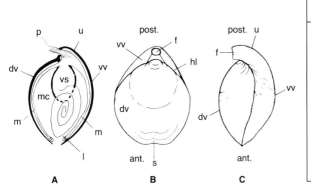

Phylum	Class	Order	Age
Brachiopoda	*Inarticulata*	*Lingulida* *Acrotretida* *Obolellida* *Paterinida*	Cambrian–Recent Cambrian–Recent Cambrian Cambrian–Ordovician
	Articulata	*Orthida* *Strophomenida* *Pentamerida* *Rhynchonellida* *Spiriferida* *Terebratulida*	Cambrian–Permian Ordovician–Jurassic Cambrian–Devonian Ordovician–Recent Ordovician–Jurassic Devonian–Recent

ductor muscles that open them. There are also pedicle muscles that move the pedicle with which the animal attaches itself to the substrate, thus allowing the organism a small degree of movement. All these muscles leave on the inside of the valves, at the point where they are inserted, muscular scars that remain visible even in fossils and that are sometimes used as distinguishing characteristics of a particular species or genus. In some forms the muscles are fixed to a spatula-shaped apparatus called the spondylium.

Brachiopods are exclusively marine animals that live attached to the sea bed, to various submerged objects, or to one another, or live imbedded in sediment, sometimes in compact groups of many individuals. In most cases, they attach themselves by means of the pedicle, which comes out of the shell through a special hole in the ventral valve, called the foramen, the size of which varies in different groups, making it a useful distinguishing characteristic. However, it has been found that in certain fossil forms the brachiopods attached themselves to the bottom in different ways: Some fixed themselves with the entire ventral valve and others used long spines located along the entire surface of the shell, or along the rear edge.

Today, brachiopods live in all the seas, but show a clear preference for those that are warm and for bottoms at depths between a few meters and 200 m. (660 ft.). Rare forms have been dredged up from 5,000 to 6,000 m. (16,500–19,800 ft.) of depth and thus show the powerful adaptability of the group. This adaptability is also demonstrated by the fossil forms, which were more abundant than modern-day forms and which have been found in deposits formed in very different environments.

Especially interesting in this sense is the existence, during the Permian, about 270 million years ago, of a few genera adapted to ancient reef environments. These brachiopods have a notable modification of the shell, with the elongation of one valve, which becomes conical, and the reduction of the opposite valve, which is transformed into a lid. These thus assume, through the phenomenon of evolutionary convergence, structures similar to those of certain coelenterates and to the ruddists, bivalves whose presence is characteristic of reefs of the Cretaceous.

The brachiopods today number about 260 species. They were much more abundant in the past, particularly the Paleozoic, when their several thousand species formed an important part of the world's marine fauna. Their abundant remains are used by paleontologists as index fossils for many geological periods, and furnish, with their many species and wide distribution area, an excellent material for correlating rocks of the same age over great distances.

An excellent index fossil for Paleozoic rocks, for example, is the genus *Paraspirifer*, of the class Articulata and the order Spiriferida, characteristic of the Devonian, which has a shell formed of convex valves with a straight and extremely elongated rear edge, ornamented by radial ribs. An index fossil for the Devonian and the Permian is the genus *Productus*, a brachiopod of the Articulata of the order Strophomenida, with a wide distribution area. Its shell is plano-convex, and its ventral valve has a much developed beak and is thickened and enlongated in correspondence to the cardinal area, where it forms two lateral ears. The two valves are ornamented with radial ribs and concentric lamellae. On the ventral valve are well developed spines with which, lacking a pedicle, the animal attached itself to the bottom. The genus *Productus* has furnished a large number of index fossils for different geological periods. Among these is *Productus giganteus*, which, with its 30 cm. (12 in.) of length, is without doubt the largest brachiopod ever to exist.

The genus *Uncites* was adapted to life on reefs during the Devonian period. An Articulata of the order Spiriferida, a widespread brachiopod with a very large shell that was biconvex, oval, ornamented by concentric growth lamellae and radial ribs, and whose ventral valve, much more developed than the dorsal, had a large hooklike beak.

The brachiopods are one of the oldest groups of invertebrates. In Precambrian strata in Montana was found what might be considered the oldest known brachiopod, an ovoid valve attributed, with some uncertainty, to the genus *Lingulella*, of 800 million years ago.

The Inarticulata were already well developed during the Early Cambrian with genera that have remained unchanged up to our own time—over a period of 570 million years. During the same period the first Articulata appeared, and these underwent great diversification, most of all during the Silurian, with roughly 300 species. For all the Paleozoic the brachiopods flourished; their decline began in the Permian and continued through the Mesozoic and Cenozoic, an era when the brachiopods progressively diminished, finally reaching the reduced state in which they find themselves today.

Deposits rich in brachiopods are found throughout the world.

(1) *Paraspirifer* sp., brachiopod of the order Spiriferida; Devonian, Ohio.
(2) *Pygites diphyoides,* brachiopod of the order Terebratulida; Late Jurassic, Alps.
(3) *Tetractinella trigonella,* spiriferid brachiopod of the Late Triassic, Italy.

(4) *Productus cora,* brachiopod of the order Strophomenida; Carboniferous of Carinthia, Austria-Yugoslavia.
(5) *Prionorhynchia quinqueplicata,* brachiopod of the order Rhynchonellida; Early Jurassic, Italy.

Below left: Disciniscia calymene, *brachiopod of the class Inarticulata; Triassic, Italy.*
Below right: Lingula cuneata, *one of the best-known inarticulate brachiopods; Silurian, New York*

They are abundant in Paleozoic rocks, for which they are often used as index fossils. An example is the genus *Composita*, Articulata of the order Spiriferida, with a small biconvex shell with an oval form. This genus is relatively abundant in Carboniferous rocks in the United States, where the species *Composita subtilita* is characteristic of the early part of that period.

The interesting Pygope, an Articulata of the order Terebratulida, is another characteristic fossil. It had a central hole formed by the fast growth of the lateral parts on the frontal margin of the shell joined on the median line. This genus is characteristic of Jurassic and Cretaceous rocks and has furnished numerous index species for other deposits of those periods, which are the *Pygope triangulus* of Jurassic rocks and the species *Pygites diphyoides*, both found in abundance in the caves of red and yellow marble of Verona.

The phylum of brachiopods is divided, based on the presence or absence of the hinge, into the two classes Articulata and Inarticulata, each of which includes in turn numerous orders, described below.

Class Inarticulata

The Inarticulata are brachiopods with chitinous or calcareous shells without a hinge, in which the valves are held together by muscles. The pedicle, when present, exits either from between valves or through a hole in the ventral valve. There is no brachial apparatus. The Inarticulata are the oldest and most primitive forms, are known from Precambrian rocks and are still alive today. They include the orders Lingulida, Arcotretida, Obolellida and Paterinida.

The members of the order Lingulida are brachiopods with chitinous or, rarely, calcareous shells that are biconvex, smooth or ornamented by slight concentric growth lines with a beaklike umbo on both valves. The pedicle exits through the line of separation between the two valves at the posterior edge. They are known from the Early Cambrian and are still found in today's seas.

The best-known genus is *Lingula*, which has a subrectangular shell, thin and elongated, and a long pedicle that exits from the pointed posterior edge. Very abundant in the Ordovician and Silurian, the genus has remained unchanged for almost 500 million years, right up to the present time.

The Arcotretida are brachiopods with a generally circular or sometimes conical chitinous or calcareous shell that is smooth or ornamented by concentric grooves, of varying depth. They have a pedicle opening on the ventral valve near the edge in the more evolved forms and in the center in those more specialized. The order is known from the Early Cambrian and it still numbers several members. The order Obolellida includes a few genera that lived only in the Cambrian and became extinct around the middle of that period. They had a calcareous, biconvex shell, subcircular or oval, with a long pedicle that exited between the two valves or from an opening whose position was very variable.

Class Articulata

The Articulata are brachiopods with a calcareous shell that has a hinge apparatus formed of teeth and sockets. There is always a brachial structure, although its shape varies. The pedicle emerges through an opening that usually involves only the ventral valve. The Articulata seem to have evolved from inarticulata brachiopods and to have become different from them slowly, with progressive modifications that, taken together, justify the distinction of the two classes. In fact, the differences between the oldest Articulata and the Inarticulata are not as marked as those between living representatives of the two classes.

The Articulata are subdivided into six orders: Orthida, Strophomenida, Pentamerida, Rhynchonellida, Spiriferida and Terebratulida.

The members of the order Orthida are characterized by a rounded or subrectangular shell, biconvex or plano-convex, with a long, straight hinge line and triangular cardinal area on both valves. The brachidium is reduced to the state of a pair of crural processes. They are known only from the Paleozoic but lived from the Early Cambrian all the way to the Late Permian.

The genus *Orthis*, which typifies this order and gives it its name, lived during the Ordovician. It had a shell with a long, straight hinge line that was squarish or almost oval, plano-convex, crossed on both valves by high ribs that spread from the beak and that give it the appearance of a scallop.

The Strophomenida are the largest order among the brachiopods, with about 400 genera that lived from the Early Ordovician to the Early Jurassic. They come in an enormous variety of forms, from those with a typical concave-convex shell to roughly semicircular forms, from those strongly modified for attachment in reefs to those that developed a spiny projection to affix themselves without the use of a pedicle. All the members of the order have a well developed hinge and an opening for the pedicle at the beak of the umbo, while they lack the spondylium and the muscles instead are anchored directly to the internal walls of the valves.

The genus *Gemmellaroia* presents an instance of the modification of a shell owing to a particular environment. This is a genus found in Permian reefs in Russia and Sicily. Its form is remarkably analogous to that of Cretaceous bivalves of the ruddist group, which millions of years later populated the same kind of marine environment. In Gemmellaroia the ventral valve has become an elongated or irregular cone that affixes itself with a form of cementation, while the dorsal valve has been transformed into an almost circular operculum or lid. The shell is thick and strong and has three layers that correspond to those of all the brachiopods. Also important is the genus *Productus*, an excellent index fossil that appeared in the Late Devonian.

The Pentamerida include brachiopods that lived from the Middle Cambrian to the Late Devonian. They were characterized by a biconvex shell with a crura and a spondylium. The most common genus is *Pentamerus*, an index species to the Silurian, which has a biconvex shell in an ovoid form that is smooth or ornamented on both valves by thin, subtle, radial ribs. The Rhynchonellida includes numerous brachiopods known since the Middle Ordovician, about 500 million years ago, some of which still exist. Their shells have rounded valves with a large sulcus on the ventral valve and a corresponding fold on the opposite valve. The posterior margin is curved, and the lophophore is supported by well developed crural processes. At one time 600 different forms were classified in the genus *Rhynchonella*; today, this name is reserved only for certain species of the Late Jurassic.

The genus *Rhynchonella* in the strict sense has a smooth, triangular shell with a high dorsal fold and a deep ventral sulcus, although it is pointed and curved. In this sense, the Rhynchonella would include only the form just described, but we must add that members of this large order of brachiopods have most often a globular, ovoid, or triangular shell ornamented with high radial ribs that lead to a zigzag anterior margin; and the deep ventral sulcus and the corresponding fold of the dorsal valve are marked on the line of contact of the valves by a pronounced curve in the same line.

The Spiriferida are articulate brachiopods that lived from the Middle Ordovician to the Jurassic. Their principal characteristic is the presence inside the valves of a spiraled brachidium that in the living animal supported a lophophore of the same form. Spirifer, which has given its name to the entire order, has a very characteristic form because of the long, straight posterior margin; the clear radial ribs; the well developed beak on both valves; and the presence on the ventral valve of a large sulcus. The Spirifer lived during the Carboniferous and is found in abundance in all the marine rocks of that period.

The Terebratulida includes very old forms, dating from the Early Devonian, together with genera still existing, including the *Gryphus* and *Argyrotheca*, very widespread in the Mediterranean, and *Magellania*, exclusive to the Pacific Ocean. All the members of this group are characterized by a brachidium in the shape of a ribbon. Many genera and species have become excellent index fossils, found in abundance in marine rocks throughout the world. Among the major genera is the *Terebratula*, characteristic most of all of the Miocene and the Pliocene.

BRACHIOPOD PLATES

PLATE III
(1) *Terebratula ampulla*, Pliocene, lower Apennines; (2) *Dictyothyris coarctata*, Middle Jurassic, France; (3) *Lobothyris vitrea*, Early Jurassic, Italy; (4) *Terebratula* sp., Pliocene, Italy; (5) *Roulleria* sp., Late Jurassic, France; (6) *Terebratula* sp., Quaternary, Italy; (7) *Triangope* sp., Late Jurassic, Apennines; (8) *Gleneothyris harlani*, Eocene, New Jersey; (9) *Roulleria* sp., Jurassic, Switzerland; (10) *Triangope* sp., Late Jurassic, Alps; (11) *Terebratula* sp., Miocene, Italy; (12) *Triangope triangulus*, Middle Jurassic, Italy; (13) *Pygope diphya*, Late Jurassic, Alps.

PLATE IV
Brachiopods of the Jurassic of Gozzano, Piedmont, Italy
(1) *Prionorhynchia serrata*; (2) *Prionorhynchia flabellum*; (3) *Spiriferina angulata*; (4) *Cirpa fronto*; (5) *Spiriferina obtusa*; (6) *Terebratula gozzanensis*; (7) *Pseudogibbirhynchia sordelli*; (8) *Quadratirhynchia quadrata*; (9) *Gibbirhynchia crassimedia*; (10) *Tetrarhynchia dumbletonensis*; (11) *Prionorhynchia aff. latifrons*; (12) *Prionorhynchia undata*; (13) *Quadratirhynchia quadrata*; (14) *Stolmorhynchia bulga*; (15) *Cirpa langi*; (16) *Spiriferina rostrata*; (17) *Prionorhynchia quinqueplicata*.

PLATE III

PLATE IV

PLATE V

PLATE VI

PLATE VII

PLATE VIII

PLATE IX

PLATE X

Worms and Other Problematic Fossils

The animals we commonly call worms are extremely varied in their anatomic organization. These animals do not constitute a homogeneous taxonomic category. Under the very general name "worms" are united organisms that belong in reality to very different groups, to independent phyla that are sometimes very distant from one another on the phylogenetic scale.

Speaking of worms in paleontology would seem a kind of absurdity since these animals, almost more than all the others, call to mind soft bodies without any hard parts and thus very hard to preserve. Yet worms are not rare in the fossil record. They are usually found in the form of impressions without much anatomic detail, the traces of their movement across the ground, or through the sediment they inhabit. Naturally, such traces furnish little information on the appearance of an animal. For this reason paleontologists sometimes tend to forget the existence of the precise classification system that concerns these organisms and to limit themselves to using the fossil traces for paleoecological reconstructions.

However, worms are not known only from traces left in sediment. In certain deposits, such as the Cambrian Burgess Shale in British Columbia, the Carboniferous Mazon Creek in Illi-

Above: *Errant polychaete. Carboniferous of Mazon Creek, Illinois.*
Below left: *Impression of a sediment-feeding worm. Tertiary limestone of the Apennines.*
Below right: Ottoia prolifica, *Siphunculoida of the Cambrian from Burgess Shale, British Columbia.*
Bottom right: Epitrachys rugosus, *Siphunculoida of the Jurassic, from Solnhofen, Germany.*

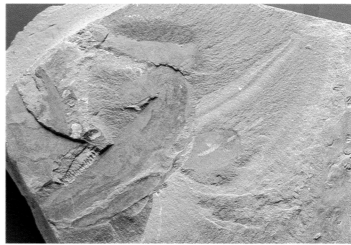

Phylum	Class	Order	Age
Nemerta Nematomorpha Nematoida Chaetognatha			Jurassic–Recent Eocene–Recent Oligocene–Recent Cambrian–Recent
Annelida	Polychaeta	Errantida Sedentarida Miskoiida	Ordovician–Recent Cambrian–Recent Cambrian–Ordovician
	Myzostomia Oligochaeta		Ordovician–Recent Carboniferous–Recent
Sipunculoida			Cambrian–Recent

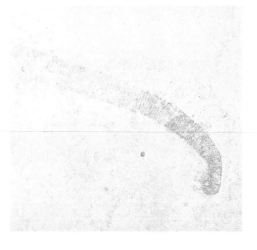

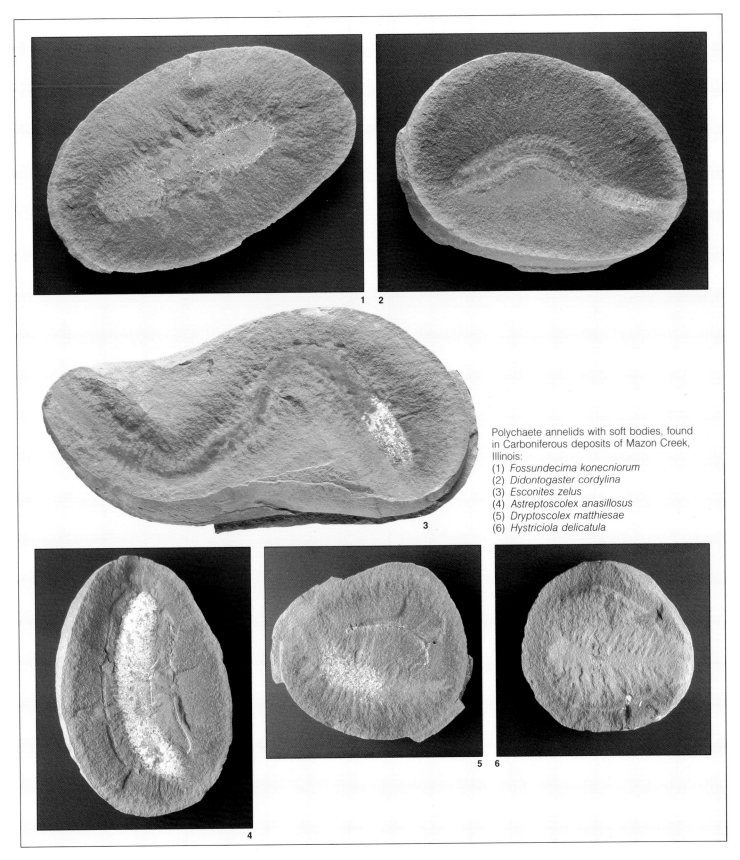

Polychaete annelids with soft bodies, found in Carboniferous deposits of Mazon Creek, Illinois:
(1) *Fossundecima konecniorum*
(2) *Didontogaster cordylina*
(3) *Esconites zelus*
(4) *Astreptoscolex anasillosus*
(5) *Dryptoscolex matthiesae*
(6) *Hystriciola delicatula*

Two rare Carboniferous forms from Mazon Creek, Illinois: Coprinoscolex ellogimus *of the phylum Echiura (below) and* Archisymplectes rhothon *of the phylum Nemertina (bottom).*

nois, the Jurassic deposits of Osteno in Italy's Lombardy, those of Solnhofen in Germany, the Cretaceous in Lebanon and the Eocene in Monte Bolca, have been found worms from various groups, with their soft bodies nicely preserved. All of these fossil specimens of soft bodies, as well as the impressions mentioned above, can be attributed to at least six different phyla.

Some of these number few fossil representatives, such as the Nemerta, the Nematomorpha and the Nematoida, known most of all from the Jurassic and the Tertiary. Others are well represented, such as the Annelida; still others are represented only by a few curious genera, as is the case with the Chaetognatha and the Sipunculoida.

Phylum Annelida

Of all the fossil worms, those that are most interesting because of their abundance in sediments are without doubt the annelids, which have, in fact, left signs of their existence in rocks of all the ages from the Cambrian to today, which is to say for a period of time that has lasted at least 570 million years. The annelids are subdivided into various classes. We will treat here only of the class Polychaeta, which appeared during the Cambrian and is in turn subdivided into the Errantia, or errant polychaetes, a group with few fossil representatives, and the Sedentaria, or sendentary polychaetes, which was much more

widespread; and the order Miskoiida, which embraces some of the strangest invertebrates known.

The errant polychaetes are soft-bodied worms known in the fossil record since the Ordovician, most of all because their mouth parts, called scolecodonts, are often found scattered in sediment. Complete examples of this group are rare. A few come from the Carboniferous deposits of Mazon Creek, others have been found recently in Jurassic deposits of Osteno (genus *Melanoraphia*), others come from the Eocene deposits of Monte Bolca (genera *Eunicites* and *Sthenelaites*), others have been found in the Jurassic deposits of Solnhofen (genus *Eunicites*) and yet others come from the Cretaceous deposits in Lebanon.

The remains of sedentary polychaetes are far more abundant. These have left important traces of their existence in the form of tubes, most often calcareous, or of burrows in the sea bottom that were used as homes. The errant polychaetes include the genera *Dickinsonia* and *Spriggina* from the Precambrian, found in South Australia's Ediacara Hills.

The sedentary polychaetes, abundant today, are known from the Cambrian. The oldest representatives, which lived 570 million years ago, are not much different from today's forms.

Among the best known is the genus *Serpula*, which has lived from the Silurian to today. This animal builds a calcareous tube, irregularly winding or almost straight, that it cements to any rigid object, such as a submerged rock, the shell of a mollusk, or another animal with a hard body. The genus *Hicetes* also builds a small tube, of variable width and form, which it attaches to the top of the coral *Pleurodictyum problematicum*, with which it lived in symbiosis during the Devonian.

The order Miskoiida includes a few genera found in Cambrian deposits and in Canada's famous Burgess Shales. Thanks to the condition of the fossils that characterize this well known deposit it has been possible to study the characteristics of these marine organisms in detail.

Phylum Nematoida

The nematoids are truly rare in the fossil record. They are, in fact, soft-body organisms that are rarely preserved. The organisms that can be attributed to this group come only from those deposits in which the soft parts of animals have been preserved (what can be called "total preservation").

Examples of complete nematoids have been found in the Carboniferous deposits of Mazon Creek and in Montana, and nematoid parasites have been found in a Carboniferous scorpion in Scotland and in insects preserved in amber from the Oligocene in the Baltic area. Also found in such amber are individual nematoids. In 1983 a new genus of nematoid (*Eophasma*) was discovered in Sinemurian deposits in Osteno in Lombardy.

Phylum Chaetognatha

The phylum Chaetognatha today includes no more than 30 marine genera that are an important part of the constitution of plankton. These are in fact worms adapted to swimming that have developed "fins." The oldest fossil representative of this group is the genus *Amiskwia* from the Cambrian, found in Bur-

(1,2) Two specimens of the polychaete *Eunicites* sp.; Cretaceous, Lebanon.
(3) *Melanoraphia maculata,* a polychaete annelid of Jurassic deposits from Osteno, Italy.
(4) Errant polychaete found in Jurassic deposits, Solnhofen, Germany.
(5) Tubular homes of the polychaete annelid Serpula; Early Jurassic, Germany.

(6) Annelid Hicetes on the coral *Pleurodictyum problematicum,* an ancient example of symbiosis; Early Devonian, Germany.
(7) Three specimens of Serpula; Eocene, Italy.
(8) Tubular homes of Serpula perfectly fossilized in a Mesozoic sediment.

gess Shale. It displays a great affinity with the modern-day Chaetognatha and seems to indicate that this group had already reached the evolutionary stage it still displays. Fossil Chaetognatha have also been found in the Carboniferous deposits of Mazon Creek.

Phylum Platyhelminthes

The Platyhelminthes, which today includes the flatworms, such as the planarians, and many parasitic worms, constitutes a poorly represented phylum for paleontology. In fact, until just recently these worms were unknown in the fossil record, but then tiny impressions were found in a layer of fine clay from the Early Permian in Val Brembana (the Collio Formation), and paleontologists recognized these to be trails left by the movement of a terrestrial planarian worm.

Traces of Movement and Habitation

In rocks, tracks are often found that paleontologists believe have been made by the movement of worms of one kind or another or on the surface of sediment. These traces are very widespread in certain sedimentary formations, but they are hard to classify. It is difficult to attribute a certain impression to a

Below left: Eophasma jurasicum, *a nematode found in Jurassic deposits at Osteno, Italy.*
Below center: *Reconstruction of the Cambrian Chaetognatha* Amiskwia sagittiformis. *The original was found in the Burgess Shale, British Columbia.*

Below right: Dictyodora liebeana, *probably the track of worms. Ordovician, from Thuringia, Germany.*
Bottom left: *Chondrites (smaller traces) and Fucoides (larger traces) on a Cretaceous rock from the Alpine foothills of Lombardy, Italy.*
Bottom right: Helminthoida labirintica, *on a Tertiary rock from an unknown area.*

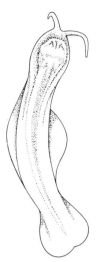
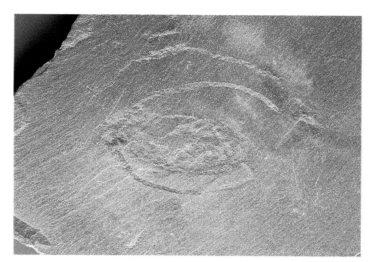

certain organism, so much so that it is often difficult to be sure whether a particular impression was left by a worm or by some other burrowing invertebrate animal.

The traces most often found in sedimentary rocks are those considered generally to be tracks or trails of movement. Because of their characteristic branching shapes these traces have sometimes been erroneously interpreted as impressions of plant remains.

Chondrites are impressions probably left by marine burrowing worms. They have a branching form and represent the refilling of the small burrows dug by the animal in mud. These have been found in fine-grain marine deposits. Fucoides are structures formed by the refilling of branching plant-shaped tubes, very similar to the chondrites and also the result of the movement of worms or echinoids. The helminthoida are made of many equidistant furrows, about 2 mm. (.08 in.) thick, sometimes arranged concentrically. According to certain au-

thors these were formed by sediment feeding worms, according to others they are trails formed by gastropods without shells and thus not preserved in the fossil record. Once held to be of inorganic origin, Zoophycos, which have a strange plantlike shape and are often found in marine sediment, have recently been discovered to be made by sedentary annelids of the family Sabellidae.

Conodonts

Similar to scolecodonts—the mouth parts of errant polychaetes—are the conodonts, microfossils a few millimeters in length believed to be formed of jaw parts and common in rock deposits from the Ordovician to the Triassic. Conodonts differ from scolecodonts in that they are made of calcium phosphate, while scolecodonts are chitinous-siliceous. Unlike Scolecodonts, conodonts have taken on considerable importance among microfossils because of their wide distribution, their abun-

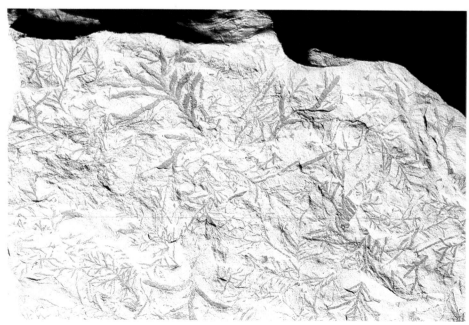
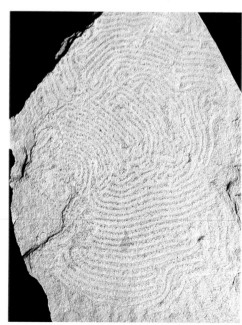

Below right: *Greatly enlarged reconstruction of two conodonts.*
Below center: *Most probably a Siphunculoida of the Ordovician from North America.*

Bottom left: Tullymonstrum gregarium, *a strange organism found at Mazon Creek, Illinois.*
Bottom right: *Reconstruction of the* Tullymonstrum gregarium.

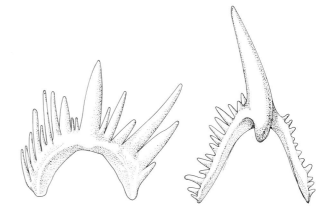

dance and their use in the determination of the relative age of rock strata.

Attributing these fossils to worms is difficult. Conodonts have, in fact, been attributed at times to mollusks because of the similarity they share with the radulae of mollusks; at times to arthropods (for example, the jaws of crustaceans or parts of exoskeletons); and at times to hard parts of primitive vertebrates, of fish or even of soft-bodied animals not yet known in their totality. A great deal about these fossils is still unknown.

Tullymonstrum Gregarium

There are numerous fossil organisms to which paleontologists cannot yet give acceptable or convincing interpretations. Among these is *Tullymonstrum gregarium,* found in thousands of nodules in the Carboniferous deposits of Mazon Creek, in Illinois.

This is a soft-bodied animal about 8 to 34 cm. (3.2–13.6 in.) long, with an elongated body and a segmented trunk, a head with a long proboscus and small jaws. Between the head and the trunk is a very strange transverse bar that some scientists believe bore eyes on its ends. The tail has fins.

The Tullymonstrum is probably a marine organism that cannot be assigned to any known animal phylum. Perhaps it is nothing but the last Carboniferous representative of a group evolved in the Early Paleozoic of which no examples have been found because it is not easily fossilized.

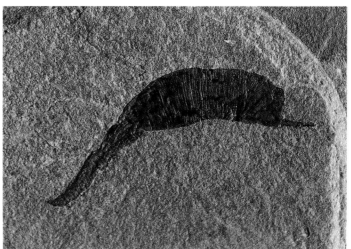

Arthropods

The phylum Arthropoda embraces an extremely large and varied group of invertebrates whose history began quite early in time, probably during the late Precambrian. The sizes of the members of this phylum vary widely, running from the microscopic to such giants as certain eurypterids, sometimes almost two meters (6.6 ft.) in length.

The arthropods are relatively common in sedimentary rocks of all geological ages, from the Cambrian to today. Some, such as the trilobites and ostracods, are found in such abundance that they are used as index fossils for numerous geologic periods. Others, such as the malacostracans and insects, have delicate structures that can be preserved only under special conditions, making them rare in the fossil form.

Arthropods are animals with a chitinous or chitinous-phosphatic external skeleton that is segmented, articulated and formed of three principal parts: the head, the thorax and the abdomen. Each of these parts is in turn formed of a certain number of segments, sometimes so tightly joined as to be no longer identifiable, each with a pair of jointed appendages. These appendages, all very similar in primitive arthropods, are differentiated in more advanced types according to the part of the body in which they are found and the functions they perform. There are thus cephalic appendices (those in the region of the head) differentiated in antennae, mandibles, and jaws; thoracic appendages (in the forward part of the body) that serve in ambulation and in movement; and abdominal appendages used for respiration and swimming.

Leaving aside internal anatomy, which is only rarely visible in fossil specimens, we can see immediately that arthropods were originally exclusively marine animals and that only later did some of them adapt to life on land while others adapted to flight.

The oldest fossil remains attributed to arthropods come from Precambrian rocks and indicate for this animal phylum a long

Far left: *Many fossil arthropods are difficult to interpret. Some believe* Phalangites priscus, *found in deposits at Solnhofen, is the larval form of a decapod crustacean; others believe it an adult pantopod.*
Left: Cyclus americanus, *Carboniferous, Mazon Creek, Illinois.*

Phylum	Subphylum	Superclass	Class	Age
Arthropoda	Protarthropoda	Onychophora		Precambrian–Recent
	Euarthropoda	Trilobitomorpha	Trilobitoidea Trilobita	Cambrian–Devonian Cambrian–Permian
		Chelicerata	Merostomata Aracnida	Cambrian–Recent Silurian–Recent
		Crustacea Myriapoda Hexapoda (Insecta)		Cambrian–Recent Devonian–Recent Devonian–Recent
		Pycnogonida		Devonian–Recent

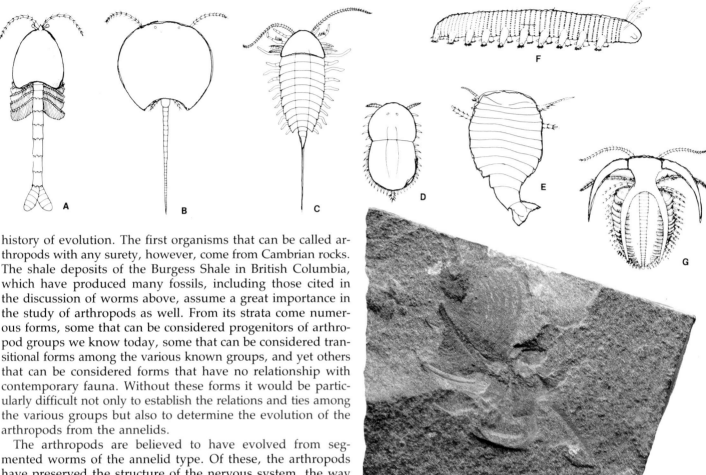

history of evolution. The first organisms that can be called arthropods with any surety, however, come from Cambrian rocks. The shale deposits of the Burgess Shale in British Columbia, which have produced many fossils, including those cited in the discussion of worms above, assume a great importance in the study of arthropods as well. From its strata come numerous forms, some that can be considered progenitors of arthropod groups we know today, some that can be considered transitional forms among the various known groups, and yet others that can be considered forms that have no relationship with contemporary fauna. Without these forms it would be particularly difficult not only to establish the relations and ties among the various groups but also to determine the evolution of the arthropods from the annelids.

The arthropods are believed to have evolved from segmented worms of the annelid type. Of these, the arthropods have preserved the structure of the nervous system, the way of growing in segments, and the characteristic elongated body form, but they have developed in addition an external skeleton that has made them lose the flexibility and an ability to contract the body that are typical of their progenitors.

Before looking at the interesting primitive arthropods it is necessary to establish that the phylum of the arthropods is divided into two principal groups: the Proarthropoda, which includes among others the onychophorans (Onychophora), known only as fossils; and the Euarthropoda, including trilobites (Trilobitomorpha), chelicerates (Chelicerata), crustaceans (Crustacea), pycnogonids (Pycnogonida), myriapods (Myriapoda), hexapods (Hexapoda) and certain other groups of little interest from the paleontological point of view.

Superclass Onychophora

In the Cambrian strata of the Burgess Shale was found the genus *Aysheaia*, attributed to the onychophorans, of which it is considered the oldest representative. It is also held to be one of the most primitive known arthropods. Not all scientists are in agreement on the taxonomic position of the onychophorans. They are considered a separate phylum or are attributed to the Protarthropoda, a primitive group with few fossil representatives. Their many-legged bodies are reminiscent of those of an annelid because of the marked segmentation and the

undifferentiated head. The head does have, however, a pair of short antennae, small eyes and a mouth with two lateral jaws. Aysheaia was a marine animal, unlike modern onychophorans, which live in the underbrush of tropical regions.

Superclass Trilobitomorpha

The Trilobitomorpha are the oldest of the Euarthropoda. They include two entire classes of primitive organisms that became extinct before the end of the Paleozoic and that we know only from fossil remains.

Class Trilobitoidea

For those who today study Paleozoic arthropods, the Trilobitoidea is not a true homogenous group, but rather a convenient class instituted to unite certain extremely diverse arthropods. The class is maintained here because the classification of these forms is far too complicated to be explained in just a few pages.

In this group, then, are united many Cambrian organisms that possessed certain morphologic characteristics that lead to their being considered progenitors of various groups of arthro-

Below: *This trilobite from the Devonian of Bundenbach clearly shows the longitudinal trilobation of the body.*
Center: *Nomenclature of trilobites: (A) dorsal side; (B) ventral side; (a) antenna; (en) endopodite; (ex) exopodite; (g) glabella; (frc) free cheek; (fc) fixed cheek; (ce) composite eye; (p) pleura; (ax) axis; (fs) facial suture.*

pods, groups that we will find well developed in later periods of the history of the earth.

Among these arthropods, for example, are the Merostomoidea, which include the genera *Sidneyia, Naraoia* and *Emeraldella.* They are considered by some paleontologists the progenitors of the merostomes, a group that developed in the Upper Silurian, because of the presence of a three-lobed dorsal shield that partially covered the body, their very primitive appendages, and a thin, elongated tail. The genus *Sidneyia,* in fact, resembles greatly the merostome eurypterids, while Naraoia is reminiscent of the Xiphosura, well known to us from their modern-day representatives, the horseshoe crabs.

The Pseudonotostraca, also called pseudocrustaceans, resemble the crustaceans, with which they were sometimes classified. Among these are the genera *Burgessia,* 10 mm. (0.4 in.) long, with a circular carapace, and *Waptia,* which resemble brachiopods, with which they might be classified if they did not have primitive appendages.

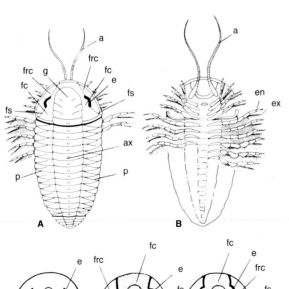

Finally, the Marrellomorpha, which include the genus *Marrella,* have a structure so unusual and strange that they cannot be placed in any known group.

Class Trilobita

The class Trilobita includes the well-known trilobites, marine arthropods that lived exclusively during the Paleozoic.

The name of these animals is derived from the appearance of their body, which is divided longitudinally into three regions. Longitudinally are visible a central part, axial lobe, and two lateral parts called pleural lobes. Transversely, the three parts include a cephalon (head), on which are found the compound, kidney-shaped eyes, a central swelling (glabella), and a line of minor resistance called the facial suture. Along that suture, which seems to divide the central part of the fixed shield from the mobile side parts, are based some of the most important systematic divisions. Behind the cephalon is the thorax, composed of from two to 22 articulated segments. The third lobe, located at the posterior end of the body, is the pygidium (tail), the result of the union of a certain number of segments that sometimes end in a long spine.

On the ventral, or lower, surface of the animal are sometimes numerous appendages of a primitive nature, compared to those of other arthropods. Each segment of the trilobite has two appendages that, with the exception of the first pair, which have been transformed into antennae, are all equal, undifferentiated, and formed each of a basic piece (protopodite), which bears an endopodite formed of various articulations, and a fringed exopodite—the first used perhaps for swimming, the second for movement. The cephalon, derived from the fusion of five segments no longer distinguishable, bears five pairs of appendages.

The trilobites appeared, already well evolved, in the Cambrian. Their structure was already perfected and indicates an evolutionary history that must go back to the Early Proterozoic era. The trilobites multiplied in the next periods, the Ordovician and Silurian, becoming much more abundant and assuming the ability to roll themselves up, as is demonstrated by many remains found in this defensive position. The trilobites began their decline during the Devonian. Only two families remained during the Carboniferous, and these disappeared at the end of the Permian, after a history that had lasted 340 million years.

Trilobites are found in marine deposits formed in various environments, indicating that these animals were adapted to differing environmental conditions. The flattened body would seem, however, to indicate for most of the types a benthic, or bottom-dwelling, existence. They are believed to have lived on the sea floor, where they could partially bury themselves, like

Left: *The facial suture on the cephalon of trilobites divides the central fixed zone from the two lateral mobile zones: (1) cephalon of the primitive type without facial suture (ipoparia); (2) cephalon with opistoparia suture, in which the lateral spines are included in the free cheek; (3) cephalon with proparia suture, in which the lateral spines are included in the fixed cheek; (fc) fixed cheek; (frc) free cheek; (e) eye; (fs) facial suture.*

Below, left to right: Ellipsocephalus hoffi, *Cambrian, Bohemia;* Para-doxides *sp.;* Olenellus clarki, *Cambrian, Nevada.*

modern-day horseshoe crabs. Others seem adapted to a nek-tonic (free-swimming) and epiplanktonic life; among these are come with giant eyes and an enlarged glabella that could have served as a flotation organ. Deposits rich with trilobites exist in Scandinavia, England, Russia, Bohemia and North Africa, all areas where Paleozoic outcroppings cover large areas, and are common in Early Paleozoic rocks throughout North America.

The class of the trilobites is divided into various orders, each with numerous minor groups. The Agnostida, probably the most primitive trilobites, lived from the Early Cambrian to the Ordovician. They had a highly developed and almost identical cephalon and pygidium, and only two or three segments in the thorax. The Redlichiida, from the lower and middle Cambrian, are characterized by well developed lateral spines (genal spines) and by an opisthoparian facial suture, a facial suture that passed behind the genal spines, which were thus included in the detachable part of the cephalon.

Also with an opisthoparian facial suture was the genus *Corynexochida*, with a generally subelliptic form and a semicircular cephalon. Very characteristic of the Postcambrian trilobites are the Phacopida, which had proparian sutures, in which the genal spines are included in the fixed part of the cephalon. Representatives of this genus are often found curled up. The Ptych-

Far left: *Track made by movement of a trilobite; Cambrian, Indiana.*
Left: Triplagnostus burgessensis, *Cambrian from Burgess Shale, British Columbia.*
Above: Phacops rana *curled up; Devonian, Ohio.*

opariida are trilobites with an opisthoparian suture, an oval and elongated exoskeleton with 12 to 17 segments in the thorax. Very widespread in the Cambrian and the Ordovician, they lived through the entire Paleozoic up until the Permian, when the two surviving families, the Proetidae and Phillipsiidae, became extinct.

The Lichida is an order with few members. It includes trilobites that lived from the Early Ordovician to the Late Devonian that are characterized by a pygidium and cephalon in unique forms, the first often spiny, the second with a particularly large glabella.

The Odontopleurida, finally, lived from the middle Cambrian to the Late Devonian and include very characteristic forms that are easily recognized because of the presence on the cephalon, thorax and pygidium of very well developed long spines.

Superclass Chelicerata

Chelicerates are terrestrial and marine arthropods known since the Cambrian and grouped in the classes of Merostomata and Arachnida. The Merostomata are very abundant in the fossil state and are exclusively marine animals; the Arachnida, more scarce, are terrestrial with rare exceptions.

(1) *Olenoides serratus*, Cambrian, Monte Stephen, Canada.
(2) *Hemirhodon amplipyge*, Cambrian, Utah.
(3) *Hemirhodon amplipyge*, Cambrian, Utah.
(4) *Albertella helena*, Cambrian, Montana.
(5) *Zacanthoides typicalis*, Cambrian, Nevada.

(1) *Calymene tristani,* Lower Silurian, Spain.
(2) *Dalmanitina socialis,* Ordovician, Bohemia.
(3) *Greenops boothi,* Devonian, Ontario.
(4) *Greenops collitelus,* Devonian, New York.
(5) *Phacops ferdinandi,* Devonian, Germany.

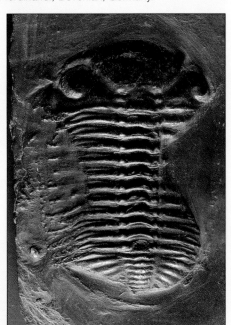

(6) *Homotelus bromidensis,* Ordovician, Oklahoma.
(7) *Dalmanites limulurus,* Silurian, New York.
(8) *Phacops corconspectans,* Devonian, Morocco.

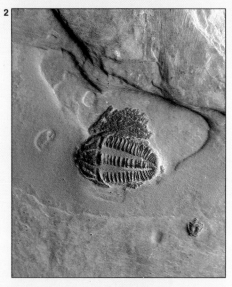

(7) *Pseudogygites latimarginatus,* Ordovician, Ontario.
(8) *Modocia typicalis,* Middle Cambrian, Utah.
(9) *Aulacopleura* sp., Silurian, Bohemia.
(10) *Homotelus bromidensis,* Ordovician, Oklahoma.
(11) *Asaphus expansus,* Ordovician, Sweden.

(1) *Lloydolithus ornatus,* Ordovician, England.
(2) *Bolaspidella housensis,* Cambrian, Utah.
(3) *Elrathia kingi,* Middle Cambrian, Utah.
(4) *Asaphiscus wheeleri,* Middle Cambrian, Utah.
(5) *Brachyaspidion microps,* Middle Cambrian, Utah.
(6) *Isotelus gigas,* Ordovician, Ontario.

Below: Eophrynus prestvici, *arachnid of the Pennsylvanian.*
Bottom: Eurypterus remipes, *Merostomata eurypterid; Silurian, New York.*

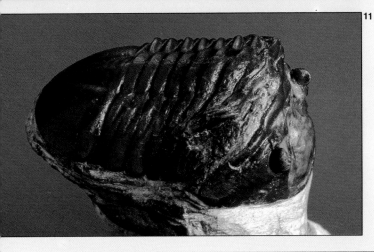

Class Arachnida

The paleontological importance of arachnids is due most of all to the fact that they include the first animal to inhabit dry land. This was the "scorpion" *Palaeophonus nuncius,* which, during the Late Silurian made its way onto still deserted continents.

Spiders are younger than scorpions and appear for the first time in strata of the Carboniferous, a period of lush vegetation in which they lived in great abundance in the immense tropical forests that eventually became the source of the deposits of coal. As we will see when discussing insects, many specimens of arachnids are preserved in amber, fossilized resin from ancient conifers, most of all from the Tertiary.

Class Merostomata

The members of the Merostomata are to us far stranger and more unusual than the arachnids. This class is divided into two subclasses, the Eurypterids and the Xiphosura.

The Eurypterids, also called giant water scorpions because of their often remarkable size, are animals that lived from the Silurian to the Permian. They had long bodies formed by a cephalic shield, with two lateral eyes and two subcentral ocelli, and six pairs of appendages; the first pair of these had chelae, the other pairs were walking legs or had paddles for swimming. The thorax was made of several segments, and the telson, or tail, was long and shaped like a spine or rounded.

(1) *Weinbergina opitzi*, Xiphosura of the Devonian, Bundenbach, Germany.
(2) Two specimens of *Mesolimulus walchii*, Upper Jurassic, Solnhofen, Germany.
(3–5) Primitive Xiphosura of the genera *Prestwichia* and *Belinurus* of the Carboniferous period.

The most famous genus was the *Pterygothus* of the Late Silurian and Devonian, which was about two meters (6.6 ft.) long. With its enormous length, this animal is the largest arthropod to ever exist. Decidedly smaller was the genus *Eurypterus,* which lived until the Carboniferous.

The Xiphosura are much more familiar to us because of the horseshoe crabs, which appeared during the Triassic, 200 to 220 million years ago. The horseshoe crab, a true living fossil, is found in seas of the Northern Hemisphere and the Indochinese peninsula. It is the only survivor of all its class.

Superclass Pycnogonida

The Pycnogonida are exclusively marine arthropods that seem to resemble the chelicerates, since the first pair of their appendages have chelae; but since they do not have a well differentiated abdomen (as with the spiders and scorpions), they have been put in a separate superclass. These are organisms known in the fossil record only from the genus *Palaeopantopus,* found in Devonian deposits in Bundenbach, Germany.

Below: *Rare Pycnogonida fossil,* Palaeopantopus maucheri; *Early Devonian, Bundenbach, Germany.*

Paleozoic ostracods:
(1) *Cythere phillipsiana*, Silurian, Sweden.
(2) *Cythere baltica*, Sweden.
(3) *Beyrichia clavigera*, Ordovician, Canada.
(4) *Leperditia canadensis*, Ordovician, Canada.

Superclass Crustacea

The crustaceans, together with the insects, or hexapods, are the most important living arthropods, since they are found in great abundance in the seas and in freshwater bodies on all continents, except Antarctica. The presence of a hard and thus often mineralized carapace has preserved them in the fossil record. Their evolutionary history, begun in the Cambrian, has continued to our day with very few changes.

The crustaceans include 10 classes (the last of which was instituted only in 1982): Cephalocarida, Branchiopoda, Mystacocarida, Ostracoda, Euthycarcinoidea, Copepoda, Branchiura, Cirripedia, Malacostraca and Thylacocephala.

Not all of these classes include abundant fossil representatives. From the paleontological point of view the most interesting are the Malacostraca, Cirripedia, Ostracoda and the Branchiopoda.

Class Ostracoda

The ostracods are crustaceans only a few millimeters long that are well preserved in the fossil record because they have a calcareous or chitinous bivalve shell.

Because of their abundance in many rocks of marine origin, and because of the great variety of known species, they are used as index fossils in dating rocks from the Paleozoic to today. Because of their small size, the methods used to gather and study these organisms are those used for foraminifers and conodonts.

Below: *Cirripedes (barnacles) of the genus* Balanus *encrusting a shell of* Flabellipecten; *Pliocene, Sicily.*
Below center: Ceratiocaris *sp., phyllocarid crustacean, Silurian, Scotland.*
Below bottom: Nahecaris *sp., phyllocarid crustacean; Devonian, Bundenbach, Germany.*

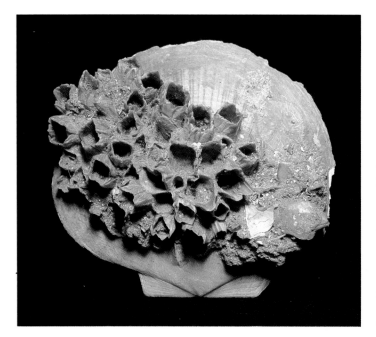

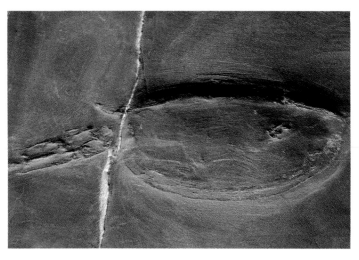

Class Cirripedia

The cirripeds are very particular crustaceans with bodies that in many groups are protected by a shell made of numerous calcareous or chitinous plates. These are essentially sessile or parasitic organisms that have undergone important modifications with respect to the classic arthropod form, with reduction of the sensory appendages, the eyes and the locomotive appendages. Although they have little use as index fossils, they are very useful in paleontology as ecological indicators: some of them, living attached to rocks or other organisms in coastal waters, indicate by their presence the nearness of the coastline.

Class Branchiopoda

The branchiopods are somewhat special crustaceans. They have, in fact, a strong bivalve carapace that in some forms takes on the appearance of a true shell that can be confused with the shell of bivalves. The branchiopods, known since the Devonian to today, fossilize well thanks to this very strong shell.

Class Malacostraca

Among the Malacostraca it is worth citing only the order of the decapods, which includes the most advanced members of the class. These well known animals include shrimp, lobster and crabs and are well preserved in the fossil record because of their tough carapace. The decapods of the Malacostraca are subdivided into macruri, with an elongated abdomen and caudal fin; the paguri, with a soft abdomen and thus rare as fossils; and brachiuri, with a reduced abdomen tucked up under the body.

Among the crabs, which appeared in the Jurassic, the genus *Marpatocarincus* from the Eocene is well known. Among the macruri, which appeared during the Triassic, about 200 million years ago, are the very interesting erionidei, excellent examples of which are found in Late Jurassic deposits at Solnhofen, Germany, a true mine of perfectly preserved fossil forms.

Fossil Malacostraca come from special deposits, those in which the fossils have been well preserved with a certain ease. In general, among these deposits are those of Solnhofen, that of the Jurassic of Holzmaden, Germany, that of the Late Cretaceous in Lebanon, and that of the Early Sinemurian at Osteno in Lombardy.

Class Thylacocephala

The class Thylacocephala was instituted in 1982 based on a fossil genus, *Ostenocaris*, found in Sinemurian deposits in Osteno in Lombardy. This is a unique crustacean with a carapace that completely covers the body of the animal except for the head, which is transformed into a cephalic sac, and three pairs of large cephalic appendages.

The Thylacocephala were animals without eyes and with reduced sense organs. They probably lived with the head fixed in sediment on the sea bottom, eating dead organisms, primarily the bodies of fish and cephalopods. They had little mobility.

Below left: Thalassina *sp., decapod crustacean of the Pleistocene, Australia.*
Below right: Palaeosculda laevis, *stomatopod crustacean, Late Cretaceous, Lebanon.*

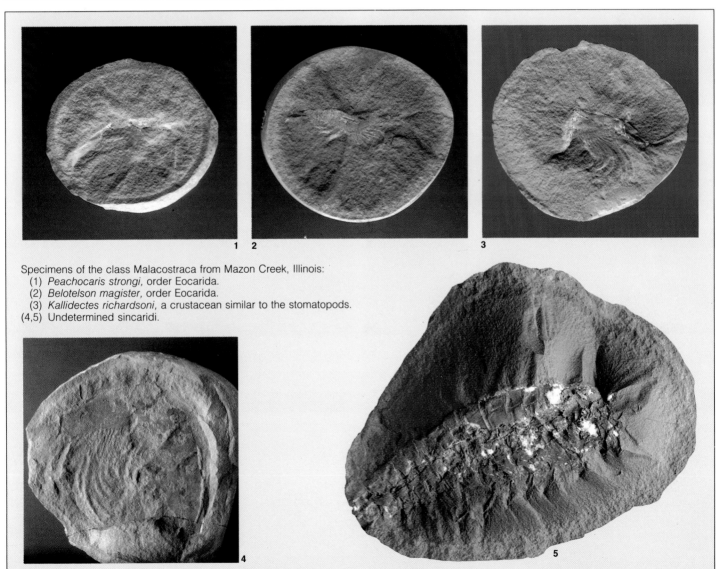

Specimens of the class Malacostraca from Mazon Creek, Illinois:
 (1) *Peachocaris strongi*, order Eocarida.
 (2) *Belotelson magister*, order Eocarida.
 (3) *Kallidectes richardsoni*, a crustacean similar to the stomatopods.
(4,5) Undetermined sincaridi.

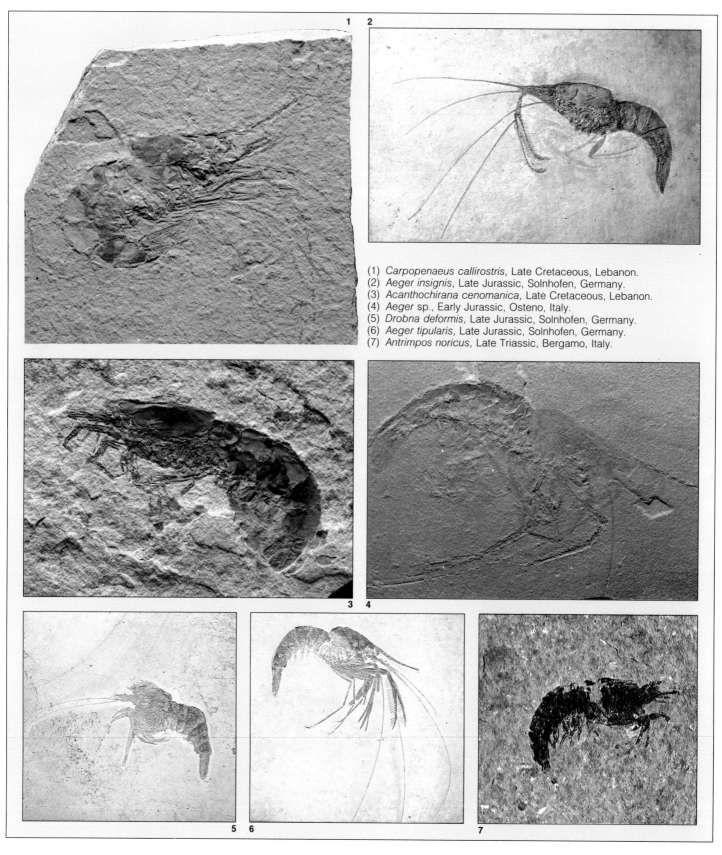

(1) *Carpopenaeus callirostris*, Late Cretaceous, Lebanon.
(2) *Aeger insignis*, Late Jurassic, Solnhofen, Germany.
(3) *Acanthochirana cenomanica*, Late Cretaceous, Lebanon.
(4) *Aeger* sp., Early Jurassic, Osteno, Italy.
(5) *Drobna deformis*, Late Jurassic, Solnhofen, Germany.
(6) *Aeger tipularis*, Late Jurassic, Solnhofen, Germany.
(7) *Antrimpos noricus*, Late Triassic, Bergamo, Italy.

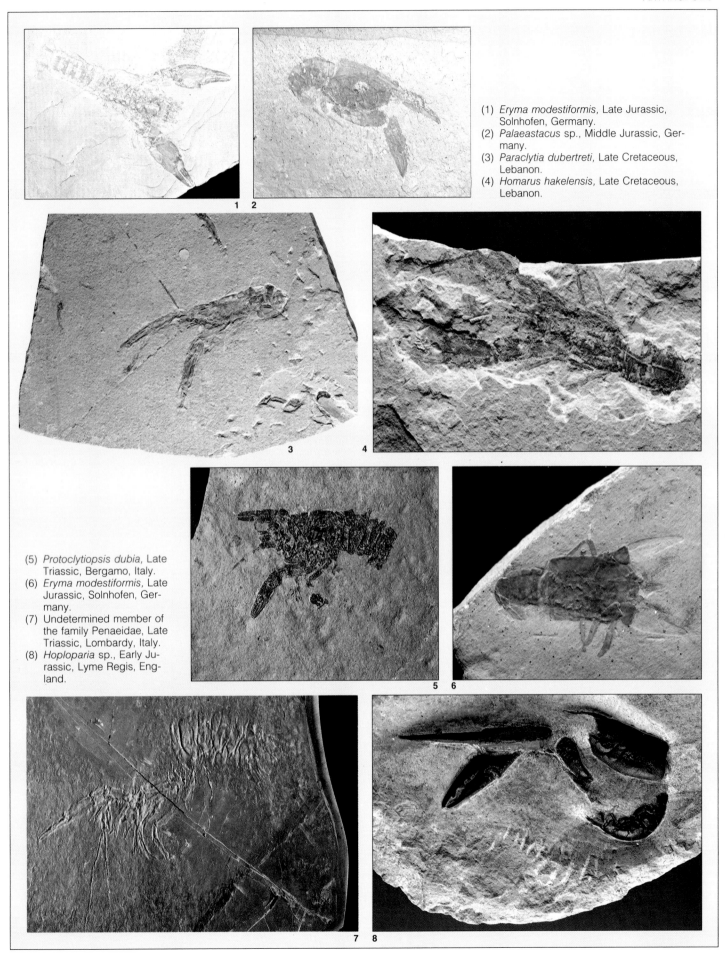

(1) *Eryma modestiformis,* Late Jurassic, Solnhofen, Germany.
(2) *Palaeastacus* sp., Middle Jurassic, Germany.
(3) *Paraclytia dubertreti,* Late Cretaceous, Lebanon.
(4) *Homarus hakelensis,* Late Cretaceous, Lebanon.

(5) *Protoclytiopsis dubia,* Late Triassic, Bergamo, Italy.
(6) *Eryma modestiformis,* Late Jurassic, Solnhofen, Germany.
(7) Undetermined member of the family Penaeidae, Late Triassic, Lombardy, Italy.
(8) *Hoploparia* sp., Early Jurassic, Lyme Regis, England.

(1) *Eryon arctiformis,* Late Jurassic, Solnhofen, Germany.
(2) *Cycleryon propinguus,* Late Jurassic, Solnhofen, Germany.
(3) *Coleia viallii,* Early Jurassic, Osteno, Italy.

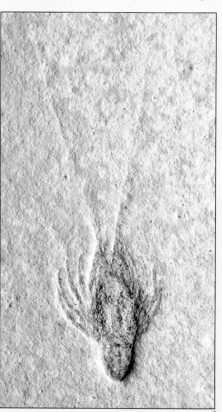

(4) *Archaeopalinurus levia,* Late Triassic, Bergamo, Italy.
(5) *Mecochirus* sp., Early Jurassic, Osteno, Italy.
(6) *Palinurina longipes,* Late Jurassic, Solnhofen, Germany.
(7) *Palinurus* sp., Eocene, Monte Bolca, Italy.

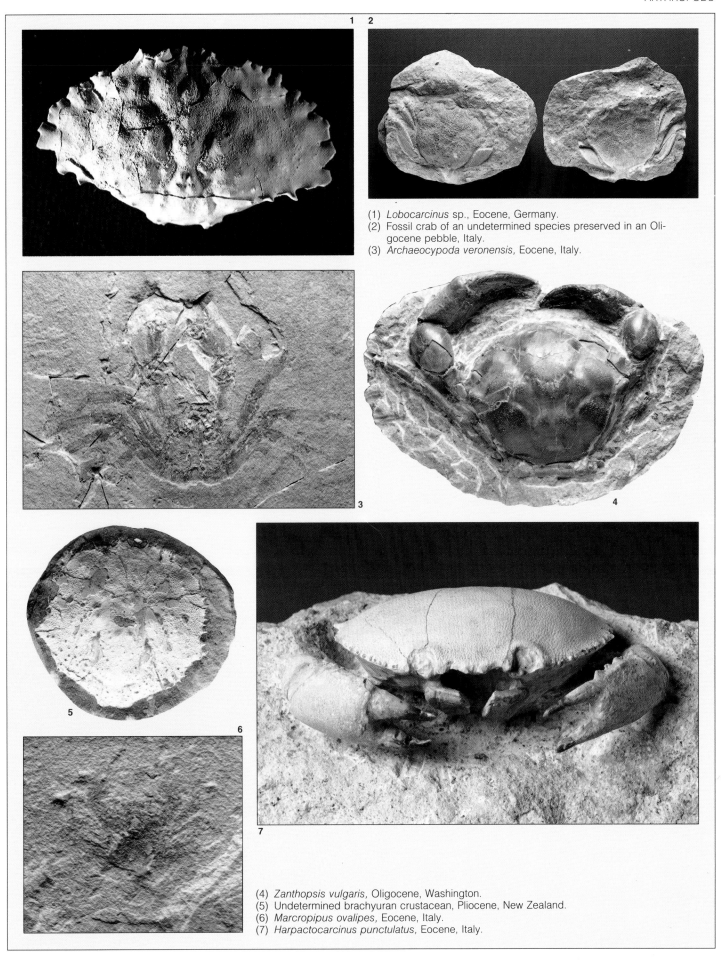

(1) *Lobocarcinus* sp., Eocene, Germany.
(2) Fossil crab of an undetermined species preserved in an Oligocene pebble, Italy.
(3) *Archaeocypoda veronensis,* Eocene, Italy.

(4) *Zanthopsis vulgaris,* Oligocene, Washington.
(5) Undetermined brachyuran crustacean, Pliocene, New Zealand.
(6) *Marcropipus ovalipes,* Eocene, Italy.
(7) *Harpactocarcinus punctulatus,* Eocene, Italy.

Representatives of the class Thylacocephala.
From top to bottom: Dollocaris ingens, Late Jurassic, La Voulte, France;
Ostenocaris cypriformis, Early Jurassic, Osteno, Italy; *Concavicaris,*
Late Devonian, Australia.

At the present time this class includes, aside from the Ostenocaris and other similar genera found in France and in other areas of Italy, certain organisms once attributed to other groups of crustaceans or those whose classification was uncertain. Examples of Thylacocephala have been found throughout the world, in various European countries, in Lebanon, in China, in Australia and in North America.

The Thylacocephala, today extinct, lived from the Silurian to the Late Cretaceous, a period of 360 million years.

Superclass Myriapoda

Little can be said about fossil Myriapoda, a group that zoologists today divide into four classes. Only rarely are their delicate bodies well fossilized. They appeared during the Devonian and developed during the Carboniferous, reaching modern times without any great changes over the course of millions of years. The best fossil specimens are from Oligocene deposits, in which these delicate animals are enclosed in drops of amber.

Superclass Hexapoda (Insecta)

The hexapods, or insects in the broad sense, are difficult arthropods to find in the fossil record because they are well preserved only in those rocks that permit, because of the presence of fine grains and quick consolidation, protection from destruction due to biological or mechanical causes. Amber offers the best fossil medium for the preservation of insects, and amber deposits are considered the most precious mines of perfectly preserved specimens. In that fossil resin, as in modern-day pine forests, numerous insects become caught in the amber, together with other invertebrates, such as miriapods and arachnids.

Most amber is from the Oligocene period (but there are mines of amber from other ages in various parts of the world). It was known to the ancients, who understood its liquid origin because of the animals enclosed in it. Amber has provided many perfect specimens of ants, termites and beetles, all groups that are still found in pine forests today.

Insect remains are also found in marine deposits, having fallen into the water after being blown by the wind, and they fossilize there together with other animals. This is the case of the Eocene deposits of Monte Bolca near Verona, where remains of insects, together with crustaceans and fish, have been found perfectly preserved due to the particular nature of that calcareous rock—sometimes even with their original colors still visible.

Even better preserved are the fossil insects of Solnhofen, where the fine-grained calcareous deposit has preserved even the most delicate structures of organisms. There in Solnhofen have been found beautiful dragonflies whose thin wing membranes have remained impressed in the rock with marvelous detail.

The first insects to appear on earth were the collembolans, found in Devonian rocks, by which time they were already as specialized as their modern-day counterparts. Their evolutionary history is controversial. Some authors hold they evolved from trilobites, others from crustaceans, yet others from the

Below left: *Insect perfectly preserved in an Eocene rock from the United States.*
Below right: *Larva of* Libellula doris; *Miocene, Italy.*

annelids or miriapods. What is known for certain is that wingless, or apterous, forms were first to appear on earth, and only later, during the Carboniferous, did the first winged, or pterous, forms appear, with the group of the Megasecoptera, to which belongs the genus *Meganeura*, a giant dragonfly with a 70 mm. (2.8 in.) wingspan. Also during the Carboniferous appeared the protoorthopterons, progenitors of today's cockroaches, but much larger; the first grasshoppers; and the hemipterans, or true bugs.

The true dragonflies, or odonates, first appeared during the Permian, together with the coleopterans (beetles), and numerous families became abundant later, during the Triassic and the Jurassic—almost all of which are now extinct. Modern coleopterans developed during the Tertiary with genera that still exist today. The lepidopterans (which today include butterflies and moths) and the hymenopterans (early relatives of bees, wasps and ants) appeared after the development of flowering plants in the Jurassic; among the latter group are the ants, which made their appearance during the Eocene. The dipterons, flies and mosquitoes appeared at the beginning of the Jurassic. To close this brief list, we will add that the isopterans, the termites, appeared for the first time in the Eocene.

Left: *Insect fossilized in Oligocene amber from the Baltic.*

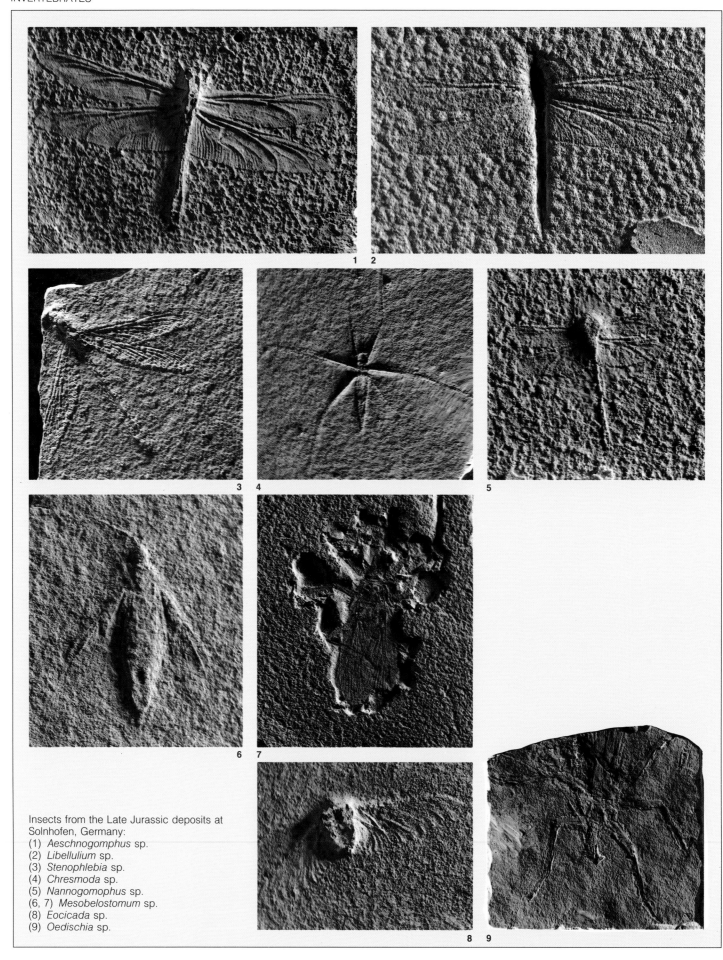

Insects from the Late Jurassic deposits at
Solnhofen, Germany:
(1) *Aeschnogomphus* sp.
(2) *Libellulium* sp.
(3) *Stenophlebia* sp.
(4) *Chresmoda* sp.
(5) *Nannogomophus* sp.
(6, 7) *Mesobelostomum* sp.
(8) *Eocicada* sp.
(9) *Oedischia* sp.

Mollusks

With the mollusks we enter a large and important phylum of invertebrates whose members have lost the segmentation typical of the arthropods and are thus defined as bilaterally symmetrical metazoans.

In most cases mollusks are characterized by the presence of an internal or external shell lined with a mantle that surrounds the body and secretes the shell itself. The soft body, which naturally does not fossilize well, is divided in three parts, the head, the foot and the visceral mass. As the soft body fossilizes only in rare cases, mollusks are known to paleontologists almost exclusively because of their shells; when the animal is alive the shell is composed of aragonite, an unstable mineral composed of calcium carbonate, which is replaced by stable calcite during the fossilization process.

The paleontological classification of mollusks is therefore based on an examination of the shell, using such characteristics of genera and species as its form, its ornamentation (usually highly varied) and its dimensions. For subdivision into larger groups, such as orders and families, the paleontologist relies on characteristics that are in some way tied to anatomic features of the soft body, such as muscular scars, siphonal canals, and so on, drawing upon useful information from living forms.

Of course, the paleontological study of less ancient forms of mollusk, of forms that still exist, or of forms similar to those still existing, is simpler because of the possible correlations that can be made; but the study of older groups, including those now extinct, whose characteristics cannot be correlated (at least, not from a distance) with living forms, becomes, instead, truly complex. This applies not only to anatomy and morphology but also, most of all, to knowledge of the life, habits and ecology of mollusks, knowledge that is of great interest in the study of the rocks of the earth's crust.

Mollusks are, in fact, organisms that can give useful information on the environment in which sedimentary rocks were formed, when, of course, one knows their habits, the limits of depth, temperature and salinity in which they could live, and the environment—ocean, land, lake, salt marsh—to which they were tied. They are thus fossils suitable for establishing paleogeographical and paleoecological reconstructions.

The evolutionary history of mollusks is long and complex because of the enormous variety of forms that have appeared over time.

The first mollusks appeared during the Early Cambrian, but the origin of these animals is probably older. Only the scarcity of fossils in Precambrian rocks—a result of the widespread metamorphism of these rocks and the consequent destruction of fossil remains in them—or the absence of hard parts in these first mollusks has prevented older finds.

The mollusks form an animal phylum subdivided into six classes, with characteristics that render them identifiable even to a novice. To these classes has been added during recent

Phylum	Class	Subclass	Order	Age
Mollusca	Monoplacophora Aplacophora Polyplacophora Scaphopoda			Cambrian–Recent Recent Cambrian–Recent Ordovician–Recent
	Bivalvia or Pelecypoda	Palaeotaxodonta Cryptodonta Pteriomorphia Palaeoheterodonta Heterodonta Anomalodesmata		Ordovician–Recent Cambrian–Recent Ordovician–Recent Cambrian–Recent Ordovician–Recent Ordovician–Recent
	Gastropoda	Prosobranchia	Archaeogastropoda Mesogastropoda Neogastropoda	Cambrian–Recent Ordovician–Recent Ordovician–Recent
		Opisthobranchia		Devonian–Recent
		Pulmonata	Basommatophora Stylommatophora	Carboniferous–Recent
	Cephalopoda	Nautiloidea Ammonoidea		Cambrian–Recent Devonian–Cretaceous
		Dibranchiata	Decapoda Octopoda	Triassic–Recent Cretaceous–Recent

Below left: Pilina *sp., monoplacophoran mollusk of the Middle Silurian;* (A) interior of the valve with muscle scars; (B) exterior of the valve.

Below center: Propilina meramecenis, *monoplacophoran mollusk, Early Ordovician, Montana.*
Below right: Gasconadeoconus ponderosus, *monoplacophoran mollusk, Early Ordovician, Montana.*

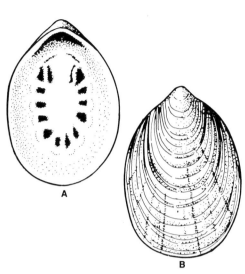

years a seventh, that of the Monoplacophora. For many years known only from fossil remains, these were once considered gastropods. The discovery of living specimens on the floor of the Pacific Ocean has permitted a more in-depth study of the soft parts of these animals and the institution of a new class of very primitive organisms.

Mollusks are today divided into these classes, with the following characteristics

• Class Monoplacophora: body protected by a univalve hood-shaped shell without torsion
• Class Aplacophora: no fossils remain
• Class Polyplacophora: body protected by a calcareous shell formed of articulated (hinged and movable) plates
• Class Scaphopoda: tubular shell
• Class Bivalvia: body protected by a bivalve shell

• Class Gastropoda: body protected by a spiral univalve shell
• Class Cephalopoda: internal or external chambered shell

Class Monoplacophora

The Monoplacophora constitute a highly interesting class because their members are believed to be the most primitive of all mollusks. These animals were known only from fossils found in rocks from the period between the Early Cambrian to the Middle Devonian (from about 570 to 384 million years ago) and were considered completely extinct. In 1952, living specimens of *Neopilina galatheae* were dredged up from the floor of the Pacific Ocean at a depth of 3,540 meters (11,682 ft.).

The Monoplacophora are characterized by a hood-shaped, nonspiraled univalve shell that protects the soft body. It is interesting to note that while the Neopilina lives today on ocean floors, its Paleozoic representatives lived in shallow water.

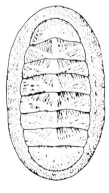

Far left: *Pebble with fossil remains of a polyplacophoran mollusk, Tertiary, Italy.*
Left: *Reconstruction of* Chiton *sp., a modern polyplacophoran mollusk.*

Below: Gervilleia socialis, *bivalve of Muschelkalk, Germany.*
Bottom: *Bivalve of the genus Pinna on a Triassic rock from Bergamo, Italy.*

Class Polyplacophora

The Polyplacophora are marine mollusks with a bilaterally symmetrical body with a ventral foot, which they use to move, protected by a calcareous or sometimes chitinous shell (which is why they are often called chitons). The shell is formed of eight articulated plates.

Because of their strong shell, chiton fossils are found in deposits from the Late Cambrian onward, usually as isolated shell plates. The genus *Chiton,* which appeared during the Cretaceous and is still alive, is the best-known representative.

Class Scaphopoda

Members of the class Scaphopoda are marine mollusks with an external univalve shell. The shell is cylindrical and slightly tapering, giving it the appearance of a tooth, or tusk, which is why these are often called tooth shells; it is open at both ends. Morphologically, the concave side of the shell is considered the dorsal, its larger opening the anterior, the smaller the posterior. The animal lives with the anterior opening buried in the mud of the sea bottom; only the posterior opening, from which excrement and reproductive shells exit, is in contact with the water.

Although their uniform appearance makes one think the Scaphopoda include few species, they are instead very numerous, both today (no fewer than 200 species are now known to exist) and in the fossil record. From the Ordovician, in fact, the period in which the first species appeared, the Scaphopoda have survived to today in the same forms: approximately 300 known fossil species are known.

Bivalvia (Pelecypoda)

The bivalves, aka pelecypods or clams, are well known to gourmets, who delight in the flavor of oysters, mussels and many other species; but they assume a fundamental importance in paleontological studies because of their widespread distribution in most marine sediments, and fresh water as well, and for the useful information they furnish to reconstruct environments of the past. Their name is derived from the two valves that compose the shell. They are also often called Pelecypoda because the ventral foot is flat and similar in shape to an axe.

These mollusks have an external shell formed of two valves, usually of the same size and shape and hinged by means of a ligamental tissue, which cover and protect the soft parts of the body of the animal. From the paleontological point of view the most interesting part, as well as the only one well preserved in the fossil record, is the shell, which we will examine in detail.

As a result of various adaptations, the two valves of some clams undergo variations that alter their growth. Thus, in the forms that do not move often, the shell becomes inequivalve because one of the valves takes on the form and function of an operculum. Even greater distortions can be noted in the forms that live attached to hard objects. In some species the growth of the two valves becomes so unequal that they reach elongated horn- or conelike forms, such as with the rudists.

The first step in studying a bivalve is determining the exact orientation of the shell, information that will permit identification of an anterior and posterior part, of a right valve and a left valve, of an anterior muscle and a posterior, and so on. The curving part of the valves, or the beak, is used to establish this orientation. This beak, in fact, is found on the upper or dorsal part of the shell and in almost every case is pointed toward the anterior part, which is less extended than the posterior. Thus the shell is oriented; from this it is easy to establish the anterior from the posterior, a right valve and a left. The right valve is that located on the right of an observer looking at the shell from its posterior part.

Externally, the valves of clams are often very different because of ornamentation, which is used to classify the various species. Two different kinds of ornamentation can be distinguished, composed of costae and ribs. In one case, the ornamentation is concentric (concentric sculpture), while in the other it spreads out in rays (rayed sculpture). In addition to this ornamentation there are often also nodes and spines that render the entire shell more varied and elegant. During growth, the shell increases in size, alternating phases of rapid growth with

(1) *Inoceramus balticus*, Late Cretaceous, Germany.
(2) *Inoceramus cripsii*, Late Cretaceous, Bergamo, Italy.
(3) *Inoceramus balticus*, Late Cretaceous, Germany.

(4) *Claraia clarai*, Early Triassic, Dolomites, Italy.
(5) *Posidonia wengensis*, bivalve of the Early Triassic, Dolomites.
(6) *Daonella moussoni*, Middle Triassic, Alps.
(7) *Halobia gigantea*, Late Triassic, California.

Below: *Bivalve of the genus Lima, Muschelkalk, Germany. In the photographs at right, from top to bottom:* Gryphaea arcuata, *Early Jurassic, France;* Gryphaea arcuata, *Early Jurassic, France;* Gryphaea arcuata, *Early Jurassic, Switzerland.*

The drawing below gives the nomenclature of the valves of a bivalve: *(ant.) anterior margin; (h) hinge; (pl) pallial line; (l) ligament; (am) anterior muscle; (pm) posterior muscle; (post.) posterior margin; (ps) pallial sinus; (b) beak.*

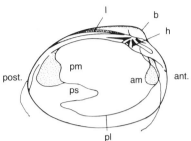

phases of little or no growth, and this is reflected on the external surface in concentric lines, called growth lines, sometimes distinguishable from the ornamentation.

Above the beak, along the dorsal margin of the shell, is the ligament that holds the valves together. Farther along is the hinge, a structure formed on each valve of teeth that fit into sockets on the opposite valve and that, by the movement of adductor muscles and with the help of the ligament, regulate the opening and closing of the valves.

The soft parts of the animal's body leave traces on the inside of the shell that paleontologists use in its classification. Scars or adductor muscles, one anterior and the other posterior in each of the valves, are visible. The two muscle scars are accompanied by a linear indentation, or pallial line, that follows the lower margin of the shell, where the edge of the mantle was attached.

These very few characteristics—muscle scars, pallial lines and the hinge—are tied to internal structures that do not undergo variations in adaptations and must be used by paleontologists to classify the bivalves.

There is much variation in the hinges, with the following characteristics:

- taxodont hinge: a large hinge area that bears numerous small, regular teeth separated from an equal number of regular sockets; teeth and sockets match from one valve to the next
- heterodont hinge: teeth differentiated into cardinal, which are perpendicular to the hinge line, and lateral, which are parallel to the dorsal margin
- schizodont hinge: very few cardinal teeth, but strong and grooved; a single tooth with two small sockets on the left valve, two teeth accompanied by a small socket on the right
- isodont hinge: small sockets and teeth that are symmetrical to the axis of the shell
- desmodont hinge: similar to the heterodont but with ribs and grooves owing to the action of the ligament

Below: *The different kinds of bivalve hinge: (A) taxodont (Glycymeris); (B) dysodont (Pecten); (C) schizodont (Trigonia); (D) heterodont (Venus); (E) isodont (Spondylus); (F) desmodont (Mya); (G₁) pachydont (Hippurites), interior of fixed valve seen from above; (G₂) pachydont, opercular valve seen from the side.*

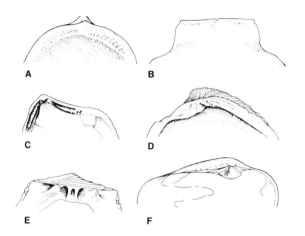

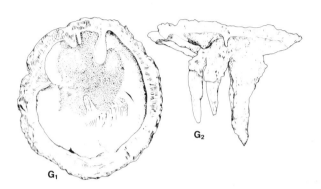

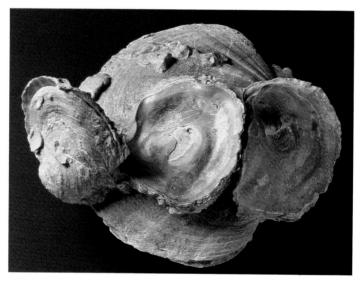

Above: *Large shell of* Pecten (Chlamys) latissimus *to which are attached several specimens of the family Ostreidae; Pliocene, Valle Andona (Alessandria, Italy). Below: Myophoria sp., bivalve of the Late Triassic of Valle Inferno (Bergamo, Italy).*

- pachyodont hinge: typical of the rudists, today extinct; teeth reduced in number but large and deformed

The last four types are in fact modifications of the heterodont hinge.

The first bivalves appeared in the Cambrian period. From these first rare forms, during the following geologic periods there was a continual diversification of new groups, some of which became extinct after short or long periods of time while others have remained almost the same up to today. As with every group of invertebrates, the evolutionary history of this class is very difficult to reconstruct, both because of the diversity of form it has assumed and because the data available are very limited.

But then why are the bivalves so important to paleontology? The reason is simple: When found in a rock formation they can provide much information about the environment of that rock and the possibility to reconstruct the paleogeography of the period in which the rocks and the fossils were deposited. In addition, many bivalves are used as index fossils to particular geologic periods.

The taxonomy of the bivalves is rather complex. It is based most of all on the character of the hinge and musculature and therefore on the scars that these have left on the inside of the shell and on the development of the siphon. The class is divided into six subclasses (see page 113), each of which in turn includes numerous orders.

Among the most interesting bivalves is the extinct group of the rudists, grouped in the order Hippuritoida, including both the superfamily of the Megalodonti, bivalves widespread in the Triassic in the Alps, and the superfamily Hippuritacea, including those that were once the true rudists. These were bivalves with pachyodont hinge that lived from the Late Jurassic to the end of the Cretaceous and underwent such extreme modifications as to no longer resemble, except distantly, the other members of the class.

Rudists lived attached to the substrate by one of their valves, which grew so excessively as to take on the form of a twisted horn or an almost upright cone. The opposite valve, on the contrary, transformed into a kind of lid that, using large deformed teeth and sockets, was hinged on the first valve. Among

(1) *Steinmannella vacaensis*, Early Cretaceous, Argentina.
(2) *Trigonia costata*, Middle Jurassic, Germany.
(3) *Trigonia navis*, Middle Jurassic, Germany.

(4) Specimens of Myophorella, a bivalve of the Early Cretaceous, Argentina.
(5) *Trigonia interlaevigata*, Middle Jurassic, Germany.
(6) *Megalodon paronai*, Late Triassic, Italy.
(7) *Megalodon guembeli*, Late Triassic, Italy.

BIVALVE PLATES

PLATE XI
Bivalves of the Pliocene from Liguria-Piedmont
(1) *Trachycardium (Dallocardia) multicostatum*, Buttigliera; (2) *Laevicardium (Laevicardium) crassum*, Valle Andona; (3) *Cardites antiquatus pectinatus*, Valle Andona; (4) *Discors acquitanicus*, Valle Botto; (5) *Cardita (Centrocardita) rudista*, Valle Andona; (6) *Glans (Glans) intermedia*, Valle Andona; (7) *Acanthocardia (Acanthocardia) aculeata*, Valle Andona; (8) *Codakia leonina*, Buttigliera; (9) *Acanthocardia (Acanthocardia) paucicostata*, Valle Botto; (10) *Lucinonia borealis*, Valle Botto; (11) *Acanthocardia (Acanthocardia) erinacea*, Valle Botto; (12) *Acanthocardia (Acanthocardia) paucicostata*, Valle Botto; (13) *Trachycardium (Dallocardium) multicostatum*, Buttigliera; (14) *Lucinonia borealis*, Valle Andona; (15) *Megaxinus (Megaxinus) transversus*, Buttigliera; (16) *Laevicardium (Laevicardium) oblongum*, Valle Andona; (17) *Megaxinus (Megaxinus) transversus*, Buttigliera; (18) *Cardium (Bucardium) hians*, Valle Botto; (19) *Cardita rufescens*, Castelnuovo; (20) *Acanthocardia (Acanthocardia) paucicostata*, Buttigliera.

PLATE XII
(1) *Lutraria lutraria*, Buttigliera; (2) *Lutraria (Eastonia) rugosa*, Buttigliera; (3) *Panopea (Panopea) glycymeris*, Buttigliera; (4) *Thracia pupescens*, Valle Botto; (5) *Paphia (Callistotapes) vetula*, Valle Andona; (6) *Lutraria (Eastonia) rugosa*, Buttigliera; (7) *Callista (Callista) chione*, Buttigliera; (8) *Chamelea gallina gallina*, Bric Barrano; (9) *Callista (Callista) chione*, Buttigliera; (10) *Callista (Callista) chione*, Valle Andona; (11) *Callista (Callista) italica*, Monale; (12) *Lutraria (Psammophila) oblonga*, Buttigliera.

PLATE XIII
(1) *Palliolum (Lissochlamys) excisum*, Valle Botto; (2) *Pecten (Flexopecten) flexuosa*, Buttigliera; (3) *Anomia (Anomia) ephippium*, Valle Andona; (4) *Chlamys (Manupecten) pesfelis*, Cortandone; (5) *Pecten (Chlamys) latissimus*, Valle Andona; (6) *Pecten (Chlamys) latissimus*, Valle Botto; (7) *Chlamys (Manupecten) pesfelis*, Cortandone; (8) *Pecten (Flabellipecten) bosniaskii*, Valle Andona; (9) *Chlamys (Aequipecten) scaporella*, Valle Botto; (10) *Chlamys (Aequipecten) opercularis*, Valle Botto; (11) *Amussium cristatum*, Asti; (12) *Isognomon (Hippochaeta) maxillatus*, Valle Botto; (13) *Chlamys (Chlamys) varia*, Valle Andona; (14) *Amussium cristatum*, Asti; (15) *Chlamys (Chlamys) varia*, Valle Andona; (16) *Pallium (Lissochlamys) excisum*, Valle Andona.

PLATE XIV
(1) *Glossus humanus*, Valmontasca; (2) *Solecurtus scapulus candidus*, Valle Andona; (3) *Glossus humanus*, Valmontasca; (4) *Tellina (Arcopagia) telata*, Valle Botto; (5) *Leporimetis papyracea*, Monale; (6) *Macoma (Psammacoma) elliptica*, Valle Botto; (7) *Tellina (Arcopagia) crassa*, Buttigliera; (8) *Solecurtus dilatatus*, Buttigliera; (9) *Tellina (Arcopagia) corbis*, Valle Andona; (10) *Solen marginatus*, Buttigliera; (11) *Tellina (Arcopagia) sedgwicii*, Cortandone; (12) *Gastrana (Gastrana) fragilis gigantula*, Buttigliera; (13) *Tellina (Arcopagia) sedgwicii*, Buttigliera; (14) *Macoma (Psammacoma) elliptica*, Buttigliera; (15) *Dosinia (Pectunculus) exoleta*, Buttigliera; (16) *Azorinus (Azorinus) chamasolen*, Monale; (17) *Ensis ensis*, Buttigliera; (18) *Solecurtus scapulus candidus*, Valle Andona; (19) *Leporimetispapyracea*, Monale; (20) *Tellina (Arcopagia) crassa*, Buttigliera; (21) *Gastrana fragilis*, Buttigliera; (22) *Gari (Psammobia) labordei*, Valle Botto; (23) *Tellina incarnata*, Valle Andona; (24) *Tellina palmata*, Monale.

PLATE XV
(1) *Barbatia (Cucullearca) candida*, Buttigliera; (2) *Anadara diluvii*, Asti; (3) *Spondylus (Spondylus) crassicosta*, Valle Andona; (4) *Arca (Arca) noae*, Valle Botto; (5) *Barbatis (Cucullearca) candida*, Valle Andona; (6) *Anadara (Anadara) diluvii*, Valle Andona; (7) *Modiolus (Modiolus) adriaticus*, Castelnuovo Don Bosco; (8) *Pycnodonta cochlear*, Valle Botto; (9) *Lima (Lima) inflata*, Buttigliera; (10) *Lima (Lima) inflata*, Valle Andona; (11) *Barbatia (Soldania) mytiloides*, Valle Andona; (12) *Modiolus (Modiolus) barbatus*, Valle Botto; (13) *Anadara (Anadara) pectinata*, Buttigliera; (14) *Nucula (Nucula) placentina*, Valle Botto; (15) *Spondylus (Spondylus) gaederopus*, Valle Andona; (16) *Nucula (Nucula) nucleus*, Asti; (17) *Barbatia (Soldania) mytiloides*, Monale.

PLATE XVI
(1) *Paphia (Callistotapes) vetula*, Monale; (2) *Callista (Callista) puella*, Buttigliera; (3) *Venus (Ventricoloidea) casina*, Valle Botto; (4) *Pelecyora (Pelecyora) brocchii*, Valle Botto; (5) *Circomphalus foliaceolamellosus*, Valle Andona; (6) *Dosinia (Pectunculus) orbicularis*, Monale; (7) *Clausinella scalaris*, Valle Botto; (8) *Callista (Callista) chione*, Valle Andona; (9) *Venus (Ventricoloidea) verrucosa*, Buttigliera; (10) *Myrosopsis pernaruna*, Buttigliera; (11) *Pelecyora (Pelecyora) brocchii*, Bric Barrano; (12) *Circomphalus foliaceolamellosus*, Monale; (13) *Venus (Ventricoloidea) verrucosa*, Buttigliera; (14) *Callista (Callista) puella*, Buttigliera; (15) *Venus (Ventricoloidea) verrucosa*, Buttigliera; (16) *Venus (Ventricoloidea) multilamella*, Valle Botto; (17) *Callista (Callista) puella*, Monale; (18) *Pitar (Pitar) rudis rudis*, Vezza d'Alba; (19) *Pelecyora (Pelecyora) gigas*, Monale; (20) *Callista (Callista) puella*, Buttigliera; (21) *Venus (Ventricoloidea) excentrica*, Buttigliera.

PLATE XI

PLATE XII

PLATE XIII

PLATE XIV

PLATE XV

PLATE XVI

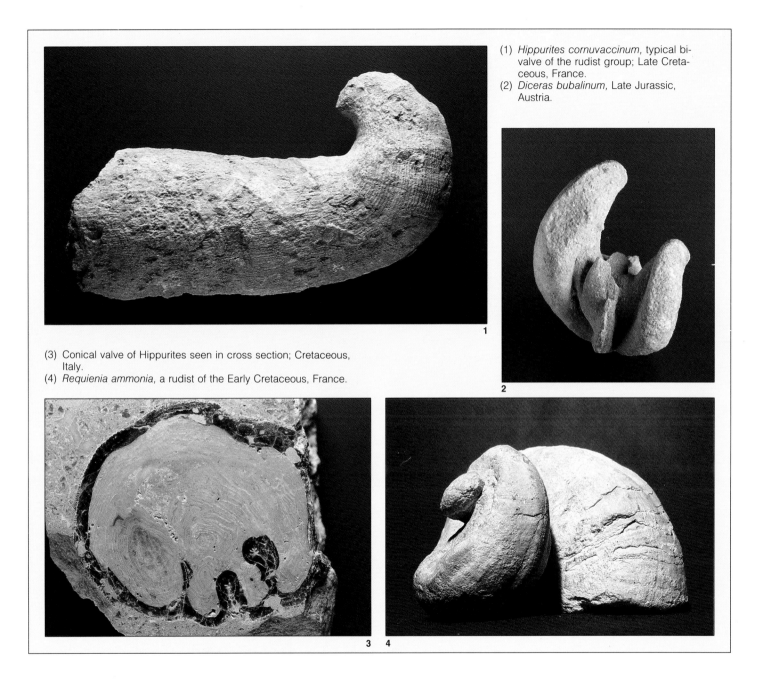

(1) *Hippurites cornuvaccinum*, typical bivalve of the rudist group; Late Cretaceous, France.
(2) *Diceras bubalinum*, Late Jurassic, Austria.
(3) Conical valve of Hippurites seen in cross section; Cretaceous, Italy.
(4) *Requienia ammonia*, a rudist of the Early Cretaceous, France.

the types richest with representatives, used as index fossils for dating reef formations, is the genus *Requienia* of the Early Cretaceous, which had twisted and pointed valves edged with a keel-shaped anatomical ridge.

In the family Hippuritidae are grouped a certain number of genera that are a bit different, among them the famous Hippurites. All of them had the right valve in a conical form, which fixed to the substrate at its apex, and the left valve was the operculum. On the larger valve were three longitudinal furrows, corresponding to three internal folds of the shell; the first was called the ligamental furrow, the others columella.

At the end of the Cretaceous the rudists became extinct, but their development revealed that, if compared to the corals and the brachiopods of reefs, animals of different phyla can reach in the same environment analogous forms in response to similar environmental pressures.

Below: *Conglomerate with several pulmonate gastropod shells of the genus* Helix; *Quaternary, Bergamo, Italy.*

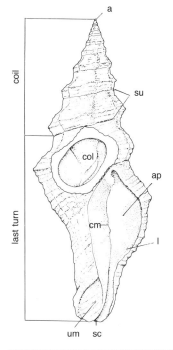

Left: *Nomenclature of a gastropod: (a) apex; (ap) aperture; (cm) columellar margin; (col) columella; (sc) siphonal canal; (l) lip; (um) umbilicus; (su) suture.*

Below left: *Block of sandstone with two specimens of* Cerithium benechi; *Eocene, France.*
Below right: *Rock with several specimens of gastropods of the genus* Turritella; *Miocene, Germany.*

Class Gastropoda

The gastropods constitute a vast group of mollusks that, unlike the bivalves, includes forms adapted to terrestrial habitats. Some gastropods are characterized by a coiled or spiraled univalve shell, some are without shells, but most display the process of torsion. These animals are much more mobile than the bivalves because they move by means of a disk-shaped, muscular foot located outside the mantle in a ventral position. None of the gastropods live permanently and completely attached.

The shell of a gastropod, which as in the other groups is only partially preserved in the fossil record, can be considered as the result of a spiral twisting of an elongated cone. This twisting is usually to the right; a twisting to the left can be the result of a malformation or can be a characteristic of a particular species. The successive whorls of the shell may be spread out or close together. In some cases the last whorl, which leads to the aperture, envelopes all the others, as in the conches.

Taking a typical shell, with whorls that are not too close together, we can define the apex, or posterior extremity, as the pointed tip of the shell. All the whorls apart from the last one are called the "spire." The spiral angle is the angle measured from the base of the spire to the apex. The line along which the whorls join together is called the suture line and has a highly variable appearance. In the forms with whorls closed toward the inside of the shell a kind of axis, called the columella, is formed. If the whorls are large, the columella is replaced by a cavity around the axis of the shell called the umbilicus.

Below: *Tube of a gastropod of the genus* Vermetus *on an Ostreidae shell; Pliocene, Italy.*
Bottom left: Chrysodomus contrarius, *a gastropod that is an indicator of warm water, with a sinistral shell; Pliocene, Suffolk, England.*

Bottom center: *Shell of Nerinea sectioned longitudinally to reveal the internal ornamentation; Cretaceous, Gosau, Austria.*
Bottom right: *Shell of gastropod of the genus* Nerinea; *Jurassic, Switzerland.*

The aperture, or opening, of the shell, which is also used in classification, appears in many different forms according to the species. Usually circular in primitive types, it becomes oval, elongated and more or less irregular in more evolved gastropods. Its edge, called the peristoma, is formed by an internal lip, or columellar lip, and by an external lip. The peristoma can be internal, in which case the animal is called olostomo; or carved out, in which case the animal is called sifonostomo. In that case there may be two openings, one anterior or branchial, and one posterior or anal, that serve as passage for the animal's two siphons.

In the forms without siphons, the lip sometimes has a middle opening that allows the passage of water into the branchial cavity. This deep opening progressively closes during the growth of the shell, leaving on the surface a characteristic furrow. This suture is present most often in the more primitive forms, since the forms with a siphon appeared only during a later period of the history of the gastropods and thus represent a more advanced stage of development.

Since the animal pulls itself back into the shell, the aperture can be closed with a movable calcareous or horny piece carried by the dorsal posterior part of the foot. This piece, called the operculum, is often preserved in the fossil record.

The ornamentation of the shell, of great importance in the classification of fossil forms, is extremely varied. The shell can be completely smooth; can be furrowed by light growth lines or by more or less marked ribs; can have large folds and varices all along the width of the whorls, spines or tubercles. There are two principal types of ornamentation: axial, in which the ornamental elements are parallel to the shell's axis; and spiral, in which the ornamental elements are parallel to the twisting

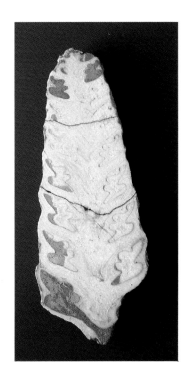

(1) *Bembexia sulcomarginata,* Devonian archaeogastropod from New York.
(2) *Polemita discors,* Silurian archaeogastropod from Dudley, England.

(3) *Oriostoma discors,* Middle Silurian from Gotland.
(4) *Platyschisma rotunda,* Permian, Australia.
(5) Specimens of *Glabrocingulum grayvillense,* Pennsylvanian, Texas.
(6) *Trepospira depressa,* Pennsylvanian, Texas.
(7) Specimens of *Ceratopea* sp., Ordovician, Arkansas.

of the spire. Observation of fossil forms reveals that even the ornamentation of the gastropods has undergone change during the course of time, having passed, in general, from less ornamented forms to those increasingly ornamented. One group of gastropods, adapted to reef life and known only as fossils, the Nerinea, had a singular ornamentation on the inside of the shell rather than on the external surface.

The classification of gastropods is based in particular on anatomical characteristics of the soft body of the animal. While this is a zoological classification, it is followed by paleontologists as well.

The gastropods are subdivided into three subclasses—Prosobranchia, Opisthobranchia and Pulmonata—based on the position of the branchia with respect to the heart in the first two and by the presence of a kind of lung in the third, which includes the terrestrial gastropods and those that live in fresh water.

The first true gastropods appeared during the Early Cambrian, 570 million years ago. These were bilaterally symmetrical mollusks with plano-spiral coiling. The torsion of the soft parts of the animal had only just been developed. These gastropods were part of the order Archaeogastropoda, which survived the Paleozoic.

The first Opisthobranchia appeared during the Devonian and have increased in number and importance right up to the present day. The first Pulmonata, last of the gastropods to appear, originated during the Carboniferous. By the beginning of the Tertiary, 65 million years ago, gastropods had already assumed the appearance they still have today. And from then on there have been no great changes. It is interesting to note that throughout the Paleozoic and the Mesozoic, the bivalves were much more abundant than the gastropods, while from the Tertiary to today the proportions have been completely reversed.

For giving relative dates to terrestrial rocks, these mollusks are not as important as other groups that came later, but they are useful, even more so than the bivalves, for the reconstruction of past environments. In fact, since we know the modern characteristics of these animals and can assume they have not changed much over the ages, we can reach important conclusions about the configuration and depth of the sea floors that existed during past epochs.

Thus, for example, the genus *Nassa* indicates a muddy sea bottom, the genera *Natica* and *Turritella* indicate sandy bottoms, the genus *Patella* indicates a rocky bottom, the genera *Patella*, *Fissurella* and *Haliotis* indicate a littoral shoreline environment, and *Helix* indicates a subaereal environment.

Other valuable information can be gathered from these organisms by considering them climatic indicators. Today, mollusks that live in warm seas and those that live in cold seas display very different characteristics. The presence of these mollusks in fossil form indicates whether in a certain epoch the climate was hot or cold.

Mollusks have proven particularly useful in providing information about conditions during the Quaternary, an epoch characterized by great climatic oscillations, alternating from cold periods (glaciations) to warm periods (interglacial periods). The

Below: *Gastropods of the genus* Bellerophon *with the characteristic plano-spiral shell.*
Bottom: *Calcareous rock with gastropods of the genus* Bellerophon, *Permian, Italy.*

mian and is very abundant in many Paleozoic rocks in North America.

Others had a regularly helicoidal shell, others a patelliform shell, such as the genus *Fissurella.* Still others have many unique forms. Among these is the genus *Haliotis,* which appeared during the Cretaceous and is still alive today; it had a series of apertures lined along the length of the suture, which was not completely closed.

The order of the Mesogastropoda appeared a little later, during the Early Ordovician. It includes certain genera that are well known today because their members are beautifully colored, but these colors, unfortunately, are not preserved in the fossil record. Indeed, colors are only rarely preserved in fossils, and mollusks lose all their color when fossilized. Even the most recent, those from the Tertiary and Quaternary, are whitish or brownish according to the type of sediment in which they were buried.

The Mesogastropoda lived in the sea, in fresh water and on land. Their shells were usually helicoidal, rarely in the form of a hood, or discoidal. They had no siphon. They included the Nerinea, which lived in reef environments during the Jurassic and the Cretaceous.

The Neogastropoda include gastropods that appeared during the Early Ordovician and had a siphonal canal. They included many types still alive today, including the murex, whelks, volutes and cones, that were already widespread during the Tertiary and are found fossilized in many marine sediments, without, of course, their pretty colors.

Subclass Opisthobranchia

The second subclass, that of the Opisthobranchia, includes marine gastropods that usually have a small shell, with simple architecture, and possess as common characteristics the position of the branchia, located behind the heart.

They are known in the fossil record since the Carboniferous, about 345 million years ago. Only the pteropods, conical-shelled nekto-planktonic (swimming and floating) mollusks in which the anterior lobes of the foot form two winglike organs used by the animal for swimming, seem to have appeared at a more distant times, during the Early Cambrian, about 570 million years ago.

Today on open sea bottoms at depths between 1,000 and 2,500 meters (3,300–8,250 ft.) sediments are formed, as in the past, composed of the accumulation of shells of these organisms. In the fossil state, they indicate a deep sea.

Very similar to the pteropods were certain strange organisms that are completely extinct today and of which we have found only the conical shell, with its elliptical or triangular cross section. These are the genera *Tentaculites* of the Ordovician and Devonian and *Hyolithes* of the Cambrian and Permian.

The best-known genus of this subclass is without doubt *Acteonella,* which had a globular shell characteristic of reef environments of the Cretaceous period. The Opisthobranchia also include the nudibranchs, gastropods with small internal shells or without shells, and therefore almost unknown in the fossil record. A single family, from the Eocene, has been discovered.

alternation of these warm and cold states has been established for marine sediments thanks to the alternation in fossil remains of warm- and cold-water mollusks. During the glaciations of the Quaternary, cold-type mollusks like those that today inhabit the North Atlantic moved into the Mediterranean; during the interglacial periods, which were much warmer even than the modern-day Mediterranean, warm-type mollusks appeared from the African coasts of Senegal, where they still can be found today.

Subclass Prosobranchia

To return to the systematics of the gastropods, the first subclass, the Prosobranchia, includes the major part of the fossil genera, which are divided in three distinct orders: Archaeogastropoda, Mesogastropoda and Neogastropoda, all of which were characterized by branchia located in front of the heart.

The first of these orders includes the most primitive gastropods, those without siphons. The shape of the shell varies a great deal: Some display plano-spiral coiling, such as the genus *Bellerophon,* which lived from the Ordovician to the Per-

Below left: *Rock with numerous shells of Tentaculites; Silurian, New York.*
Below right: *Specimens of* Hyolithes cecrops; *Middle Cambrian, Utah.*
Bottom left: *Sectioned specimens of* Acteonella *sp., Late Cretaceous, Austria.*

Bottom right: *Slab with numerous specimens of* Hyolithes cecrops; *Middle Cambrian, Idaho.*

Subclass Pulmonata

The gastropods included in the subclass of the Pulmonata are characterized by the absence of branchia and by the presence of a pulmonary sac, or lung, formed by fusing the mantle to the visceral sac.

The second largest group of gastropods, this includes more than 7,000 species, of which 6,300 are alive today and 700 are known in fossil form. The Pulmonata include terrestrial gastropods with or without shells, including snails and slugs and many freshwater gastropods.

The first Pulmonata appeared during the Paleozoic, but only during the Late Cretaceous, about 70 million years ago, did they reach the distribution and importance that they still have today. The Pulmonata are classified in two orders based on the position of their eyes: basommatofori, eyes located at the base of tentacles on the head; and stilommatofori, whose eyes are located at the end of the tentacles.

Among the basommatofori, all inhabitants of fresh water, was the genus *Planorbis*, which appeared during the Jurassic and is widespread in Tertiary sediments and in contemporary freshwater bodies. Among the stilommatofori is the genus *Helix*, which includes the common snail and which appeared in the Cretaceous and is frequent in terrestrial sediments, such as the fossil dunes of the Tertiary and Quaternary.

GASTROPOD PLATES

PLATE XVII
Gastropods of the Pliocene from Liguria-Piedmont
(1) *Bursa (Ranella) nodosa*, Valle Botto; (2) *Semicassis laevigata*, Valle Botto; (3) *Cymatium tuberculiferum*, Buttigliera; (4) *Strombus coronatus*, Vezza d'Alba; (5) *Lunatia catena*, Valle Botto; (6) *Cymatium tuberculiferum*, Buttigliera; (7) *Naticarius dillwyni*, Valle Andona; (8) *Cymatium (Monoplex) doderleini*, Valle Botto; (9) *Neverita josephinia*, Monale; (10) *Zonaria (Zonaria) pyrum*, Valle Botto; (11) *Trivia europaea*, Valle Botto; (12) *Strombus coronatus*, forma giovanile, S. Stefano Roero; (13) *Cymatium (Lampusia) affine*, Valle Botto; (14) *Cymatium (Monoplex) distortum*, Valle Botto; (15) *Naticarius hebraeus*, Valle Botto; (16) *Naticarius millepunctatus*, Valle Botto; (17) *Payradentia intricata*, Valle Andona; (18) *Gyrineum (Aspa) marginatum*, Monale; (19) *Natica (Natica) pseudoepiglottinus*, Valle Botto; (20) *Cymatium (Monoplex) partenopaeum*, Valle Botto; (21) *Zonaria (Zonaria) porcellus*, Valle Botto; (22) *Sinum haliotoideum*, Monale; (23) *Cassidaria echinophora*, Valle Botto.

PLATE XVIII
(1) *Subula (Subula) fuscata*, Valle Andona; (2) *Terebra (Terebra) acuminata*, Valle Andona; (3) *Conus brocchii*, Valle Botto; (4) *Mastula (Mastula) striata*; (5) *Mitra fusiformis*, Valle Botto; (6) *Clavus (Drillia) brocchii*, Valle Andona; (7) *Strioterebrum (Strioterebrum) reticulare*, Valle Botto; (8) *Conus mediterraneus*, Valle Botto; (9) *Hastula (Hastula) farinei*, Monale; (10) *Gemmula (Gemmula) rotata*, Piea; (11) *Strioterebrum pliocenicum*, Valle Andona; (12) *Clavatula (Clavatula) interrupta*, Valle Andona; (13) *Epalxis (Batytoma) cataphracta*, Valle Botto; (14) *Expalxis (Batytoma) cataphracta*, Pliocene, Asti: (15) *Turricula (Surcula) lathyriformis*, Valle Botto; (16) *Clavus (Drillia) oblongus*, Valle Andona; (17) *Clavus (Drillia) brocchii*, Buttigliera; (18) *Raphitoma (Homotoma) stria*, Valle Botto; (19) *Conus aldrovandii*, Buttigliera; (20) *Conus antediluvianus*, Rio Torsero; (21) *Conus mercatii*, Valle Andona; (22) *Turris (Turris) turricula*, Valle Andona; (23) *Conus striatulus*, Valle Botto; (24) *Conus pyrula*, Valle Andona.

PLATE XIX
(1) *Mitra (Mitra) tracta*, Valle Botto; (2) *Alectrion (Desmoulea) conglobatus*, Valle Botto; (3) *Hinia (Hinia) musiva*, Valle Botto; (4) *Mitra (Mitra) junior*, Valle Botto; (5) *Ovatella myotis*, Valle Andona; (6) *Narona (Sveltia) altavillae strictoturrita*, Valle Botto; (7) *Bulla (Bulla) subampulla*, Valle Andona; (8) *Sphaeronassa mutabilis pliomagna*, Valle Andona; (9) *Alectrion semistriatus*, Valle Botto; (10) *Mitra (Mitra) tubuliformis*, Valle Botto; (11) *Hinia prismatica*, Valle Andona; (12) *Narona (Tribia) uniangulata*, Valle Botto; (13) *Fasciolaria fimbriata*, Valle Botto; (14) *Trigonostoma umbilicare*, Valle Botto; (15) *Fusinus rostratus*, Valle Botto; (16) *Narona (Solatia) hirta*, Valle Botto; (17) *Mitra (Mitra) astensis*, Monale; (18) *Fusinus rostratus cinctus*, Valle Botto; (19) *Narona (Sveltia) varicosa*, Valle Botto; (20) *Alectrion (Alectrion) turritus*, Valle Botto; (21) *Mitra (Tiara) alligator*, Valle Botto; (22) *Narona (Sveltia) varicosa*, Monale; (23) *Sphaeronassa longoastensis*, Monale; (24) *Fusinus clavatus* morfotipo *magnicostatus*, Valle Botto; (25) *Cancellaria (Bivetiella) cancellata*, Valle Andona; (26) *Hinia clathrata*, Valle Andona; (27) *Alectrion (Alectrion) turritus*, Valle Botto; (28) *Bulia (Bulia) striata*, Valle Botto.

PLATE XX
(1) *Petaloconchus intortus*, Valle Botto; (2) *Gibbula magnus*, Valle Andona; (3) *Cerithium (Thericium) crenatum*, Valle Botto; (4) *Capulus hungaricus*, Valle Botto; (5) *Diodora italica*, Valle Botto; (6) *Crepudula (Janacus) crepidula*, Valle Botto; (7) *Crisotrema cochleia*, Buttigliera; (8) *Opalia crenata*, Buttigliera; (9) *Cerithium vulgatum*, Vezza d'Alba; (10) *Niso (Niso) terebellum*, Valle Botto; (11) *Architectonica (Architectonica) simplex*, Valle Andona; (12) *Capulus (Brocchia) laevis*, Valle Botto; (13) *Turritella (Zaria) subangulata*, Valle Botto; (14) *Capulum (Brocchia) laevis*, Valle Botto; (15) *Calliostoma conulum*, Valle Botto; (16) *Thais biplicata*, Valle Andona; (17) *Triton affine*, Monale; (18) *Pseudosimmia carnea*, Valle Botto; (19) *Diloma (Oxystele) patulum*, Buttigliera; (20) *Cerithium (Thericium) varicosum*, Monale; (21) *Aporrhais pespelecani*, Valle Andona; (22) *Aporrhais uttingeriana*, Valle Botto; (23) *Calyptraea chinensis*, Valle Andona; (24) *Crepidula unguiformis*, Valle Botto; (25) *Astraea rugosa*, Buttigliera; (26) *Petaloconchus intortus*, Valle Andona; (27) *Xenophora crispa*, Valle Botto; (28) *Turritella (Haustator) vermicularis*, Buttigliera.

PLATE XXI
(1) *Argobuccinum giganteum*, Valle Botto; (2) *Muricopsis cristata*, Valle Botto; (3) *Heteropurpura polymorpha*, Valle Andona; (4) *Ocinebrina imbricata*, Valle Andona; (5) *Ocinebrina (Ocinebrina) funiculosa*, Valle Botto; (6) *Murex brandarius torularius*, Valle Botto; (7) *Murex (Tubicauda) spinicosta*, Vezza d'Alba; (8) *Mitrella (Macrurella) elongata*, Valle Andona; (9) *Hexaplex (Phyllonotus) rudis*, Valle Andona; (10) *Hadriania craticulata*, Buttigliera; (11) *Cantharus dorbignyi*, Valle Botto; (12) *Ocenebra polymorpha*, Valle Andona; (13) *Trunculariopsis rudis*, Buttigliera; (14) *Ficus reticulatus*, Valle Botto; (15) *Malea orbiculata*, Valle Botto; (16) *Mitrella erithrostoma*, Valle Botto; (17) *Buccinulum (Euthria) corneum*, Valle Botto; (18) *Hexaplex (Phyllonotus) rudis*, Valle Andona; (19) *Mitrella (Macrurella) semicaudata*, Valle Botto; (20) *Trunculariopsis truncula conglobata*, Asti; (21) *Hexaplex (Phyllonotus) hoernesi*, Valle Botto; (22) *Mitrella (Macrurella) nassoides*, Valle Botto; (23) *Ocenebra erinacea*, Buttigliera.

PLATE XXII
Gastropods of the Pliocene of Barton (England)
(1) *Voluta athleta*; (2) *Volutocorbis scabriculus*; (3) *Turricula rostrata*; (4) *Murex minax*; (5) *Turricula exorta*; (6) *Voluta solandri*; (7) *Trochus monilifer*, (8) *Globularia patula* f. *brabantica*; (9) *Fusus errans*; (10) *Voluta digitalina*; (11) *Volutospira luctator*; (12) *Volutospira ambigua*; (13) *Murex tricarinatus*; (14) *Sycostoma pyrus*; (15) *Conorbis dormitor*; (16) *Voluta luctatrix*; (17) *Fusus regularis*; (18) *Strepsidura turgida*; (19) *Fusinus porrectus*; (20) *Sassia arguat*; (21) *Volutospira scalaris*; (22) *Clavilithes longaevus*; (23) *Globularia grossa*; (24) *Euthriofusus regularis*; (25) *Fusus bulliformis*.

PLATE XXIII
Gastropods of the Eocene of Roncà (VI)
(1) *Lutraria oblonga*; (2) *Cyrena* cfr. *sirena*; (3) *Elire damatus*; (4) *Arca cobellii*; (5) *Cyrena* sp.; (6) *Volutolyra subspinosa*; (7) *Cerithium menegurioides*; (8) *Ampullina* cfr. *ausonica*; (9) *Cardita pachydonta*; (10) *Capsidia cypraeformis*; (11) *Cardium fragiforme*; (12) *Rostellaria corvina*; (13) *Nerita conoidea*; (14) *Chemnitzia lactea*; (15) *Hipponyx* cfr. *dilatatus*; (16) *Strombus fortisi*; (17) *Cerithium castellinii*; (18) *Cerithium conoideum*; (19) *Natica cepacia*.

PLATE XVII

PLATE XVIII

PLATE XIX

PLATE XX

PLATE XXI

PLATE XXII

PLATE XXIII

Below left: *Different forms of nautiloids: (A) orthocone shell; (B) cirtocone shell; (C) girocone shell; (D) evolute coil; (E) involute coil.*
Below right: Lituites lituus, *a nautiloid with a partially coiled shell; Ordovician, Holland.*

Class Cephalopoda

The Cephalopoda constitute an ancient group of highly specialized mollusks that have long passed the period of their maximum development. Today's 400 living species are a small fraction of those that lived from the Late Cambrian, about 570 million years ago. The few modern-day species that have a chambered external shell, descendants of the genus *Nautilus*, are all that remain of a vast group that populated the oceans for millions of years. The Cephalopoda are exclusively marine animals and the most advanced mollusks. They are found today worldwide, while their fossil remains, widespread in sedimentary rocks of all ages, are used as index fossils for correlations among distant marine strata.

The class's name is derived from the fact that the foot—which, as we have seen, assumes various forms and functions in the different mollusk classes—is in these animals partly transformed into a head with a series of tentacles that surround the mouth, used both for locomotion and for the capture of prey. The "head" also contains the siphon, an organ that the animal uses to move by ejecting water through it.

Unlike the other mollusks we've examined up to now, in the Cephalopoda the head is clearly differentiated and has two large, camera-type eyes. The mouth has chitinous jaws that are sometimes fossilized. The major characteristic in almost all the Cephalopoda is the presence of an external or internal shell, a shell that is usually easily fossilized. This shell, as we will see, is different from those we have examined up to now because of the presence of numerous septa that divide it internally into chambers. Based on this characteristic, certain other fossil forms without soft parts, of such extinct animals as the ammonites, have been attributed to the Cephalopoda.

The class Cephalopoda is divided into three subclasses; the nautiloids (Nautiloidea), the members of which were very abundant during the Paleozoic and of which the genus *Nautilus* is the only living remainder; the ammonoids (Ammonoidea), of which we have fossil remains only from the Devonian to the Late Cretaceous; and the coleoids (Coleoidea), or Dibranchiata, to which belong, together with several exclusively fossil forms, most of the modern-day Cephalopoda, including cuttlefish, squid and octopuses.

Together with these three principal subclasses there are two groups of minor importance that include only Paleozoic forms once classified among the nautiloids—the Endoceratoidea and Actinoceratoidea.

Subclass Nautiloidea

The nautiloids are the most ancient shelled cephalopods. They appeared suddenly during the Late Cambrian, and their relationships with other groups of invertebrates are unknown. Although their origins remain obscure, they constitute a group of extreme importance in paleontology since in subsequent periods they led, in all probability, to the subclasses of ammonoids and dibranchiats. Furthermore, unlike other groups that became completely extinct, they have survived up to our time, although with very few representatives, after an evolutionary history that has lasted more than 500 million years.

In today's seas there are still a few species of the genus *Nautilus*, confined to the western portion of the South Pacific Ocean. Observing the oldest nautiloids we can see that they have not remained unchanged in time and that today's species are not identical to the oldest representatives. In the course of evolution important changes took place in terms of the form of the shell, part of the internal anatomy, and habits and way of life.

The first Cambrian nautiloids were very primitive types with a straight or slightly curved shell. During the periods following the Cambrian, an explosive evolution took place, with an incredible multiplication of forms and a tendency of the shell toward plano-spiral coiling. This coiling became complete around the beginning of the Silurian, the period during which the nautiloids reached their peak, after having passed intermediate stages with cirtocone, or slightly coiled, shells; gyrocone shells, coiled without contact between the successive whorls; evolute shells, with whorls that just touched one another; and involute shells, in which the last whorl enclosed more or less completely all the preceding whorls, which can be seen in today's *Nautilus*.

At the end of the Paleozoic, the nautiloids began a decline, perhaps as a result of increased competition from the ammonoids, which were derived from the nautiloids and which at that moment in the history of the earth began an impressive development. During the Jurassic, about 195 million years ago, the period of maximum expansion of the ammonoids, the nau-

Bottom left: *Section of* Cenoceras striatum. *The phragmocone is visible, as is, at center, the small embryonic chamber (protoconch); Early Jurassic, England.*
Bottom center: Ceroceras striatum, *a nautiloid similar to modern members of the group; Early Jurassic, Italy.*

Bottom right: *Thin section of limestone with Orthoceras. The straight chambered shell is typical of primitive nautiloids; Silurian, Fluminimaggiore, Italy.*

tiloids were reduced to a few genera, among them the genus *Nautilus*, which exists in a similar form today, unchanged by the passage of 150 to 160 million years.

Of most interest to paleontologists is the presence of an external calcareous shell, the shape of which varies but which can be divided in two principal parts: the phragmocone (the chambered portion) and the body chamber.

The phragmocone is the most developed part of the shell and is divided internally into chambers by septa perpendicular to the longitudinal axis of the shell. These septa leave on the inside wall of the shell, below the first layers of which it is formed, characteristic lines known as sutures, which can be simple or wavy. Each septum bears a hole through which passes the siphuncle, the soft tubular elongation of the mantle that extends through the chambers up to the beginning, or protoconch, located at the center of the coil. The chambers are known as camerae and contain, along with fluids, a gaseous mixture similar to atmospheric air but richer in nitrogen, which, when made more or less dense by the animal, changes its buoyancy and permits vertical movements in the water.

The animal lives in the body chamber, which is closed to the rear by the last septum and open to the outside in front in a way that varies in the different groups. Lateral formations of the peristoma, which is the edge of the aperture, can in fact close off this opening, giving rise to some unusual apertures, such as the T-shaped openings that characterize certain genera of the Silurian and the Carboniferous.

On the external surface of the shell there is sometimes ornamentation of varying intensity, formed by simple growth lines, by ribs or by grooves parallel or longitudinal to the axis of the shell, sometimes zigzagging. In certain rare specimens, the external coloration of the shell has been preserved, formed most of all by longitudinal or transversal bands or lines of darker or lighter gray or black.

The nautiloids thus had an evolution that lasted many millions of years and had an enormous flourishing, most of all during the Paleozoic, with the production of innumerable different species characterized by wide distribution and very short lifespans. These species are used as index fossils for Paleozoic rocks and assume at times an importance similar to that of the ammonoids in the following era.

The subclass Nautiloidea is subdivided by paleontologists into several orders, most of which lived exclusively during the Paleozoic. Among the most ancient and common groups are the orthoceratids, which had straight shells and body chambers that reached two meters (6.6 ft.) in length in the giant forms and were ornamented by longitudinal or transversal ribs. Representatives of this group lived from the Ordovician to the Triassic, or from about 590 million to 230 million years ago, and are found frequently in Paleozoic rocks in the central and western United States. The family Nautilidae appeared in the Late Triassic. It comprises the most modern members of the group, including the genus *Nautilus*, the first fossil remains of which come from Jurassic deposits.

The only living genus of the nautiloids has furnished us with excellent information on how these animals lived. The Nautilus, an excellent swimmer, lives in warm seas and it seems that its environment is closely tied to temperature and the salinity of the water. They usually live at about 500 meters (1,650 ft.) of depth, but each night migrate toward shallower depths, probably following the movements of the plankton on which they feed. After death, the shell floats and can be carried by currents into areas far distant from where the animal lived. This has resulted in the great distribution of the nautiloids in rocks of all environments and explains why they can not be used as paleoecological indicators.

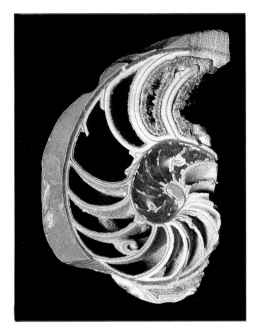

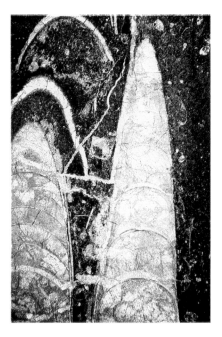

PLATE XXIV

Below: Ammonite in a section of the red "marble" of Verona. The chambers of the phragmocone are visible; Late Jurassic, Italy.

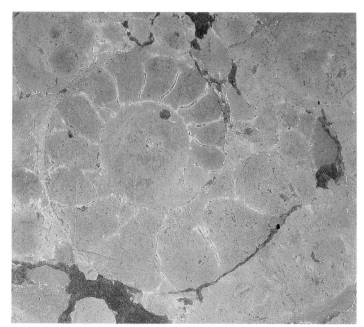

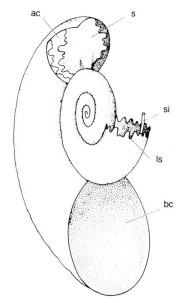

Nomenclature of ammonoids:
(bc) body chamber;
(ac) air chamber;
(ls) lobe of suture;
(s) septum;
(si) siphuncle.

Subclass Ammonoidea

An external shell similar to those of the nautiloids was present in the ammonoids, cephalopods that, owing to the abundance of the specimens and the variety of their forms, represent a great enigma to paleontologists. Ammonoids form an immense group that, after populating the Paleozoic and Mesozoic seas, became extinct at the end of the Cretaceous, about 70 million years ago, and up to now it has been impossible to determine the exact causes of this sudden decline. Various hypotheses have begun to appear plausible, hypotheses that avoid the notion of an immense catastrophe and are based, instead, on normal ecological models.

Ammonoids appeared during the Early Devonian with forms that seem to be derived from the orthocerid nautiloids of the Paleozoic. They began their great evolutionary development during the Late Devonian, replacing the nautiloids and reaching, during the Mesozoic, the complexity so well known today. The subclass Ammonoidea includes the single order Ammonitida, subdivided into the suborders Anarcestina,

Goniatitina, Ceratitina, Phylloceratina, Lytoceratina and Ammonitina, each of which includes in turn numerous superfamilies, families and genera.

The shells of ammonoids, which because of their solid calcareous structures fossilize well, are the only part of the animal that we can describe with certainty. The soft parts of the body, sometimes thought to be similar to those of today's Nautilus, are completely unknown, as they probably decayed rapidly after the moment of death.

The shell of an ammonoid is constructed of a single valve, usually plano-spiral, that can be considered as the result of the coiling of a straight, elongated cone around an axis. It is divided into three parts: the protoconch or first chamber, formed at the beginning of the animal's juvenile life, representing the earliest growth stage; the phragmocone, the long part, partitioned by septa toward the aperature into numerous chambers probably filled, like the Nautilus, by a gaseous and fluid mixture; and finally the body chamber, open to the outside, in which the animal lived.

The animal could withdraw completely into the shell, closing the opening with a calcareous operaculum, or disk, carried by the ventral part of the mantle. The animal was connected to the chambers by a siphuncle, a tube-like extension of the mantle that passed through holes in the septa in the various chambers. It then extended to the protoconch with a thickening (caecum) tied to the bottom by a calcareous cord, the prosiphon.

The phragmocone, the part most readily preserved in the fossil record, constituted the most developed part of the shell and was divided in very complex forms, into chambers by septa that left on the surface of the shell, below the first layer, characteristic lines, called suture lines.

The shells of ammonoids are usually covered by very marked ornamentation, formed by radial, straight, curved or winding

---

PLATE XXIV
Cephalopods
(1) *Atractites orsini*, belemnite cephalopod with a phragmocone very similar to those of many coiled nautiloids; (2) *Aturia* sp., Miocene, Italy; (3) *Nautilus archincianus*, Late Cretaceous, France; (4) *Gomphoceras pyriforme*, Silurian, England; (5) *Metacoceras mutabile*, Pennsylvanian, Montana; (6) *Orthoceras* sp., Devonian, Algeria; (7) *Dolorthoceras sociale*, Ordovician, Iowa; (8) *Planetoceras globatum*, Carboniferous, England; (9) *Nautilus* sp., Early Jurassic, Italy; (10) *Nautilus distefanoi*, Early Jurassic, Italy; (11) *Mooreoceras normale*, Pennsylvanian, Montana; (12) *Dolorthoceras sociale*, Ordovician, Iowa; (13) *Aturia aturi*, Miocene, Italy; (14) *Cyrtoceras lineatum*, Middle Devonian, Germany; (15) *Epphioceras* sp., Pennsylvanian, Montana; (16) *Nautilus* sp., Early Jurassic, Italy; (17) *Orthoceras planorectatum*, Jurassic, Germany; (18) *Orthoceras inflata*, Devonian, Germany; (19) *Eutrephoceras maruconensis*, Early Cretaceous, Peru.

A perfect ammonite from the Jurassic in England, with the suture lines evident along the entire length of the phragmacone.

ribs, by tubercles (or knobs) of various forms and sizes, and by spines that must have reached great sizes. This ornamentation is often used as the basis for the subdivisions both into genera and species.

For subdivisions such as suborders and families, great importance is given to the sutures. These sutures are formed where the internal partitions made by the septa in the phragmocone meet the inside of the shell of the ammonoid. Since the septa were not arranged linearly the sutures are often strongly curved into lobes and saddles. Saddles curve toward the aperture of the shell while lobes curve away from the aperture. The suture line has undergone in the course of evolution progressive complication, passing from simple, straight or gently curved to highly convoluted sutures. These progressive complexities can be observed even during the development of each individual, so that in the early stages the suture is simple and tends to become increasingly complex during growth. It is believed, but not yet proved, that this tendency toward complex sutures had the function of strengthening the thin shell, thus rendering it more resistant to blows and to the water pressure of great depths.

Another characteristic used in the classification of these fossils is the appearance of the shell, which, as in the case of the nautiloids, is found in very different forms. It seems that the first ammonoids, those which appeared in the Middle Paleozoic, had straight shells. These began to coil later, during the Early Devonian, and by the end of that period the shells were fully coiled in a plano-spiral form.

This subclass went into decline during the Cretaceous. The ammonoids then began to develop aberrant, irregular forms:

straight, hooked, partly coiled and partly uncoiled, turreted, coiled without a precise direction. The Cretaceous saw the entire group move toward extinction, and after an existence of 330 million years, from the Early Devonian to the Late Cretaceous, it became completely extinct about 65 million years ago, leaving as testimony of its existence only fossilized shells.

Very little is known of the life of ammonoids. Research is hampered by two obstacles: the total absence of soft parts and the probable postmortem transport of the shells. This transport, in particular, makes the establishment of a relationship between the fossils and the environment in which they were deposited very difficult. This transport was in all probability very common since the shells of ammonoids, like those of the nautiloids, were very light and the chambers were full of gas, so they must, with the loss of the soft parts, have floated well and been transported by currents for great distances.

In reconstructing the lives of these animals, the most valuable information concerns their mobility. Following experiments using models, it has been established that ammonoids moved holding the shell with the coils vertical above them and the aperture near the ground. This seems to be demonstrated by the finding, in Jurassic deposits at Solnhofen, of ammonite shells fossilized near impressions of their backs which were made when they fell to the sea floor.

Other information, although very scarce, on the way of life of the ammonoids has come from the study of other animals that were their contemporaries. Thus it is known that the ammonoids, notwithstanding their shell, were a tasty and abundant food for the marine reptiles of that period. Some specimens, in fact, have been found in the stomachs of these fossilized animals, and a large North American ammonite found in the Pierre Shale of South Dakota bears the signs of bites produced by a mosasaur, a giant marine reptile of the Late Cretaceous.

The importance of ammonoids to paleontologists is due most of all to the fact that they are used in special ways as index fossils. Each species is generally characterized by a great expansion that lasted only a brief time. Using ammonoids it has thus been possible to divide the Mesozoic into numerous "biozones," each of which corresponds to a period of time in which were present one or more characteristic species. Because of the ammonoids' wide diffusion such zones can be correlated across wide areas with a considerable accuracy.

A few words must be added about aptychi, the calcareous or chitinous operculums of ammonoids that are usually found individually in sediments. Fortunately, rare specimens of ammonoids with the aptychi in place have been found and permit the recognition of these strange fossils, whose function once seemed very obscure.

The aptychi can be divided into two large groups: the anaptychi, contained in sediments deposited from the Late Devonian to the Cretaceous, formed of a single valve ornamented with concentric and radial ribs; and the true aptychi, limited to Jurassic and Cretaceous rocks, formed of two strongly ornamented valves.

Since aptychi are usually found isolated, only in rare cases

Right: Crioceratites emerici, *a Cretaceous ammonite with the shell twisted into a spiral whose successive whorls do not touch.*
Far right: *Ammonite with a typically twisted shell,* Ancyloceras matheronianum *of the Early Cretaceous.*

Below: Hyphantoceras reussianum, *Late Cretaceous, Germany. Bottom: Block with aptychi of the Laevaptychus type, Jurassic, Tierra del Fuego, Argentina.*

can the genera of ammonoids to which aptychi belong be determined, so the different types of aptychi have been assigned specific generic names of their own.

Subclass Coleoidea

The subclass Coleoidea includes most of the cephalopods—the most advanced group of mollusks—alive today. These animals are well known to most people, for the group includes cuttlefish, squid and octopuses common worldwide. During past geologic eras, this subclass was very well represented, but without reaching the diffusion enjoyed by the nautiloids and the ammonoids, during the Paleozoic and the Mesozoic, respectively. As indicated by their name, the Coleoidea, or Dibranchiata, have only two branchia, two fewer than the nautiloids and, probably, the ammonoids.

Leaving aside the anatomy of the soft parts of the body, we must note that these animals are characterized in most cases by the presence of an internal shell (for example, the pen of the squid and the cuttlebone of the cuttlefish). In most cases, this is the only part of the animal preserved as a fossil. Very rare, in fact, are instances of fossilized Coleoidea that have no shell, such as octopuses, or of Coleoidea in which the soft parts are preserved. Although this internal shell is different from those of the other cephalopods, it has the same general structure and can be divided into three parts that correspond more or less to those described for the other subclasses.

The Coleoidea include two large orders: the Decapoda, which have 10 tentacles around the mouth and are divided into the extinct suborder of the Belemnoidea and the still living Sepioidea and Teuthoidea; and the Octopoda, which have eight tentacles and which include the extinct suborder of the Palaeoc-

AMMONOID PLATES

PLATE XXV

(1) *Cadomites humphresianum*, Middle Jurassic, Germany; (2) *Emileia multiforme* var. *micromphalum*, Middle Jurassic, Argentina; (3) *Tornoceras simplex*, Late Devonian, Germany; (4) *Grammoceras* sp., Early Jurassic, Germany; (5) *Coeloceras grenouillowi*, Early Jurassic, Germany; (6) *Cycloceras valdani*, Early Jurassic, Germany; (7) *Arietites turneri*, Early Jurassic, Germany; (8) *Leioceras opalinum*, Middle Jurassic, Germany; (9) *Oxyparoniceras telemachi*, Early Jurassic, France; (10) *Arietites raricostatum*, Early Jurassic, Germany; (11) *Macrocephalites macrocephalus*, Middle Jurassic, Germany; (12) *Oistoceras crescens*, Early Jurassic, England; (13) *Aegoceras planicosta*, Early Jurassic, Germany; (14) *Ceratites* sp., Triassic, Germany; (15) *Dactylioceras athleticum*, Early Jurassic, England; (16) *Plenoceras costatum*, Jurassic, Germany; (17) *Rasenia uralensis*, Late Jurassic, England; (18) *Pseudofarrella garatei*, Jurassic, Argentina; (19) *Amaltheus* (Pleuroceras) *costatus*, Early Jurassic, Germany; (20) *Perisphinctes* (Mantelliceras) *plicatilis*, Middle Jurassic, Germany; (21) *Pleuroceras spinatum* var. *buckmanni*, Early Jurassic, Switzerland.

PLATE XXVI

(1) *Arcestes muensteri*, Middle Triassic, Italy; (2) *Peltoceras annularis*, Middle Jurassic, Germany; (3) *Perisphinctes parabolis*, Middle Jurassic, Germany: (4) *Mantelliceras* sp., Late Cretaceous, England; (5) *Polyptychites* sp., Late Jurassic, Germany; (6) *Perisphinctes convolutus*, Middle Jurassic, Germany; (7) *Olcostephanus astierianus*, Lower Cretaceous, France; (8) *Proarcestes subtridentinus*, Middle Triassic, Italy; (9) *Bullatimorphites* sp., Middle Jurassic, France; (10) *Kosmoceras (Lobokosmoceras) proniae*, Late Jurassic, England; (11) *Hoplites deluci*, Early Cretaceous, France; (12) *Oxynoticeras* (Gleniceras) *guibalianum*, Early Jurassic, France; (13) *Goniatites* sp., Devonian, Morocco; (14) *Hoploscaphites* sp., Late Cretaceous, U.S.A.; (15) *Acanthoceras rothomagensis*, Jurassic, England; (16) *Nigericeras gignouxi*, Late Cretaceous, Nigeria.

PLATE XXVII

Ammonoids of the Early Jurassic (Sinemurian) of Monte Albenza (Bergamo)

(1) *Juraphyllites quadrii* f. *solidula*; (2) *Arnioceras* cfr. *insolitum*; (3) *Arnioceras hartmanni*; (4) *Eoderoceras* sp.; (5) *Arietites* cfr. *bucklandi*; (6) *Arnioceras* cfr. *ceratitoides*; (7) *Coroniceras bisulcatum*; (8) *Coroniceras bisulcatum*; (9) *Arnioceras* sp.; (10) *Geyeroceras cylindricum*; (11) *Juraphyllites* sp.; (12) *Coroniceras bisulcatum*; (13) *Pararnioceras truemanni*; (14) *Agassiceras nodulatum*; (15) *Pararnioceras truemanni*; (16) *Arnioceras insolitum*; (17) *Coroniceras* cfr. *primitivus*; (18) *Pararnioceras meridionale*; (19) *Juraphyllites quadrii*; (20) *Arnioceras geometricum*.

PLATE XXVIII

Ammonoids of the Early Jurassic (Domerian) of Alpe Turati (Como)

(1) *Lioceratoides fucinianum*; (2) *Lytoceras francisci*; (3) *Fuciniceras bonarellii*; (4) *Fuciniceras intumescens*; (5) *Arieticeras accuratum*; (6) *Arieticeras expulsum*; (7) *Arieticeras domarense*; (8) *Reynesoceras ragazzonii*; (9) *Protogrammoceras meneghinii*; (10) *Arieticeras retrorsicosta*; (11) *Aveyroniceras acanthoides*; (12) *Arieticeras lottii*; (13) *Fuciniceras fortisi*; (14) *Arieticeras ruthense*; (15) *Meneghiniceras lariense*; (16) *Paltopleuroceras* sp.; (17) *Harpophyllites eximium*; (18) *Phylloceras emeryi*; (19) *Protogrammoceras celebratum*; (20) *Uptonia* cfr. *obsoleta*.

PLATE XXIX

Ammonoids of the Early Jurassic (Toarcian) of Passo del Furlo (Pesaro)

(1)*Mercaticeras* sp.; (2) *Lillia chelussii*; (3) *Chartronia* sp.; (4) *Lillia* sp.; (5) *Brodieia bayani*; (6) *Phymatoceras mavigliai*; (7) *Phymatoceras iserense*; (8) *Brodieia* sp.; (9) *Chartronia* sp.; (10) *Phymatoceras muelleri*; (11) *Phymatoceras merlai*; (12) *Phymatoceras erbaense*; (13) *Pseudomercaticeras* sp.; (14) *Dumortieria meneghinii*; (15) *Dumortieria insignisimilis*; (16) *Phymatoceras meneghinii*.

PLATE XXX

Ammonoids of the Early Jurassic (Toarcian) of Passo del Furlo

(1) *Nodicoeloceras angelonii*; (2) *Catacoeloceras puteolum*; (3) *Dactylioceras holandrei*; (4) *Telodactylites renzi*; (5) *Platystrophites latus*; (6) *Collina gemma*; (7) *Nodicoeloceras hungaricum*; (8) *Nodicoeloceras lobatum*; (9) *Peronoceras* cfr. *vortex*; (10) *Orthodactylites mediterraneum*; (11) *Nodicoeloceras verticosum*; (12) *Orthodactylites merlai*; (13) *Nodicoeloceras verticellum*; (14) *Peronoceras bollense*; (15) *Nodicoeloceras acanthus*; (16) *Peronoceras andraei*; (17) *Nodicoeloceras baconicum*; (18) *Catacoeloceras* cfr. *mucronatum*; (19) *Nodicoeloceras crassoides*; (20) *Mesodactylites sapphicum*.

PLATE XXXI

Ammonoids of the Early Jurassic (Toarcian) of Passo del Furlo

(1) *Hammatoceras tenuinsigne*: (2) *Hammatoceras planiforme*; (3) *Hammatoceras perplanum*; (4) *Rarenodia* sp.; (5) *Hammatoceras costulosus*; (6) *Rarenodia* sp.; (7) *Hammatoceras perplanum*; (8) *Hammatoceras* gr. *insigne*; (9) *Hammatoceras clavatum*; (10) *Erycites intermedius*; (11) *Erycites* aff. *reussi*; (12) *Erycites rotundiformis*; (13) *Hammatoceras victorii*; (14) *Hammatoceras planinsigne*; (15) *Hammatoceras planinsigne*.

PLATE XXXII

Ammonoids of the Early Jurassic (Toarcian) of Passo del Furlo

(1) *Costileioceras* sp.; (2) *Phylloceras selinoides*; (3) *Pseudogrammoceras subfallaciosum*; (4) *Hildoceras bifrons*; (5) *Hildaites serpentiniformis*; (6) *Hildoceras bifrons*; (7) *Phylloceras heterophyllum*; (8) *Phylloceras ausonium*; (9) *Hildaites exilis*; (10) *Harpoceras exaratum*; (11) *Glyptarpites diplois*; (12) *Hildaites proserpentinus*; (13) *Polyplectus policostatus*; (14) *Lytoceras* cfr. *fimbriatus*; (15) *Lytoceras dorcadis*; (16) *Leukadiella* sp.; (17) *Callyphylloceras nilssoni*; (18) *Lobolytoceras* cfr. *siemensis*; (19) *Hildoceras semipolitum*; (20) *Hildoceras sublevisoni*; (21) *Phylloceras loczy*.

PLATE XXXIII

Ammonoids of the Late Jurassic (Kimmeridgian-Titonic) of Passo del Furlo

(1) *Aspidoceras acanthomphalum acanthomphalum*; (2) *Spiticeras spitiense*; (3) *Aspidoceras* cfr. *zeuchneri*; (4) *Aspidoceras acanthicum*; (5) *Aspidoceras acanthicum*; (6) *Physodoceras* cfr. *montesprini*; (7) *Phanerostephanus dalmasiforme*; (8) *Aspidoceras (Pseudowaagenia)* cfr. *micropilum*; (9) *Phylloceras isotypum* subsp. *apenninica*; (10) *Neocosmoceras bitubercolatum*; (11) *Simoceras volanense*; (12) *Neocosmoceras ambiguum*; (13) *Physodoceras cyclotum cyclotum*; (14) *Phanerostephanus* sp.

PLATE XXXIV

Ammonoids of the Late Jurassic (Kimmeridgian-Titonic) of Passo del Furlo

(1) *Notostephanus kurdistanensis*; (2) *Katroliceras* cfr. *sowerbii*; (3) *Callyphylloceras* aff. *kochi*; (4) *Paraberriasiella* cfr. *blondeti*; (5) *Lytoceras orsinii*; (6) *Pectinatites* cfr. *inconsuetus*; (7) *Katroliceras* sp.; (8) *Protetragonites quadrisulcatum*; (9) *Taramelliceras* cfr. *nodogioscutum*; (10) *Lytoceras montanum*; (11) *Haploceras verruciferum*; (12) *Phylloceras empedoclis* subsp. *furlensis*.

PLATE XXXV

Ammonoids of the Late Jurassic (Kimmeridgian-Titonic) of Passo del Furlo

(1) *Spiticeras* sp.; (2) *Lytoceras polycyclum*; (3) *Haploceras verruciferum*; (4) *Calliphylloceras leiokoclos*; (5) *Parapallasiceras* cfr. *pseudocontingens*; (6) *Blanfordiceras uhligi*; (7) *Simoceras (Lytogyroceras) subbeticum*; (8) *Ptychophylloceras ptychoicum*; (9) *Berriasiella privasensis*; (10) *Parapallasiceras praecox*; (11) *Phylloceras isotypum* subsp. *apenninica*; (12) *Phylloceras serum*; (13) *Spiticeras bulliformis*; (14) *Pavlovia* aff. *iastriensis primaria*; (15) *Parapallasiceras praecox*; (16) *Spiticeras spitiense*; (17) *Lytoceras montanum*; (18) *Simoceras subbeticum*; (19) *Neolissoceras grasi*; (20) *Paraberriasiella* sp.; (21) *Hemispitceras steinmanni*; (22) *Spiticeras spitiense*.

1

2

3

4

5

6

7

8

9

10

11

12

13

14

15

16

17

18

19

20

21 **PLATE XXV**

PLATE XXVI

PLATE XXVII

PLATE XXVIII

1

2

3

4

5

6

7

8

9

10

11

12

13

14

15

16

PLATE XXIX

PLATE XXX

1

2

3

4

5

6

7

8

9

10

11

12

13

14

15

PLATE XXXI

PLATE XXXII

PLATE XXXIII

PLATE XXXIV

PLATE XXXV

Below left: *Section of belemnite in a rock from the Middle Jurassic of Franconia, Germany. Visible are the elongated rostrum and, in the upper part, the chambered phragmocone.*

Below center: *Section of* Megateuthis giganteus, *belemnite of the Middle Jurassic, Germany. The rostrum is very developed, and above is the conical phragmocone, of which part of the conoteca is preserved.*

Below: *Nomenclature of belemnites:*
(A) frontal section; (B) side section; (ph) phragmocone; (pr) proostracum; (r) rostrum; (si) siphuncle; (se) septum.

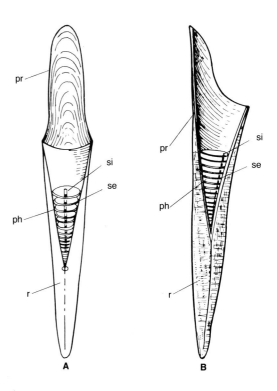

topoda, the Cirroteuthoidea, which are unknown in the fossil record, and the Polypodoidea, with numerous members, both fossil and living.

In marine sediments of the Mesozoic it is not rare to find strange, elongated, cigarlike fossils that are very strong and completely calcified. For a long time these presented paleontologists with a true dilemma. Detailed studies of their internal structure and the fortunate finding of impressions of the soft parts of the animals that lived in these fossils have led to the conclusion that the "cigars" were remnants of the internal shell of certain extinct cephalopods, which were called belemnites and were grouped in the suborder of the Belemnoidea.

Unlike the ammonoids, whose soft parts are still completely unknown, in the case of the belemnites scientists were aided by the discovery of certain impressions left by the body of the animal while falling, after death, on the fine layer of slime that covered the bottom of tranquil marine basins. Using reconstructions based on these findings the belemnites are believed to have been animals similar to cuttlefish; they had an ink sac and a number of tentacles that, according to the impressions, varied from eight to six, located in the cephalic area around the mouth, which had small jaws.

Within the body of this animal was the shell composed of three distinct parts: the rostrum, phragmocone, and proostracum. The rostrum is the hardest portion and that which is best preserved in the fossil state. It is made of small prisms of calcite located radially with respect to the longitudinal axis. It is usually elongated, but in some species is flattened. It ends sometimes with a point, sometimes with a protuberance,

sometimes more or less rounded. The external surface is often covered by granulations and furrows; the latter, developed most of all on the ventral and dorsal parts, are used as characteristics for identifying genera or species, since they are believed to be traces of muscle scars.

On its end the rostrum has a conical cavity in which was located the phragmocone. This is the part of the shell divided by septa that corresponds to the chambered portion of the shell of the nautiloids and ammonoids. Because of its extreme fragility it is preserved more rarely than the rostrum. The phragmocone was formed of a number of septa crossed, near the ventral end, by the siphuncle. In the best preserved specimens it is possible to see the phragmocone's very delicate external

PLATE XXXVI
Belemnites
(1) *Hybolites* sp., Middle Jurassic, France; (2) *Dactyloteuthis digitatus*, Early Jurassic, France; (3) *Belemnitella americana*, Cretaceous, New Jersey; (4) *Belemnites sulcatus*, Middle Jurassic, Italy; (5) *Belemnitella quadrata*, Late Cretaceous, France; (6) *Belemnitella mucronata*, Late Cretaceous, France; (7) *Megateuthis giganteus*, Middle Jurassic, Germany; (8) *Paxillosus hastatus*, Jurassic, Germany; (9) *Pachyteuthis densus*, Jurassic, Wyoming; (10) *Duvalia* sp., Late Jurassic, Italy; (11) *Belemnites pacillosus*, Early Jurassic, Germany; (12) *Megateuthis giganteus*, Middle Jurassic, Germany; (13) *Gastrobelus umbilicatus*, Early Jurassic, Germany; (14) *Duvalia dilatata*, Early Cretaceous, France; (15) *Duvalia dilatata*, Early Cretaceous, Sicily; (16) *Pachyteuthis densus*, Jurassic, Montana; (17) *Duvalia dilatata*, Early Cretaceous, Castellane; (18) *Hybolites* sp., Late Jurassic, Alpine foothills, near Vicenza, Italy; (19) *Belemnites elongatus*, Early Jurassic, Germany; (20) *Belemnites pacillosus*, Jurassic, Germany.

PLATE XXXVI

Below left: *This slab contains fossilized tentacles of Teuthoidea cephalopods of the genus* Acanthoteutis *that can clearly be seen to bear hooks; Late Jurassic, Eichstatt, Germany.*

Below center: Trachyteuthis hastiforme, *a Teuthoidea cephalopod; Late Jurassic, Solnhofen, Germany.*

Below right: Plesioteuthis prisca; *Late Jurassic, Solnhofen, Germany.*

wall (conotheca). Even more delicate and therefore harder to preserve is the proostracum, derived from an elongation of the conotheca toward the front of the animal.

The first belemnites appeared at the beginning of the Mesozoic, in the Early Triassic, about 230 million years ago. They had a shell with a well developed phragmacone. There followed a progressive reduction of the phragmacone compared to the rostrum, and then of the rostrum compared to the proostracum. Thus, in the Aulacoceratidae, the most primitive belemnites of the Triassic and Jurassic, the phragmacone is much more developed than the rostrum, and there is no proostracum; in the Atractitidae, the phragmacones of which are often found in Early Jurassic rocks, there seems to be a sign of the proostracum. In Jurassic belemnites the phragmacone is notably reduced, while the rostrum is well developed. Because of this change, the belemnites, so abundant in Jurassic and Cretaceous rocks, have furnished numerous index fossils.

In the Belemnoteutidi, already present in the Late Triassic but most diverse in the Jurassic and the Cretaceous, the proostracum begins to develop, while at the same time one notes a curving of the phragmacone. In the neobelemnitidi, finally, are grouped forms that lived from the Cretaceous to the Tertiary and that mark a transition to representatives of the suborder Sepioidea and show an even more marked tendency of the phragmocone to curve. At the beginning of the Tertiary, in the Paleocene, the Belemnitida became extinct, making room for the Sepioidea and the Teuthoidea, from which are probably derived most of the forms living today.

The suborder Sepioidea includes the modern-day cuttlefish and certain fossil forms very similar to them. Among these are the Spirulirostridae, which lived from the Eocene to the Miocene, which demonstrate a strong tendency toward coiling of the phragmocone. The Spirulidae, with a spiraled phragmacone and, without a siphon, have been found as fossils only in Miocenic rocks, while the only living representatives live confined to the oceans at a depth of from 100 to 200 meters (330–660 ft.). The Sepiidae, to which belongs the common cuttlefish, appeared during the Eocene. Their shell is composed of a small rostrum, barely visible, a relatively well developed phragmacone that forms the central, spongy part of the bone of the cuttlefish, and by a large proostracum.

The Teuthoidea are the suborder of the squid, whose very reduced shell, or pen, is composed of a well developed proostracum. The squid appeared during the Early Jurassic.

Finally, to end our discussion on mollusks, we should turn briefly to the Octopoda, the cephalopod order to which belongs the octopus. These appeared during the Late Cretaceous with the genus *Palaeoctopus,* known from a single specimen for which this separate suborder was created. The suborder Polypodoidea includes the genus *Argonauta,* in which the female has a kind of plano-spiraled shell. It is used however, as a container for eggs and not for protection. The earliest fossil records of the Argonauta date to the Cenozoic.

Echinoderms

The echinoderms (phylum Echinodermata) are exclusively marine animals that have well defined characteristics. They are subdivided into 14 classes (excluding the Stylophora and Homoiostelea by classifying the two as part of the chordates and thus separate from the true echinoderms). Some of these classes appeared in the seas of the Early Cambrian and were extinct before the end of the Paleozoic, while others, which appeared only slightly later, count a large number of still living members. Among the echinoderms that still populate our seas are the Crinoidea, Asteroidea, Echinoidea and Holothurioidea, best known by the names sea lilies, sea stars (starfish), sea urchins and sea cucumbers.

The echinoderms are distinguishable by the presence of an exoskeleton composed of calcareous plates, a body with a five-sided radial symmetry, and an internal water-vascular system that circulates water through the body by means of five radial canals formed by porous plates, along which the current of water, full of particles of food, moves toward the mouth. A mouth opening and an anal opening are sometimes located on opposite surfaces of the body, sometimes on the same side. In the second case there is development of bilateral symmetry, very clear most of all in the more mobile echinoderms.

The body of many echinoderms is divided into five radial extensions that take on the appearance of arms in the Asteroidea, of fixed areas in the Echinoidea and of internal compartments in the Holothuroidea. These extensions, called ambulacra, follow the course of the water-circulation canals and are visible on the exoskeleton as five radial canals. The ambulacral areas are separated by groups of plates without pores (called nonporous plates) that constitute the interambulacra.

The part of these animals that is best known to the paleontologist is the exoskeleton, which encloses the internal organs and is formed of calcareous plates, usually ornamented by spines and/or tubercles, and loosely articulated or solidly fused together to form, in most cases, a very strong shell. These plates are formed in the living animal by a net of spicules fused together whose empty areas are filled by organic material. In fossils, the original high magnesium calcite of the spicules transforms into low magnesium calcite, which is much more resistant, while the empty areas fill with the same mineral, which, crystalizing, leaves a strong skeleton that can be readily preserved.

Echinoderms are of great importance in paleontology, as are other index fossils such as echinoids and crinoids, in providing ecological indicators. Since the echinoderms are strictly marine animals and only rarely adapted to salt marshes, the finding of so much as a single plate is a sure indication of a marine environment. Furthermore, many of them are specially adapted. Some are adapted to life on rocky bottoms, others live on muddy or sandy bottoms, and many others furnish valuable information about the depth of the ocean in the various geologic periods.

The phylum Echinodermata, often divided into Pelmatozoa, or stalked echinoderms, and Eleutherozoa, or mobile echino-

Top: Gogia palmeri, *eocrinid echinoderm, Middle Cambrian, Idaho.* Above: Halocystites murchisoni, *paracrinid echinoderm, Ordovician, Canada.*

Phylum	Class	Age
Echino-dermata	*Cystoidea*	Ordovician–Devonian
	Paracrinoidea	Middle Ordovician
	Edrioblastoidea	Middle Ordovician
	Parablastoidea	Early and Middle Ordovician
	Blastoidea	Silurian–Permian
	Eocrinoidea	Cambrian–Silurian
	Crinoidea	Cambrian–Recent
	Stelleroidea	Ordovician–Recent
	Helicoplacoidea	Early Cambrian
	Edrioasteroidea	Cambrian–Carboniferous
	Ophiocistoidea	Ordovician–Devonian
	Cyclocystoidea	Ordovician–Devonian
	Echinoidea	Ordovician–Recent
	Holothuroidea	Ordovician–Recent

Below left: Cincinnatidiscus stellatus, *edrioasteroid echinoderm, Ordovician, Kentucky.*
Below center: Isorophus cincinnatiensis, *edrioasteroid echinoderm, Upper Ordovician, Kentucky.*
Below right: *Reconstruction of Edrioasteroidea.*

Bottom left: *Edrioasteroidea,* Isorophus cincinnatiensis, *attached to the shell of a brachiopod, Ordovician, Ohio.*
Bottom right: *Rock with edrioasteroids of the species* Agelacrinites hanoveri *and* Temeischytes carteri, *Late Devonian, Iowa.*

derms, appeared suddenly during the Cambrian, during which period many representatives already displayed strong specialization. Among these classes were the Eocrinoidea and the Edrioasteroidea, both of which became extinct long before the end of the Paleozoic, and the Crinoidea, which is thus the oldest class to survive up to modern times. For this reason the origin of the echinoderms is believed to reach back to the Precambrian (over 600 million years ago).

With the exception of the Blastoidea (which appeared during the Silurian), almost all the other groups appeared during the next period, the Ordovician, about 70 million years later. Some of these groups became extinct before the end of the Paleozoic, while others, such as the Crinoidea, Asteroidea, Echinoidea and Holothuroidea, reached our age in full bloom after an evolutionary history that has lasted at least half a billion years.

Among the different classes listed on page 163 we will deal here only with those that have importance in stratigraphic studies and those that have the largest number of fossil representatives.

Class Edrioasteroidea

The Edrioasteroidea, which lived from the Cambrian to the Carboniferous, were echinoderms with spherical bodies, more or less flattened, that lived attached to the sea bottom with their underside, without the use of a pedicle, or to other solid objects, such as, for example, the shells of brachiopods.

The flexible exoskeleton was formed of irregular plates, and on the upper surface were five sinuous ambulacral areas formed by smaller and regular plates at the center of which was the mouth. The anal opening, located in the area between two ambulacra, was covered by a pyramid of small plates.

Class Cystoidea

The Cystoidea, today extinct, lived from the Ordovician to the Devonian. They lived attached to the sea floor by means of a stem formed of layered plates that ended with a branching similar to roots. At the other end the stem supported a spherical body or calyx, slightly elongated or flattened, that could reach a maximum of 46 cm. (18.4 in.) in height. The calyx was

Below left: *Rock with cystoids of the species* Echinosphaerites auran-
tium, *the inside of which is covered with calcite crystals, Ordovician,
Sweden.*

Below right, from top to bottom: *Nodule with numerous cystoids, Ordovician, Morocco;* Holocystites scutellatus, *cystoid of the Silurian from Indiana;* Echinosphaerites infaustus, *Ordovician, Bohemia;* Caryocrinites
sp., *Silurian, United States.*

formed of an arrangement of small hexagonal, pentagonal, or
irregularly shaped plates aligned in alternate circles. On the
plates were either single pores, paired pores on the bottom of
small depressions, or rhomboidal pores aligned symmetrically
on each side. The classification of Cystoidea is based on the
position of the pores.

On the upper part of the calyx were the mouth and anal
openings. From the mouth, in the more advanced forms, spread
out the ambulacral areas, simple or forked, formed of small
plates covered by other plates to constitute a true canal. On
the edges of each ambulacral canal were thin appendages, called
brachioles (arms), that gave the whole the appearance of a
flower. With their movement, the brachioles produced a current of water that directed food to the mouth.

Class Blastoidea

The Blastoidea constitute a class of stemmed (stalked) echinoderms that appeared during the Silurian and became extinct
before the end of the Permian, after an existence of about 200
million years.

The Blastoidea lived fixed to the sea floor by means of a
flexible stem formed of a series of layered plates that ended in
a series of branchings. The other end of the stem was attached
to the ovoidal theca, or calyx, composed of three series of five
large plates each, closed in the upper part by a flattened disk
in the center of which was the mouth. From this spread the
five ambulacral areas, similar to the petals of a flower, formed
of a series of small and regular plates. These covered a very
complex internal apparatus that probably had both respiratory
and reproductive functions. Around the mouth were five holes,
one of which was the anal opening. On the marginal plates of
each area were inserted the brachioles.

Above: *Reconstruction
of a cystoid.*

PLATE XXXVII

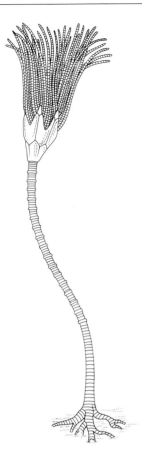

Left: *Reconstruction of a blastoid.*
Below center: *Rock with numerous remains of blastoids of the species*
Cryptoblastus melo; *Mississippian, Missouri.*
Below right: *Nodule of siderite with complete specimen of the holothuroid*
Achistrum welleri; *Pennsylvanian, Mazon Creek, Illinois.*

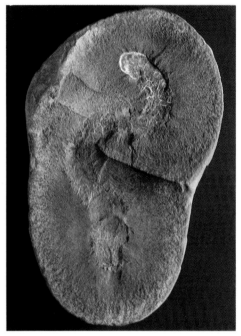

Class Holothuroidea

The Holothuroidea, well known because they are widespread in modern-day seas, constitute a special class among the echinoderms. They are different from the other echinoderms because they lack a hard exoskeleton. The body of the Holothuroidea is covered by a tough, noncalcareous, spiny skin in which are spread numerous calcareous spicules called sclerites, which vary in appearance. These are the only elements that, because of their calcareous nature, are adapted to preservation in the fossil state. Because of their microscopic size, sclerites are gathered and studied with the methods developed for analyzing microfossils. Complete impressions of these animals are very rare and have been found only in rocks particularly adapted to the preservation of the soft structures of animals.

Class Crinoidea

The crinoids are one of the most interesting groups of echinoderms, both because of the great variety of species that have arisen in the course of the geologic time and because of the abundance of the fossil finds attributed to them. Furthermore, the crinoids are more important than the other echinoderm groups discussed thus far because their remains are widespread in Paleozoic rocks, which appear sometimes in such abundance as to lead to great accumulations that are called crinoidal limestone.

The crinoids are exclusively marine animals that live most often fixed to the bottom by means of a stem. Many forms live attached during early stages and become mobile as adults. These latter are without stem, but they can adhere briefly to the sea bottom or to submerged objects.

A complete crinoid has three distinct parts: the calyx, which encloses the vital organs; the arms, which are used to carry food toward the mouth; and the stem, which serves to fix the animal to the sea floor.

The stem is formed of numerous layered plates (ossicles) that are often found scattered in sediment and indicate with certainty to the paleontologist the marine origin of the rock in which they are found. Their form varies greatly from species to species; there are circular, square, elliptical, pentagonal and stellate. Some have a smooth surface, other are covered by radial ribs, yet others have petaloid designs. At the center of each plate is a hole opening on to a canal that runs almost the entire length of the stem. At the end are appendages in the form of roots or, more rarely, anchors, that help the animal adhere to the bottom.

The other end of the stem leads to the calyx, composed of a series of pentagonal plates joined in a rigid form or articulated. The calyx is generally in the shape of a cup and contains the vital organs, protected from above by a circular cover, at the center of which is the mouth. From the mouth, five ambulacral canals connect to the arms. These are formed of plates aligned in simple or double series. They are more frequently very branched to augment the area used to find food. On the ventral side of each plate is an appendage, called a pinnule, on which the ambulacral canals continue.

PLATE XXXVII
Blastoids
(1) *Pentremites welleri*, Mississippian, Illinois; (2) *Pentremites pyriformis*, Mississippian, Alabama; (3) *Pentremites* sp., Mississippian, Illinois; (4) *Pentremites* sp., Mississippian, Illinois; (5) *Pentremites godoni*, Mississippian, Kentucky; (6) *Pentremites rusticus*, Mississippian, Oklahoma; (7) *Deltablastus delta*, Permian, Timor; (8) *Pentremites sulcatus*, Mississippian, Alabama; (9) *Pentremites cherokeeus*, Mississippian, Illinois; (1) *Pentremites angustus*, Mississippian, Oklahoma; (11) *Pentremites symmetricus*, Mississippian, Illinois; (12) *Pentremites obesus*, Mississippian, Illinois; (13) *Pentremites pryiformis*, Mississippian, Indiana; (14,15) *Pentremites sulcatus*, Mississippian, Tennessee.

Below left: *Nomenclature of crinoids: (a) arms; (f) filament; (c) calyx; (pi) pinnule; (pe) peduncle; (r) root.*

Below center: *Block of rock with numerous fragments of peduncles of crinoids of the genus* Encrinus.

Below right: *Specimen of the crinoid* Cyathocrinites goniodactylus, *complete with part of the peduncle, calyx and arms.*

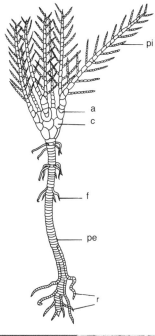

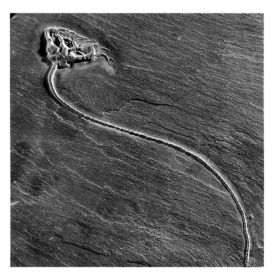

Above left: *Rock with fragments of peduncles (stems) of the crinoid* Schyphocrinites elegans; *Devonian, Morocco.*

Above right: *Block with numerous crinoid stems preserved still anatomically connected; Devonian, England.*

Far left: *Complete specimen of* Codiacrinus schultzeri; *Devonian, Germany.*

Left: *Crinoid of the order* Comatulida *genus* Saccocoma; *late Jurassic, Germany.*

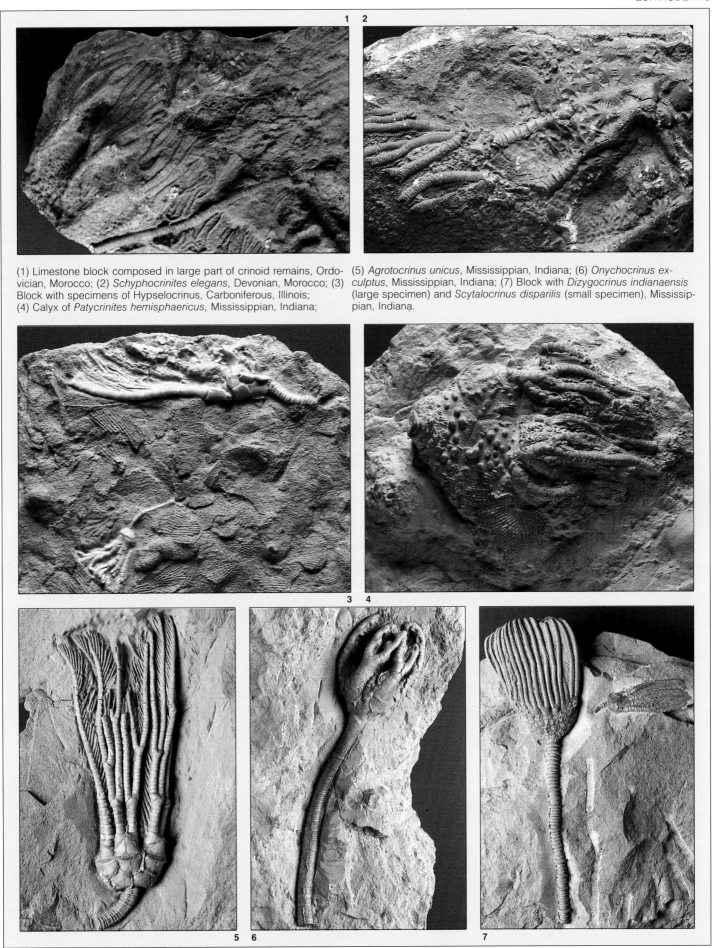

(1) Limestone block composed in large part of crinoid remains, Ordovician, Morocco; (2) *Schyphocrinites elegans,* Devonian, Morocco; (3) Block with specimens of Hypselocrinus, Carboniferous, Illinois; (4) Calyx of *Patycrinites hemisphaericus,* Mississippian, Indiana;

(5) *Agrotocrinus unicus,* Mississippian, Indiana; (6) *Onychocrinus exculptus,* Mississippian, Indiana; (7) Block with *Dizygocrinus indianaensis* (large specimen) and *Scytalocrinus disparilis* (small specimen), Mississippian, Indiana.

Below left: Encrinus lilliformis, *Muschelkalk, Württemberg, Germany,*
Below center: *Limestone with numerous crinoid calyxes that in section show a typical star shape; Jurassic, France.*
Below right: *Block with numerous specimens of Pentacrinus; Early Jurassic, Germany.*

Bottom left: *Crinoid of the order Comatulida, genus* Pterocoma; *Late Cretaceous, Lebanon.*

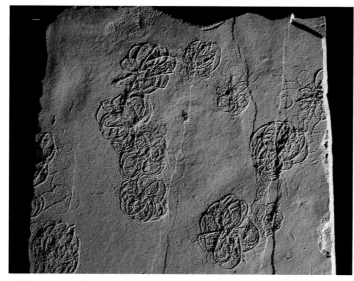

The crinoids were so well developed when they appeared during the Cambrian, about 570 million years ago, that their origin, still obscure, must have been even earlier in time. They are grouped into five subclasses. Among these the Echmatocrinea lived only during the Cambrian; during the Middle Ordovician can be found the subclasses Camerata, Inadunata and Flexibilia, which became extinct before the end of the Triassic period, when the Articulata appeared.

The subclass Camerata includes crinoids whose tightly joined plates formed a rigid calyx, while the mouth and the ambulacral canals were covered by a vault formed by numerous plates. The arms were formed by one or two series of plates and bore well developed pinnules. These forms, which lived from the Middle Ordovician to the Middle Permian, constitute a well defined group, whose representatives, however, have little stratigraphic value.

The subclass Inadunata includes several genera that lived during the period of time between the Early Ordovician and the Triassic. The calyx is formed by rigidly joined plates, and with presents the mouth and ambulacral canals covered by big plates. The only Mesozoic group attributed to this subclass is the family Encrinidae, whose genera have had a role of primary importance in the formation of Triassic sediments in the Alps. Among the most common is the genus *Encrinus*, of which the species *Encrinus lilliformis* is typical of the Middle Triassic and is found both in the form of complete calyxes and as scattered osides. Encrinus has a depressed calyx, supported by a long stem formed by circular, completely equal osicles, ornamented by radial ribs. The calyx has long arms formed by a double series of plates.

The subclass Flexibilia includes crinoids whose calyx is made of movable plates. This subclass includes only a few genera that lived from the Middle Ordovician to the Permian.

PLATE XXXVIII
Crinoids
(1) *Dorocrinus gouldi,* Mississippian, Iowa; (2) *Cactocrinus reticulatus,* Mississippian, Iowa; (3) *Encrinus lilliformis,* Muschelkalk, Germany; (4) *Hypocrinus schneideri,* Permian, Timor; (5) *Rhipidocrinus crenatus,* Devonian, Germany; (6) *Rhipidocrinus crenatus,* Devonian, Germany; (7) *Hesencrinus elongatus,* Mississippian, Iowa; (8) *Eutrochocrinus christyi,* Mississippian, Iowa; (9) *Timorocrinus mirabilis,* Permian, Timor; (10) *Dizygocrinus rotundus,* Mississippian, Iowa; (11) *Cupressocrinus abbreviatus,* Devonian, Germany; (12) *Actinocrinites coplowensis;* (13) *Batocrinus subequalis,* Mississippian, Iowa; (14) *Actinocrinites* sp., Carboniferous, Wales.

PLATE XXXVIII

Below left: Salteraster solwinii, *echinoderm of the subclass Asteroidea, Silurian, Australia.* Below right: *Block with numerous specimens of ophiuroids, Jurassic, France.*
Center left: *Ophiuroid of the genus Bundenbachia, Devonian, Bundenbach, Germany.* Center right: *Euzonosoma sp., asterozoid ophiuroid, Devonian, Bundenbach.*

Bottom left: Furcaster decheni, *asterozoid ophiuroid, Early Devonian, Bundenbach.* Bottom center: Helianthaster rhenanus, *asterozoid asteroid, Early Devonian, Bundenbach.* Bottom right: Ophiura primigenia, *Early Devonian, Bundenbach.*

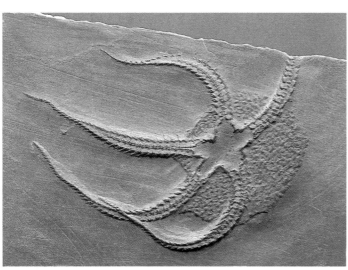

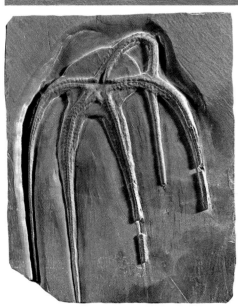

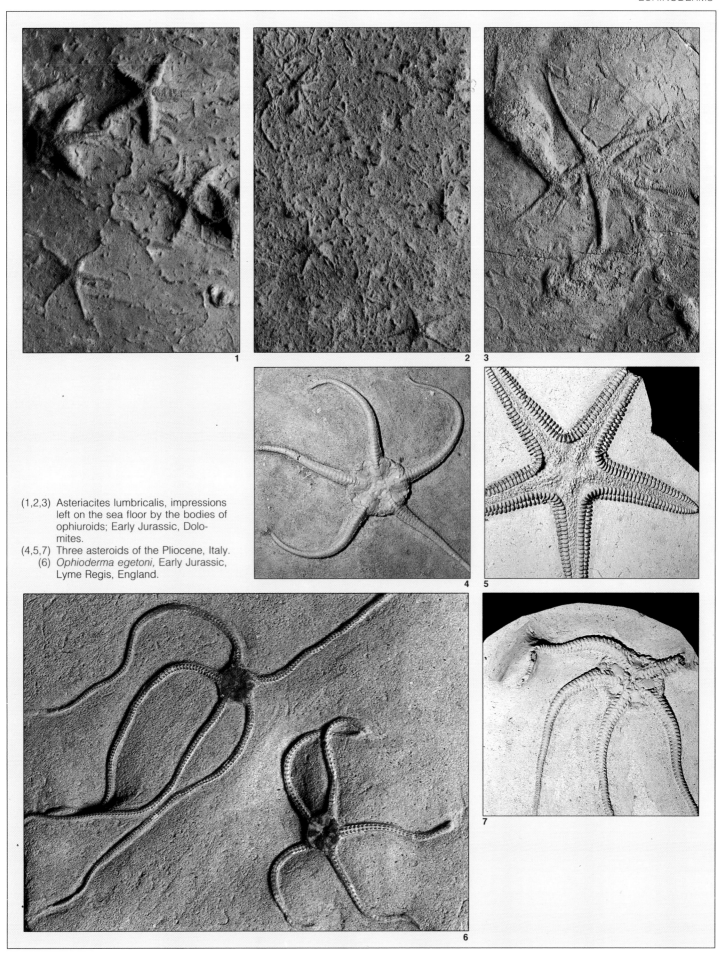

(1,2,3) Asteriacites lumbricalis, impressions left on the sea floor by the bodies of ophiuroids; Early Jurassic, Dolomites.
(4,5,7) Three asteroids of the Pliocene, Italy.
(6) *Ophioderma egetoni,* Early Jurassic, Lyme Regis, England.

Below left: *Nomenclature of Echinoidea: (A) cross section; (B) top view; (aa) ambulacral area; (anap) anal aperture; (tf) tube feet; (m) mouth; (rwc) radial water canal; (sc) stone canal; (g) gonads; (sh) shell; (ia) interambulacral area; (fs) foot-stalks; (mp) madreporite plate.*
Below right: *Block of rock with echinoids of the species Tripneustes parkinsoni,* Miocene, France.

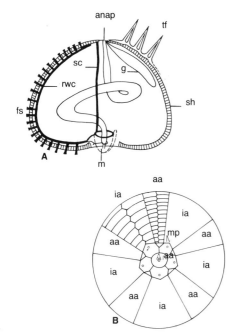

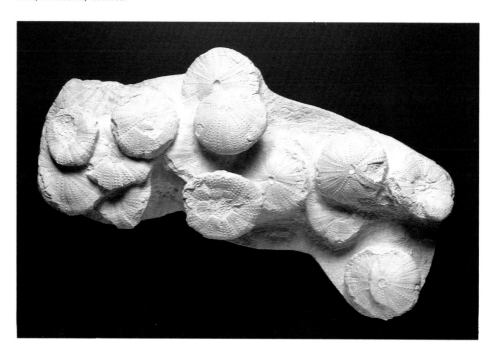

The subclass Articulata includes the largest number of post-Paleozoic crinoids as well as all the modern-day forms. These are characterized by a calyx formed of clearly articulated plates, with exposed mouth and ambulacral canals, and with arms formed of a single series of plates. Many genera and species of this subclass are used as index fossils for Mesozoic rocks. Well known is the genus *Pentacrinus*, whose stem was formed of pentagonal osicles that are found in abundance in Triassic and Jurassic deposits. Complete specimens of this animal, which has a very reduced calyx, have been found in rocks from the Jurassic in Holzmaden and reach the size of several meters.

Finally, the family Comatulidae, which appeared during the Jurassic, still exists today. The representatives of this group live fixed during youth and become free-swimming as adults.

Class Stelleroidea

The Stelleroidea, to which belong the starfish that are abundant even today, are mobile echinoderms with a body formed of a central disk from which spread five arms—the number of these arms can increase in multiples of five in certain cases and has been known to reach, on rare occasions, 40. Inside the central disk are all the organs of the animal. These organs continue along the arms (which are actually extensions of the body rather than appendages), permitting the regeneration of the entire animal from only a single fragment. The anal and mouth openings are on the underside of the disk, from which spread five ambulacral canals that run along the length of the arms.

The skeleton, distinguishable in ventral and dorsal sides, is formed by numerous plates not joined but held together by flexible tissue. These echinoderms are found in the fossil record only rarely, since the body decomposes rapidly after death,

freeing the plates, which are usually found scattered in sediment.

Because the Stelleroidea live today, as in the past, at all depths and at all latitudes, they can provide paleontologists with little specific information.

The Stelleroidea appeared during the Early Ordovician with the subclass Somasteroidea, which includes the most primitive representatives, with a body only approximately pentagonal. During the Late Ordovician appeared the subclass Ophiuroidea, with very mobile organisms, and the subclass Asteroidea, which includes the classic starfish with their slow movements.

Class Echinoidea

The echinoids, known as sea urchins and sand dollars, are echinoderms whose body is closed in a shell without arms or a stem, composed of numerous regular plates. The shape of the shell is variable: spherical, hemispherical, conical or disk-shaped. While the animal is alive, the shell encloses the soft parts, including the contorted visceral sac, which is exposed to the outside through the anal opening on the top surface and the mouth on the bottom surface. The position of these two openings determines the symmetry of the echinids, which are divided into two groups: regular echinids with a five-fold symmetry, with the two openings located at opposite sides of the shell; and irregular echinids with bilateral symmetry as a result of the marked migration of the anal opening toward the shell margin.

From the mouth spread five ambulacral canals that run along the internal walls of the shell in correspondence with the plates in the ambulacral areas. Tube feet, extending through holes in the ambulacra, are used for movement and respiration.

Below left: *Spine of an echinoid of the genus* Cidaris; *Late Jurassic, Germany.*
Below center: *Isolated spines of an echinoid.*
Below right: *Spines of* Cidaris *sp., Late Cretaceous, Germany.*

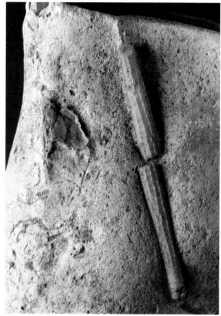

As with every animal group, the only part of the echinoids that fossilizes is the calcareous shell, thus it is on the structure and form of the shell that classification is based. This skeleton is formed by a great number of tightly fused plates. These are aligned in vertical series and form 10 zones, or areas, each of which is composed of two series of plates. There thus exist, in regular alternation, five ambulacra made of plates with holes and five interambulacra without holes.

The mouth is on the underside and is composed of various calcareous pieces that form a complex known as Aristotle's lantern, used for chewing. Several important systematic subdivisions are based on the presence and, sometimes, absence of the Aristotle's lantern, and its appearance. On the top, the anal opening has moved toward the lateral edge of the shell and, in some extreme cases, onto the lower side.

The first echinoids appeared in the seas during the Ordo-

Left: *Perfectly preserved specimen of* Plesiocidaris durandi; *Late Jurassic, France.*
Above: *Slab with various specimens of* Lenticidaris utahensis; *Early Triassic, Utah.*

175

PLATE XXXIX

(1) *Cidaris coronata*, Jurassic, Germany; (2) *Cidaris coronata*, Jurassic, Germany; (3) *Cyphosoma koenigi*, Late Cretaceous, Dover, England; (4) *Glypticus hieroglyphus*, Late Jurassic, Germany; (5) *Stenonaster tuberculata*, Late Cretaceous, Italy.

vician period, about 500 million years ago. These were Paleo-echinoids, very primitive regular echinoids that lived throughout the Paleozoic era and became extinct in the Permian. In that period appeared the modern, regular echinoids. The great diffusion of these echinoids began only during the Triassic, with the cidarids, a group very similar to today's spiny sea urchins, species of which are used as index fossils for certain stretches of time in the Mesozoic.

The irregular echinoids appeared later, during the Jurassic, and reached during the Cretaceous such a vast expansion that they furnish numerous index fossils for that period. At the beginning of the Cenozoic, about 65 million years ago, the regular echinoids began to diminish in importance, while the irregular echinoids assumed greater stratigraphic value.

Even from the ecological point of view, these animals offer the paleontologist valuable information on the appearance of the sea floor in the past. The regular echinoids are organisms adapted for life on rocky bottoms at various depths, while the irregular echinoids live on sandy or muddy bottoms at slight depths. The finding of these animals thus offers a general indication of the sea floor on which they lived.

PLATE XXXIX
Spines of Echinoids
(1) Large spines of echinoids, Early Jurassic; (2) *Cidaris acicularis*, Miocene, Italy; (3) *Cidaris marginata*, Late Jurassic, France; (4) *Cidaris glandifera*, Jurassic, Italy; (5) *Cidaris blumenbachi*, Late Jurassic; (6) *Cidaris glandifera*, Jurassic, France; (7) *Hemicidaris* sp., location unknown; (8) Spine of echinoid of the Triassic, Bergamo, Italy; (9) *Cidaris blumenbachi*, Late Jurassic, Germany.

(1) *Clypeus ploti*, Middle Jurassic, Switzerland.
(2) *Heteraster* sp., Late Cretaceous, Germany.
(3) *Eupatagus antillarum*, Eocene, Florida.
(4) *Holasteropsis credneri*, Late Cretaceous, Westphalia.
(5) *Hemiaster fournelli*, Late Cretaceous, Algeria.
(6) *Offaster pilula*, Late Cretaceous, England.
(7) *Schizaster* sp., Eocene, Italy.

(1) *Isomicraster senonensis* of the Late Cretaceous, Europe.
(2) *Echinolampas affinis,* Tertiary fossil species of a genus of echinoid still living, France.
(3) *Holaster planus,* Late Cretaceous, Egypt.
(4) *Hemipneustes radiatus,* Late Cretaceous, Crete.

(5) *Micraster coranguinum,* Late Cretaceous, England.
(6) *Collyrites elliptica,* Late Jurassic, England.
(7) *Holectypus depressus,* Middle Jurassic, England.
(8) *Echinocorys tipica,* Late Cretaceous, location unknown.

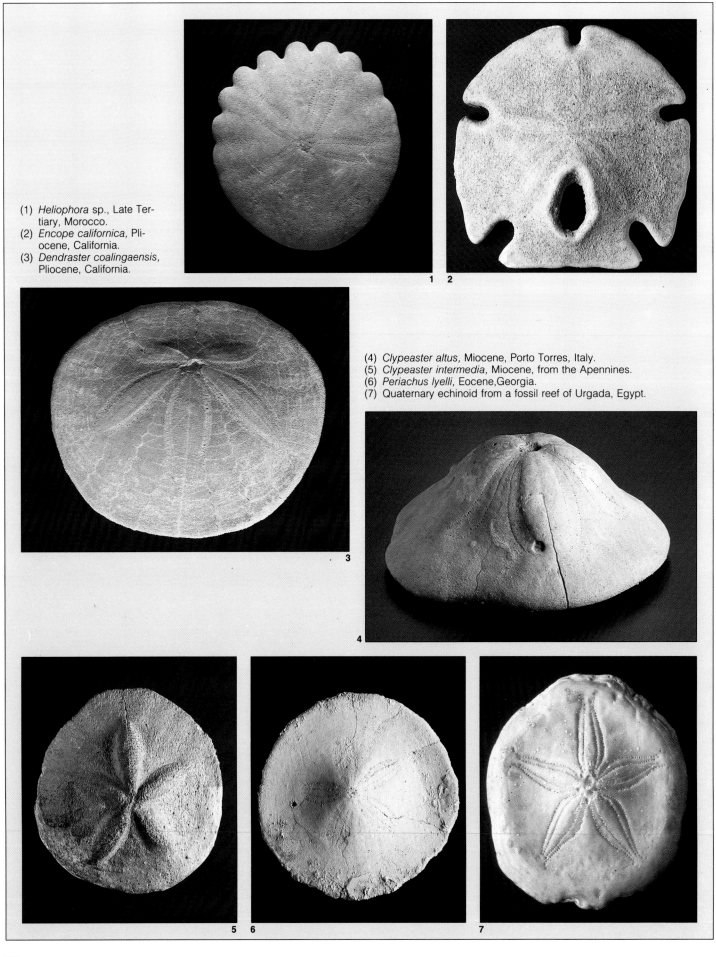

(1) *Heliophora* sp., Late Tertiary, Morocco.
(2) *Encope californica,* Pliocene, California.
(3) *Dendraster coalingaensis,* Pliocene, California.

(4) *Clypeaster altus,* Miocene, Porto Torres, Italy.
(5) *Clypeaster intermedia,* Miocene, from the Apennines.
(6) *Periachus lyelli,* Eocene, Georgia.
(7) Quaternary echinoid from a fossil reef of Urgada, Egypt.

Protochordates or Stomochordates

In this group can be found certain animals that seem to occupy a position between the lower invertebrates and the chordates, which is to say between the organisms without a notochord, or flexible dorsal supporting rod, and those in which that cord runs the entire length of their bodies, serving as their chief internal skeletal support.

The stomochordates, interesting precisely because they lead in certain aspects toward the chordates, have characteristics common with both chordates and other invertebrates. Like chordates, they have a series of gill clefts located in the pharynx region and have a nerve cord located in the dorsal position. They have a stomochord instead of a notochord, which are similar to each other only in appearance.

The stomochordates include three very different groups: the enteropneusti, the pterobranchs and the graptolites.

Enteropneusta

The Enteropneusta have one living member, the genus *Balanoglossus*, and are almost unknown in the fossil record. Indeed, only one specimen is known, which was found a few years ago in Jurassic deposits at Osteno in Lombardy; on the basis of this specimen the species *Megaderaion sinemuriense* was established.

This is a small animal, just 2.5 cm. (1.8 in.) long, very similar to modern-day representatives of the group, with the body divided in three parts: an initial nasal portion (the proboscis); an elongated rectangular portion (the collar); and a vermiform end portion (the trunk).

Above: Megaderaion sinemuriense, *a rare Enteropneusta of the Early Jurassic, Italy.*
Below: Monograptus chimaera, *Silurian, Germany.*
Bottom: *Thin section of* Monograptus *sp., Silurian, Italy.*

Pterobranchia

The pterobranchs include a few modern-day species and are more interesting than the preceding group from a paleontological point of view. The modern-day genus *Rhabdopleura* is in many ways analogous to certain organisms known exclusively from fossils whose classification has been uncertain for many years. These are graptolites that are today classified, because of their resemblance to Rhabdopleura, in a special group of stomochordates.

Rhabdopleura is a colonial animal formed by a chitinous tube made of circular or semicircular rings from which extend shorter secondary tubes that house the individuals of the colony, called zooecia. Both the principal tube and the secondary branches are connected along their length by a cord, called the stolon, that connects the various individuals of the colony.

Graptolites

Like Rhabdopleura, graptolites, in the subphylum Hemichordata, are colonial animals that lived from the Middle Cambrian to the Late Carboniferous (Pennsylvanian) and disappeared completely during that period, about 280 million years ago, leaving behind the fossilized remains of their small, flat bodies, clues to an enigmatic past.

Before they were compared to the pterobranchs, the graptolites represented a great problem for paleontologists. At first considered either plants or even inorganic in origin, they were then classified, with little certainty, near the cephalopods and coelenterates. Only the discovery of fossil specimens in partic-

Below: *Nomenclature of graptolites: (A) detail of rhabdosome; (B) group of rhabdosomes in a floating colony; (g) gonotheca; (h) hydrotheca; (p) pneumatofore; (r) rhabdosome; (s) sicula; (v) virgella.*

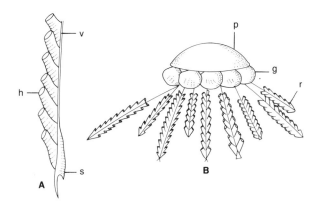

ularly good condition—not flattened but preserved round and altered to pyrite—permitted the study and comparison that led paleontologists to consider them similar to living stomochordates.

Like the pterobranchs, the graptolites are colonial organisms, forming small colonies enclosed in a chitinous exoskeleton. A graptolite colony, called a rhabdosome, is formed of small, overlapping semiannular segments. These are connected to an empty conical chamber, called a sicula, that multiplies by gemmation. The extremity of the sicula becomes longer, forming the axis of the graptolite, called the virgella. This rigid stem, branching or simple, straight or curved, bears along it a series of small hydrothecas, linked by a canal and each inhabited, as in the Rhabdopleura, by an individual member of the colony.

All graptolite colonies are built on this base, but they appear in an enormous variety of growth patterns. This abundance of patterns, which differentiates species, is found in the rocks of the Early Paleozoic and has made this group extremely complex, although very useful to the paleontologist, who, precisely because of their variety and widespread distribution, can use graptolites as index fossils.

The class of graptolites (if indeed it is a class) is divided into five orders, each with a distinct characteristic. Some graptolites are in fact sessile organisms (attached to rocks or other substrate), benthic (living on the sea bed) or epiplanktonic (floating, like seaweed). Among these are graptolites, irregular branching forms with a pedicle with which the rhabdosome fixes itself to the sea bottom or the floating object. Those are the oldest graptolites, but also the longest-lived, appearing before all the others, during the Middle Cambrian, and existing until the Early Mississippian.

In planktonic graptolites the rhabdosome is much simpler, sometimes formed of a single axis that is straight or curved, sometimes slightly branching. In planktonic graptolites many rhabdosomes may unite, joined together by a disk-shaped pneumatofore, formed like a cupola, which served as a flotation organ. Just under the base of the pneumatofore is a series of small spheres, each of which contains a certain number of sicules, the embryonal chambers where entire rhabdosomes originate. Thus, these spheres must have been reproductive organs.

Planktonic graptolites lived most of all during the Ordovician and Silurian periods, which are referred to together as the "graptolite era."

1

2

Graptolites are used as index fossils for defining various stratigraphic levels from the Ordovician to the Silurian. Numerous different species of graptolites are known, each of which had a wide distribution and a short life.

Graptolites from the Silurian in England:
(1) *Dichograptus* sp.
(2) *Leptograptus* sp.
(3) *Dicranograptus* sp.
(4) *Didymograptus* sp.
(5) *Orthograptus* sp.
(6) *Phyllograptus* sp.
(7) *Nemagraptus* sp.

THE CHORDATES

The chordates are called advanced animals because they are the phylum in which the vertebrates are placed.

The chordates constitute a phylum that includes physiologically complex organisms that are morphologically different from each other, but they are all characterized by the presence of the notochord, an elastic rod that runs along the principal axis of the body, above the visceral cavity and beneath the nerve cord, or central nervous system. Another characteristic of the chordates is that the organs of sight, hearing, equilibrium and smell are joined in the front part of the body, near the mouth and around the "head." They also have a series of openings along the sides of the body that expose the internal body to the external environment.

In vertebrates, which are the most advanced representatives of the chordates, the notochord is present in embryonic stages and is the main component of the spinal column. In other chordates, for example the cephalochordates, the notochord does not evolve into a spinal column but is present even in the adult stage and constitutes the body's only support.

All of these characteristics are more or less developed in the various chordates. They are thus found in organisms morphologically and physiologically so different as to make necessary the subdivision of the phylum into several subphyla, each including, except for the vertebrates, very few representatives.

The phylum Chordata is subdivided into four groups: the subphylum Urochordata, which includes several organisms with sac-like bodies, a few sessile organisms (attached to rocks or substrate), such as the sea squirts (class Ascidiacea), and others that are pelagic (or free-swimming), such as the salps; the subphylum Cephalochordata, of which the lancelets, or amphioxus, are the best-known representative; the subphylum Hemichordata, which contains the graptolites; and the subphylum Vertebrata.

One of the most interesting problems in biology and paleontology concerns the origin of the chordates. From which group of lower invertebrates did these organisms develop? And when? The problem is the subject of much debate, which applies to the vertebrates as well, since the origin of one group bears significantly on the origin of the other.

Until some years ago, the annelids and arthropods were believed to be the invertebrate groups closest to the chordates because the segmentation of their bodies seemed comparable to the segmentation of the cephalochordates. There are, however, substantial differences: The bodies of arthropods and annelids are truly segmented in rings, while the segmentation of chordates is only superficial and incomplete. Furthermore, the anatomical organization of the chordates is different from that of the two groups of invertebrates; in the chordates the nerve cord is in a dorsal position, while in the annelids and arthropods it occupies a ventral position.

Aside from the differing anatomical organization, yet another characteristic separates chordates from annelids and arthropods: their process of embryonic development.

Opposite: Homeosaurus pulchellus, *a rhynchocephalian reptile of the Late Jurassic, Solnhofen, Germany.*

It seems clear, therefore, that the chordates originated from neither the annelids nor the arthropods. Studies have demonstrated that they are derived from another group of invertebrates, one whose representatives are extremely different from the morphological point of view—the echinoderms.

The derivation of the chordates from the echinoderms was discovered thanks to studies that revealed a great similarity between the embryos of the two groups regarding the development of the coelom, or body cavity. It is the same in echinoderms and chordates, but different in the other invertebrates. Quite recently paleontological "proof" has been added to these studies to suggest an echinoderm-chordate evolution. In marine rocks ranging in age from the Middle Cambrian to the Middle Devonian are certain fossil organisms whose armor, composed of polygonal calcite plates, is similar to that of echinoderms, thus leading paleontologists to classify them in that group of invertebrates.

These organisms, members of the class Stylophora, are unusual echinoderms. They are flattened, as though adapted to life on the sea bottom, they display no rayed symmetry, nor do they have a stem or a pedicle. The body is formed of a theca and a cord that, like the theca, is covered by calcareous plates. The Stylophora have certain characteristics atypical of the echinoderms and include two groups with distinct forms, the horned and the mitred, which seem to be derived one from the other.

The bodies of Stylophora are composed of two distinct parts, a true body rounded and flattened dorso-ventrally and a long tail divided in turn into three parts. These two parts of the body, once called theca and pedicle in conformity with similar parts in the echinoderms, contain a series of structures comparable to those present in the chordates. The head is composed of a series of marginal plates to which are attached the flexible dorsal plates and on the surface of which open the gills, the anus, the mouth and the gonads. Inside is a reduced encephalon, located at the point where the head joins the tail and to which are attached the cranial nerves, in turn attached with the sense organs. The tail is also covered by calcareous plates and at its anterior end are a neural cord, which thickens toward the front, forming a kind of encephalon, and the notochord. A series of muscles run parallel to the notochord and blood vessels.

Because of this unique anatomy, the Stylophora cannot be said to be true echinoderms. Thus, a new classification has been established. They are grouped in the subphylum Calcichordata, considered a member of the phylum of the chordates.

Since these organisms also possess characteristics of the chordates, the Calcichordata may be transitional organisms between the echinoderms and the chordates. Some scientists speculate that they represent the point of origin of the chordates, and thus also of the vertebrates.

The Vertebrates. The vertebrates are the most advanced of all animals. They are organisms with a spinal column, and although they include animals that are very different from mor-

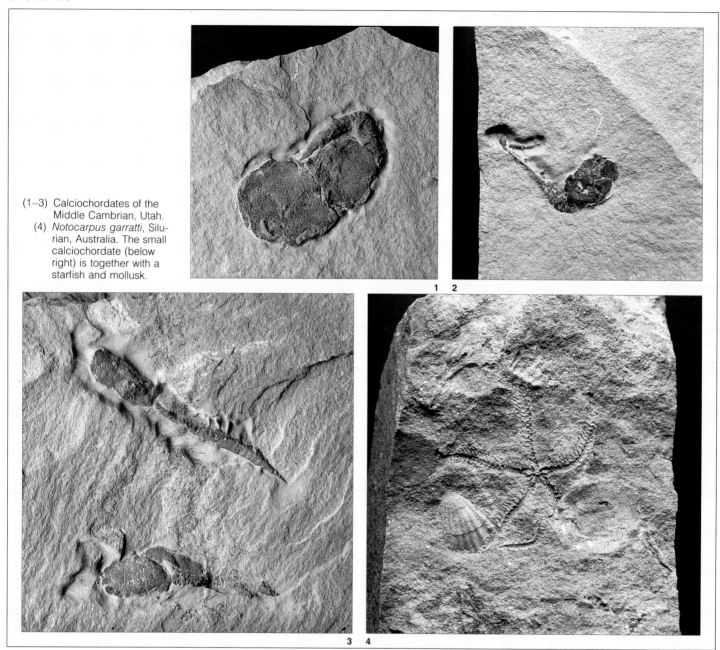

(1–3) Calciochordates of the Middle Cambrian, Utah.
(4) *Notocarpus garratti*, Silurian, Australia. The small calciochordate (below right) is together with a starfish and mollusk.

1 2

3 4

phological (external) and adaptive points of view, they are all substantially alike from the anatomical (internal) point of view. Included in the vertebrates are fish, amphibians, reptiles, birds and mammals. Paleontologists divide the subphylum Vertebrata into nine classes. Some of these are now extinct, others have many fossil representatives but few modern-day forms, and still others are extremely widespread today.

Since all vertebrates have a strong internal skeleton, many fossilized specimens have been found. This abundance of fossil remains has permitted paleontologists to reconstruct the evolutionary history of the vertebrates, a history that links the various classes together in an almost continuous succession.

The vertebrates, which today dominate our planet, from sea water to fresh water, on dry land and even in the air, appeared during the Early Ordovician, 500 million years ago, with marine forms that are grouped in the class of the Agnatha.

Subphylum	Class	Age
Vertebrata	*Agnatha* (agnathans)	Ordovician–Recent
	Acanthodii (acanthodes)	Silurian–Permian
	Placodermi (placoderms)	Devonian
	Chondrichthyes (chondrichthyans)	Devonian–Recent
	Osteichthyes (osteichthyans)	Silurian–Recent
	Amphibia (amphibians)	Devonian–Recent
	Reptilia (reptiles)	Carboniferous–Recent
	Aves (birds)	Jurassic–Recent
	Mammalia (mammals)	Triassic–Recent

Agnatha

The class of the Agnatha, or "jawless fish," the oldest and most primitive known vertebrate, is represented today by very few living forms. These are the lampreys (order Petromyzontiformes) and the hagfish (order Myxiniformes), called cyclostomes (Cyclostomata) because of their round mouth, characteristic of these animals. They are clearly distinguished from all other vertebrates most of all because they do not have jaws or paired lateral appendages, two characteristics that, in the light of the evolutionary history of vertebrates, make them very primitive. Furthermore, cyclostomes have a weak cartilaginous skeleton and neither teeth nor a bony skeleton, and are thus not preserved in the fossil record.

During the interval between the Ordovician and the Devonian, the agnathans were very widespread. They appeared much different than today's cyclostomes, although they did have the fundamental characteristic of the class—the absence of jaws and appendages.

Paleozoic agnathans were characterized by the presence of strong external armor formed of bony plates, which permitted their preservation as fossils and led to the name ostracoderms ("shell skins"), which is sometimes used for them.

The agnathans reached their maximum expansion during the Late Silurian and the Devonian. During this period of time they were represented by various groups: the orders Osteostraci, Anaspida and Heterostraci.

The Osteostraci, well represented by the genera *Cephalaspis* and *Hemicyclaspis,* were animals that could reach 30 centimeters (12 in.) in length and had a compact head shield, while the rest of the body was covered by a mosaic of small plates. The eyes, a single nostril and three sensory areas were situated centrally on the upper part of the head shield, while the mouth and the gills were on the ventral side. The flattened body, dorsal position of the eyes and nostril, and ventral position of the mouth are all indications of an animal adapted to bottom-dwelling habits. The Osteostraci probably lived in the shallow waters of lakes, rivers and estuaries, scraping the bottom and sucking up food through the mouth, which had no chewing apparatus.

The Anaspida, among which the genus *Birkenia* is included, had a less flattened body, the eyes were placed in a more lateral position, and the armor was less extensive—signs that they must have had greater mobility and been adapted to life in more open waters.

The Heterostraci were more varied. Some were adapted to free swimming, far from the sea bottom. These had a cylindrical body with a developed tail, and eyes laterally positioned (genus *Pteraspis*). Others, adapted to life on the bottom, had a flattened body, as in the genus *Drepanaspis*. The Heterostraci, which include the oldest agnathans, lived both in fresh water and salt water. In more evolved forms the mouth has a series of mobile plates that may have allowed it to chew food. This possibility was fully realized in the next group, the Acanthodians, which, due to this characteristic and to the development of appendages in the form of paired fins, had radically changed habits and gained significant advantages.

The agnathans of the Silurian and Devonian were strongly armored animals, like the placoderms (as we will see), their contemporaries during the Devonian. The presence of this armor poses an interesting question: Why did these first vertebrates, which must have been superior to all of the other existing invertebrates, need such strong defensive structures? What enemies might these first vertebrates have had in the waters of the Middle Paleozoic?

Paleontological research has revealed an association of animals characteristic of freshwater lacustrine environments of the Devonian period. This was an association of armored fish, both agnathans and placoderms, and large size arthropods, eurypterids of the class Merostomata. They are also called giant sea scorpions because of the enormous sizes they could reach (some were two meters [6.6 ft.] long).

The eurypterids were predators, and since they lived in the same areas as the primitive vertebrates, the relationship they had with these may have been based on predation. Thus, it seems that eurypterids preyed upon the first vertebrates, most of all the agnathans, which, tied to their bottom-dwelling habitat, had no other defense than the development of strong armor.

Drepanaspis gemuendensis, *an agnathan; Early Devonian, Bundenbach, Germany.*

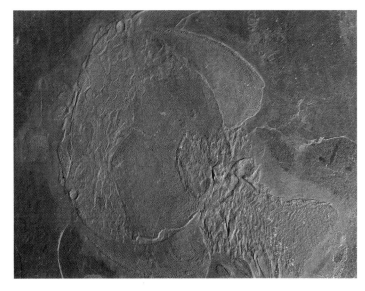

Acanthodii

Together with the jawless agnathans, which led a slow life on the bottom of bodies of water, during the Silurian appeared the first vertebrates with jaws (that is, the first gnathostomes). These were of the class Acanthodii, the so-called spiny sharks, characterized by their small size, an elongated body, laterally placed eyes, an heterocercal tail (into which the vertebral column extended) and fins supported by a long spine.

The acanthodians thus present two important anatomical innovations: the presence of a mouth with mobile jaws and the presence of paired fins, or appendages.

These two innovations are important to the evolutionary history of the vertebrates. The development of jaws opened new possibilities for adaptation, greatly increasing the power of vertebrates, which went from being simple "suckers" of food to being predators. The development of the fins was indispensable in permitting a departure from the sea bottom. With these two new structures the vertebrates became fast swimmers, able to adapt themselves to more open waters.

The appearance of jaws in vertebrates took place with the transformation of certain anatomical elements that originally had nothing whatsoever to do with feeding. The jaws were, in fact, derived from the transformation of gill (or branchial) arches. These bony, V-shaped supports, aligned horizontally in series along the gill slits, strengthened the gill region and provided a rigid support for the muscles that controlled the closing and opening of the slits. In the course of evolution, the first three arches, called respectively the premandibular, mandibular and hyoid, transformed and led to the origin of jaws and the mandible.

The premandibular arch became the trabeculae, two cartilaginous bones located at the base of the neurocranium; the mandibular arch formed with its upper branch (called the palatoquadrato, the jaw) and with its lower (called the cartilagine of Meckel), the mandible; the hyoid joined to the mandibular, causing the joining between the palatoquadrato (and that is the jaw) and the skull.

In the Devonian genus *Acanthodes* one can observe the mandibular arch, which forms with its upper expanse the jaw and with its lower part the mandible, with numerous teeth. Behind the mandibular arch is the hyoid arch, not yet particularly transformed with respect to the normal gill arches.

The acanthodians lived from the Silurian to the Permian, from about 435 to 230 million years ago, and are thus the first vertebrates to have jaws and appendages. Although they demonstrate the evolution of jaws, they do not furnish any other information on the development of the appendages, which is revealed instead by the structures of other groups of fish, the Cladoselache, which we will examine later.

Placoderms

During the Devonian, a third group developed, together with the agnathans and the acanthodians: the placoderms.

The placoderms, vertebrates with jaws and paired fins, were

Spines of acanthodes, Listracanthus *sp., Pennsylvanian, Montana.*

very strange animals, most with armor formed of dermal plates that covered the head and the front part of the body. They first appeared in fresh water and then later migrated to marine environments where, because of their fins and jaws, they became more active. The class Placodermi is subdivided into three orders: Arthrodira, Antiarchi and Rhenanida.

The most common and certainly the most spectacular were the members of the Arthrodira. Their head was protected by a large shield hinged, by way of a flexible joint, to a bony belt that covered part of the body. Rows of large plates served as teeth. This order includes the most fearsome of all the Devonian predators, the genus *Dinichthys*, the bony armor of which, the only part preserved as a fossil, can reach up to three meters (9.9 ft.) in length. The appearance of the rear part of this animal, not covered by armor, is unknown, so its total length may have been enormous.

The members of the order Antiarchi were small, generally lived in fresh water and had paired front fins covered by a

Class	Order	Age
Agnatha	Osteostraci Anaspida Heterostraci Cyclostomata	Silurian–Devonian Silurian–Devonian Ordovician–Devonian Recent
Acanthodii		Silurian–Permian
Placodermi	Arthrodira Antiarchi Rhenanida	Devonian Devonian Devonian

Below left: Pterichthyodes *sp., placoderm of the Middle Devonian, Scotland.*
Below center: Gemuendina sturtzi, *placoderm of the Early Devonian, Bundenbach, Germany.*
Below right: Bothriolepis canadensis, *placoderm of the Late Devonian, Canada.*

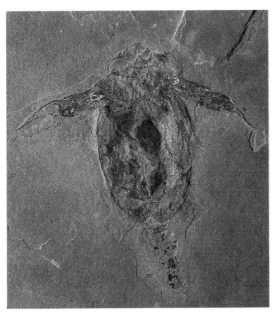
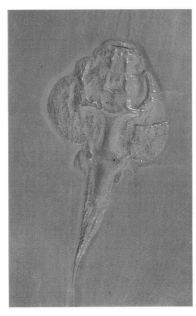

mosaic of small plates. The best known of the Antiarchi are the genera *Pterichthyodes* and *Bothryolepis.*

The representatives of the order Rhenanida were only distantly similar to today's skate. They were flattened, with the mouth located toward the rear, had jaws and mandible furnished with small teeth, and enlarged rear fins.

The body of these animals, as clearly demonstrated in the genus *Gemuendina* from the Devonian of Germany, was totally covered by a mosaic of small plates.

Chondrichthyes

A group of fish is more evolved than their predecessors, with more developed fins and jaws, appeared in the waters of the Devonian period. This was the class Chondrichthyes, the cartilaginous fish whose members still populate in great abundance the seas of today with the two orders of the Selachii (sharks) and the Batoidea (rays).

The chondrichthyans underwent rapid development during the interval of time between the Devonian and the Permian, or about 360 to 226 million years ago. By the end of the Paleozoic era (245 million years ago) many of the groups that had evolved became extinct, and the chondrichthyans survived up to our time in a relatively reduced variety of forms. The modern-day members of the group are divided in two subclasses: the Elasmobranchii, which includes, for example, the sharks, rays and skates, and the Holocephali, including the chimaeras. Except for the Batoidea, the chondrichthyans are fast swimmers that now live in the open sea.

The principal characteristic of the chondrichthyans was the nonbony internal skeleton. The external covering, which was particularly strong in the preceding groups, consisted only of toothlike scales that give the chondrichthyans the characteristic roughness seen, for example, on the skin of sharks.

Since they lack strong external armor and do not possess an internal bony skeleton, fossil chondrichthyans are not easy to find. Usually, the only parts preserved are teeth and, more rarely, the scales.

The subclass Elasmobranchii, the most primitive, appeared during the Devonian (between 408 and 360 million years ago) with the order Cladoselachii, which survived until the end of the Paleozoic. The genus *Cladoselache* has been useful in the study of evolution. This Devonian animal, of which a few complete specimens are known, is particularly important because the structure of its paired fins is such that it indicates how these important anatomical structures originated. The paired fins of Cladoselache were constituted of a piece of cartilage, elongated backward and parallel to the body, from which parted at a right angle several subparallel rays. These fins thus had a very large base and evidently were incapable of rotation on their axis, as occurs in more evolved fish. Such structures served only as stabilizers and were not used for swimming. The structure of the fin of this ancient Devonian shark led to the belief that fins originated as lateral cutaneous folds within which later appeared pieces of cartilage—and still later, bone—for support.

Not only is the cartilaginous skeleton of Cladoselache known but also the outline of its entire body, due to the perfect preservation of several specimens in carbonaceous clay. This animal was in many ways similar to today's sharks: It was tapered, about a meter long and had an heterocercal tail, two dorsal fins, pectoral fins and pelvic fins.

The primitive structure of the skeleton of Cladoselache leads one to believe that it represents the group of cartilaginous fish from which all the others originated, both the Elasmobranchii and the Holocephali. From the Cladoselachii, the Elasmobranchii evolved in two directions, corresponding to the orders Pleuracanthiformes and Selachii.

The order Pleuracanthiformes, named for the genus *Pleuracanthus,* lived in fresh water during the Carboniferous and Per-

Below: *Teeth of the Paleozoic shark* Xenacanthus texensis, *Early Permian, Oklahoma.*
Bottom: *Perfect specimen of Rhinobatos, a batoidea of the Late Cretaceous, Lebanon.*

in appearance to a modern shark. Modern-type sharks appeared at the beginning of the Mesozoic, about 245 million years ago. During this era the Selachii broke into two separate evolutionary lines, one that would lead to the aggressive, fast-swimming predators that we know, and the other that would lead to the skate, torpedo fish and the Batoidei in general, specialized for life on the sea bottom.

Some representatives of the first evolutionary line, grouped in the suborder Galeoidea, are found in abundance in Mesozoic and Cenozoic rocks, particularly marked by sharp, triangular teeth with one or more points, which are attributed to numerous genera, including *Lamna, Carcharias, Hemipristis* and *Carcharodon.* Some of these genera are still living today, but during the Tertiary they reached enormous sizes, far larger than those of their modern-day representatives.

The Batoidea, representatives of the second line of development of the Selachii, include, as we have said, forms adapted most of all to life in proximity to the sea bottom. The bodies of these animals are thus flattened, the pectoral fins are very enlarged and are used almost as though they were wings to "fly" in the water, while the tail is reduced to a simple sharpened point. The oldest representatives of the Batoidea appeared during the Jurassic, about 195 million years ago. These were forms still intermediate between the Selachii and the true Batoidea; their pectoral fins were already very much enlarged while the body was still tapered and there were well-developed dorsal and caudal fins. Unlike sharks, the Batoidea are not fast predators, and the two groups have very different teeth. The Batoidea have flattened teeth aligned in rows to create two chewing plates, one above and one below, adapted for breaking the shells of the mollusks or other organisms on which these animals fed.

These characteristic teeth are often found fossilized in Mesozoic and Cenozoic rocks, sometimes scattered, sometimes still attached in complete plates. Among the best known genera

mian. The Pleuracanthiformes had an elongated body with a long dorsal fin, which ran the entire length of the back, and a pointed caudal fin. The paired fins were more evolved than those of Cladoselache because they were aligned on a median axis from which the fins radiated to each side. However, the most obvious characteristic of the genus *Pleuracanthus*, which lived during the Carboniferous, was a long spine that jutted out from the base of the cranium and swept backward. This spine is often the only part of this organism that is preserved in the fossil state.

While the Pleuracanthiformes inhabited the fresh waters of the Carboniferous, during the same period another order of Elasmobranchii had become adapted to life in the seas. This is the order of the Selachii, which evolved from the Cladoselachii around the end of the Devonian.

The first Selachii, which appeared during the Late Devonian, are of the group called Ibodontidi and can be considered an intermediate form between the Cladoselachii and the modern Selachii. The genus *Hybodus*, which appeared during the Permian and survived until the Cretaceous, already was close

PLATE XL
Fossil teeth of chondrichthyans and osteichthyes
(1) *Ceratodus* sp., Paleocene, Mali; (2) *Hemipristis serra*, Miocene, Maryland; (3) *Isurus oxyrhynchus hastalis*, Tertiary, Italy; (4) *Odontaspis* sp., Oligocene, Italy; (5) *Odontaspis taurus*, Tertiary, Italy; (6) *Oxyrhina* sp., Late Jurassic, Italy; (7) *Notidanus primigenius*, Miocene, Antwerp; (8) *Odontaspis taurus obliqua*, Tertiary, Italy; (9) *Carcharodon* sp., Late Tertiary, Argentina; (10) *Hemipristis serra*, Tertiary, Italy; (11) *Myliobatis* sp., Paleocene, Mali; (12) *Chrysophrys cincta*, Miocene, Italy; (13) *Sparus cinctus*, Tertiary, Italy; (14) *Notidanus primigenius*, Tertiary, Germany; (15) *Otodus obliquus*, Teritary, Italy; (16) *Odontaspis* sp., Miocene, Italy; (17) *Galeocerdo* sp., Miocene, Florida; (18) *Carcharodon megalodon*, Tertiary, Italy; (19) *Odontaspis* sp., Miocene, Germany; (2) *Myliobatis* sp., Paleocene, Mali.

PLATE XL

Below: Protospinax *sp., batoidea of the Late Jurassic, Germany.*

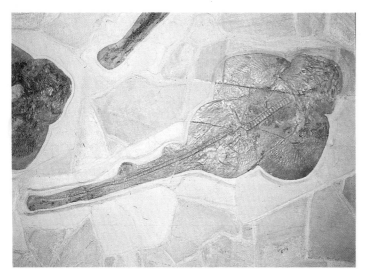

mals, deposits famous for the complete preservation of the organisms they contain. There are, for instance, the celebrated Selachii and Batoidea found in Eocene rocks of Monte Bolca (Italy), Batoidea preserved in the Cretaceous limestone of Lebanon and the Selachii perfectly preserved in the Jurassic deposits of Solnhofen, Germany.

The class of the chondrichthyans includes two groups of organisms joined in the subclass Holocephali. These are the Bradiodonts and the Chimaeriformes, the first of which lived from the Devonian to the Permian and is known only from its teeth, the second of which is still alive today in deep sea water.

Paleontologists are not in agreement on the chimaera, and the classification of this strange animal is the subject of much discussion. These animals, of which beautiful fossil specimens remain, have such primitive characteristics that some scholars believe they are not related to the chondrichthyans but are instead the last representatives of the placoderms, though without the characteristic armor.

can be cited the *Ptychodus,* whose almost square teeth, ornamented by transverse furrows, are used as index fossils for rocks of the Late Cretaceous; the *Myliobatis,* which appeared during the Cretaceous and is still alive, with hexagonal teeth grouped very close to form a continuous covering on the palate and the mandible; and *Rhinobatos,* which appeared during the Jurassic.

Besides their teeth, other parts of both the Selachii and the Batoidea have been found in the fossil record. Some deposits have preserved numerous complete specimens of these ani-

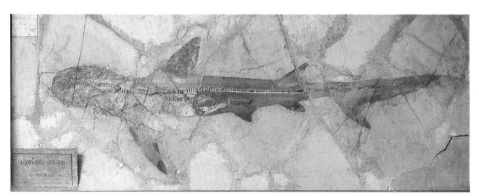

Above: *Shark preserved with the impression of its soft body parts in an Eocene deposit at Monte Bolca, Italy.*
Right: Platyrhina bolcensis, *batoidea in Eocene deposit at Monte Bolca, Italy.*

Class	Subclass	Order	Age
Chondrichthyes	Elasmobranchii	Cladoselachii Pleuracanthodi Selachii Batoidea	Devonian–Permian Carboniferous–Permian Devonian–Recent Jurassic–Recent
	Holocephali		Devonian–Recent

Osteichthyes

The Osteichthyes, the most evolved class of fish, are of great importance in the evolutionary history of vertebrates. Indeed, a group of Osteichthyes began the amphibians, the evolution line destined to lead to the formation of terrestrial vertebrates, which in turn led to all the other tetrapods, or four-legged vertebrates. The Osteichthyes are without doubt the most numerous vertebrates in existence today and populate abundantly all the freshwater and marine environments.

The Osteichthyes are also called bony fish because they have an internal bony skeleton. The external covering is made up of scales, of which there are two principal kinds: ganoid scales, typical of Acintopterygii (ray-finned), and ctenopid or cycloid scales, typical instead of Sarcopterygii (lobe-finned). An interesting characteristic of the Osteichthyes is the presence in the gill area of certain flattened bones, operculan bones, that cover the gill slits. These are exposed to the exterior with a single opening, not separate openings as is the case with the

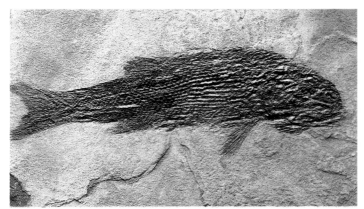

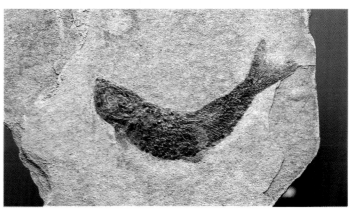

Top: Palaeoniscus blainvillei, *a chondrostean of the Carboniferous period, France.*
Above left: Albertonia clupidinia, *Triassic, British Columbia.*
Above right: *Undetermined member of the order Pholidophoriformes from Triassic deposits at Bergamo, Italy.*
Left: *Group of small fossil fish in a Cretaceous deposit from Lebanon.*

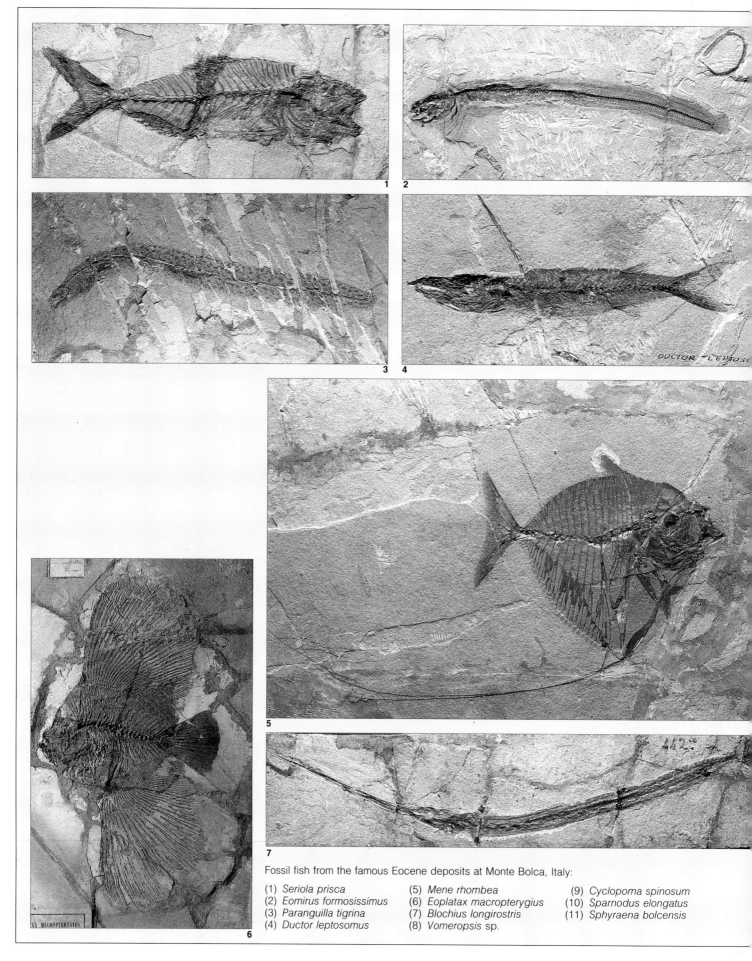

Fossil fish from the famous Eocene deposits at Monte Bolca, Italy:

(1) *Seriola prisca*
(2) *Eomirus formosissimus*
(3) *Paranguilla tigrina*
(4) *Ductor leptosomus*
(5) *Mene rhombea*
(6) *Eoplatax macropterygius*
(7) *Blochius longirostris*
(8) *Vomeropsis* sp.
(9) *Cyclopoma spinosum*
(10) *Sparnodus elongatus*
(11) *Sphyraena bolcensis*

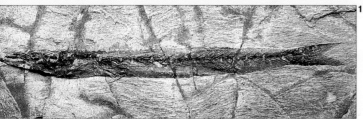

chondrichthyans. The paired fins are articulated in the Osteichthyes with a scapular belt often fused to the cranium. The oldest bony fish probably had respiratory sacs, a kind of lung, that were then transformed in most of the forms into the modern-day swim bladder, an organ that serves to facilitate vertical movements in the water.

The first Osteichthyes appeared during the Devonian, at which time they were already divided in two subclasses: Actinopterygii, or ray-finned fish, and Sarcopterygii, or lobe-finned fish.

The first of the actinopterygians belonged to the order Paleonisciformi, of a type represented by the genus *Cheirolepis.* This was a small fish with large eyes, a large mouth, a heterocercal tail (containing an extension of the vertebral column) with an upper lobe more developed from the lower, a dorsal fin located toward the rear, an anal fin located ventrally, and pectoral and pelvic fins that were decidedly modern.

The group of the paleonisciformi, the first actinopterygians, together with the sturgeon, the modern Polipteriformes, and the Acipenseriformes, which appeared in the Permian and are still living, comprise the superorder Chondrostei. This superorder constitutes the first evolutionary level of the bony fishes; the other two superorders in which the subclass of the actinopterygians are divided represent, in fact, two successive stages from this first level.

These two superorders are the Holostei and the Teleostei. The first, which appeared during the Triassic and survived with a certain abundance until the Cretaceous, includes a few freshwater species, such as the gar and sturgeon, which live in American rivers. The Teleostei, which appeared during the Jurassic, have reached today their maximum development. Modern modern fish belong to this group. The oldest known teleost is the genus *Leptolepis,* which lived during the Jurassic and is known from specimens from the deposits of Solnhofen.

More interesting from the point of view of the evolution of the vertebrates is the subclass Sarcopterygii, since the first amphibians evolved from a group of this subclass. The sarcopterygians appeared during the Devonian (between 408 and 360 million years ago), already differentiated in two orders, the Crossopterygii and Dipnoi. These groups were rather abundant during the Paleozoic, a period during which their members were adapted to life in fresh water, but they were never as populous as the actinopterygians. The Crossopterygii and Dipnoi have survived up to modern times, but with very few representatives.

The differences between actinopterygians and sarcopterygians are marked: The sarcopterygians have spiny (cosmoid) scales different from those of the actinopterygian, a pineal hole in the cranium, and a choane (from which they take the name choanati), which serves as a second means of communication between the external atmosphere and the respiratory sac.

Although there are noteworthy affinities between Crossopterygii and Dipnoi, there are also differences, most of all in the construction of the axial skeleton and the head. These differences have led certain scholars to classify these two groups of vertebrates not as orders of the same subclass but as two distinct classes.

Below left: Paralepidotus ornatus, *a holostean from the Late Triassic, Italy.*
Below right: Colobodus bassanii, *a chondrostean of the Middle Triasic, Besano Italy.*
Bottom: Amia kermeri, *Eocene, Germany.*

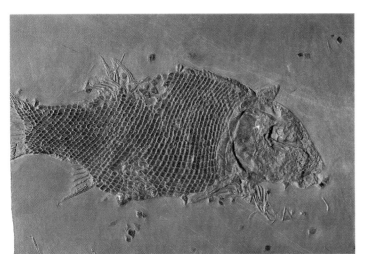

The Dipnoi appeared at the beginning of the Devonian with the genus *Dipterus,* a form that was already specialized, characterized by a long, tapering body, with an heterocercal tail, two dorsal fins, and paired fins formed on a central axis from which spread bony rays. The body of Dipterus was covered by cosmoid scales, while the cranium was covered by bony plates.

This ancient Dipnoi was adapted to life in fresh water and was not unlike modern members of the group, called lungfish. Today, these are separated into three genera, the Australian *Neoceratodus,* the African *Protopterus* and the South American *Lepidosiren.* They live in fresh water and can survive long periods of drought or lack of oxygen in the water, which happens when pools get smaller during the dry season. To survive the lack of oxygen, the Neoceratodus comes out of the water and breathes atmospheric air; Protopterus and Lepidosiren can survive out of the water for entire months, hibernating in hard clay balls and breathing air. To do this, Neoceratodus has, aside from gills, a single lung, while Protopterus and Lepidosiren have double lungs.

Since modern-day Dipnoi can breathe on land and in water, it is possible that the Devonian forms had this ability. This would prove that the formation of lungs, and thus of the ability to breathe atmospheric air, was acquired by fish in order to face unfavorable environmental conditions and before they tried to inhabit dry land. Notwithstanding their ability to adapt themselves to breathing air, it was not the Dipnoi that gave origin to terrestrial vertebrates, but the Crossopterygii.

The Crossopterygii today have but one living member, the genus *Latimeria,* which lives in the Mozambique Channel. This is the last representative of a group of Crossopterygii that had nothing whatsoever to do with the origin of tetrapods (which are derived from an extinct suborder that was widespread in the fresh waters of the Devonian and is called the Rhipidistia).

During the Devonian these animals lived in fresh water on the plains of the Laurasian continent. Some of these, of the genera *Eusthenopteron* and *Osteolepis,* for example, had anatomical traits that put them in a direct line toward the origin of amphibians.

Eusthenopteron was a carnivorous Rhipidistia whose remains have been found in Canada, Russia and Scotland. It was slightly more than a half-meter (.16 ft.) in length. The anatomical characteristics of the skull, backbone and paired fins place this animal very near the primitive amphibians. The skull was, in fact, large and flattened with bones aligned in a way very much like the skull bones of the genus *Ichthyostega,* which is, as we will see, the oldest known amphibian.

On the vault of the skull were two large parietal bones between which was the pineal opening; on the mandible and jaws were labyrinthodont teeth made of an interflexion of enamel and dentin. The internal nostrils were developed on the surface of the palate, between the vomer and the palatine bone, which permitted the animal to use its "nose" as an organ of sense and shows that Eusthenopteron was probably capable of pulmonary breathing.

Even more evolved toward amphibians were certain characteristics of the postcranial skeleton. The internal bones of the paired fins were aligned in a way approaching that of the appendages of amphibians; they were formed of a proximal bone articulated with a scapular bone and with two large bony elements articulated in turn with the proximal bone, one longer than the other. From the shorter of these two bones spread other distal bones. While the proximal bone is comparable to the humerus in terrestrial vertebrates, and the two intermediate bones with the ulna and the radius, the distal bones can

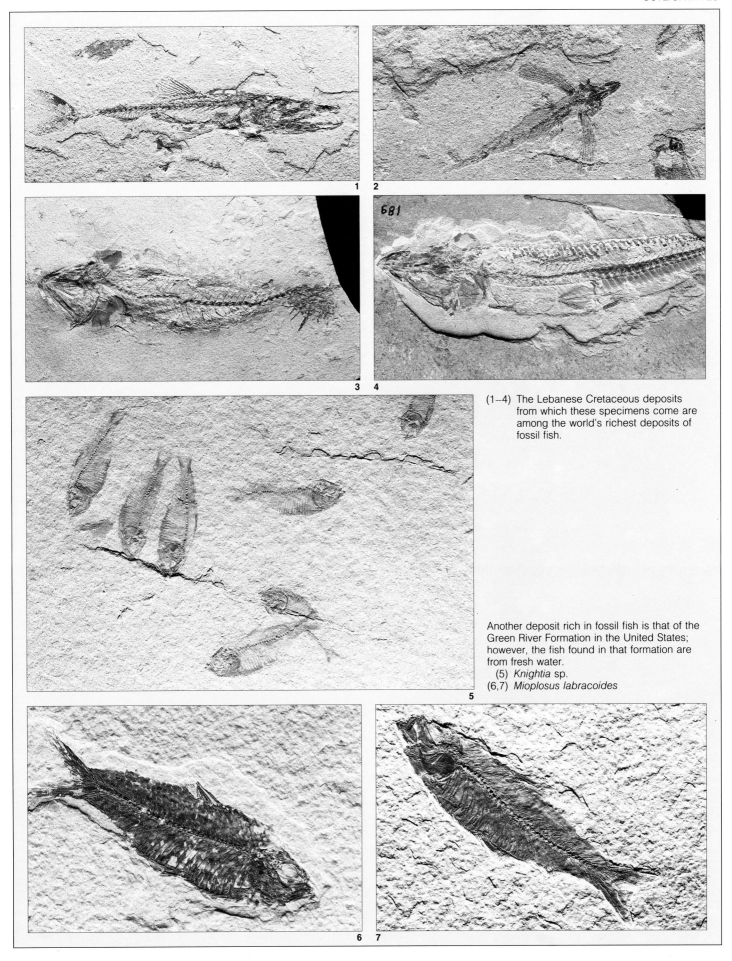

(1–4) The Lebanese Cretaceous deposits from which these specimens come are among the world's richest deposits of fossil fish.

Another deposit rich in fossil fish is that of the Green River Formation in the United States; however, the fish found in that formation are from fresh water.
(5) *Knightia* sp.
(6,7) *Mioplosus labracoides*

Below left: Paleorhynchum latum, *a Tertiary fish found in Switzerland.*
Below right: Syngnathus *sp., Late Miocene, Italy.*

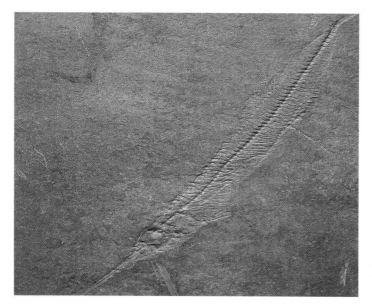

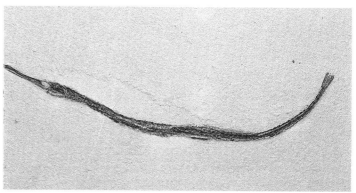

Below left: Gyroptychius *sp., a crossopterygian fish of the Middle Devonian, Scotland.*
Below right: Osteolepsis *sp., a crossopterygian of the Middle Devonian, Scotland.*

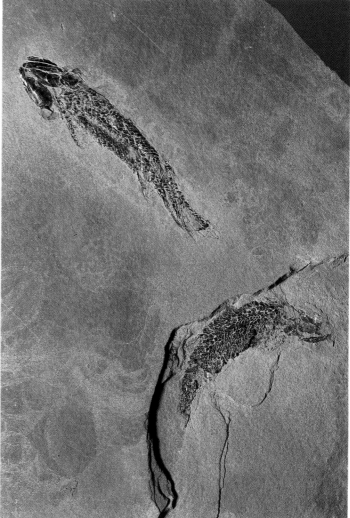

Below: Microdus alternans, *Middle Jurassic, Switzerland.*
Below center: *This specimen comes from the celebrated Italian deposit of fossil fish of the Cretaceous at Petraroia in Campania.*

be considered the first rough outline of the bony elements of the hand. The fin had, as in other fish, a series of rays that greatly amplified its surface area.

The spinal column of Eusthenopteron was even more advanced. The vertebra were the most developed of all the fish, strongly bony, formed like rings, and furnished each one with a long neural spine folded backward; and behind this was a small interdorsal bone. The ribs, short and triangular, were articulated with the ventral arches of the vertebral body. These traits place the Rhipidistia on the evolutionary line that leads to the amphibians, in particular to Ichthyostega.

Although the evolution of amphibians from *Crossopterygii Rhipidistia* seems well established, it is not easy to understand what factors led the Crossopterygii to establish themselves in the subaerial environment. It is believed that the desire for more water was the incentive that led the Crossopterygii to make their first excursions on dry land. During the Devonian, the continent of Laurasia, in the lakes of which the Crossopterygii and Dipnoi lived, went through alternating dry and rainy periods. The lakes were thus subject to periods of low levels that could lead even to their drying up. During these periods of drought the Crossopterygii and Dipnoi had to breathe air to survive: The Dipnoi, capable of pulmonary respiration, buried themselves in mud and awaited the new rainy season, while the Crossopterygii, probably also capable of pulmonary respiration—but in possession of stronger fins and backbone—must instead have sought new bodies of water. These impulses were the drive toward the conquest of dry land.

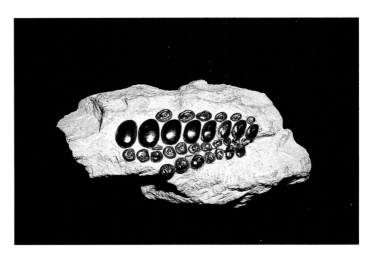

Left: Leptolepsis knorrii, *one of the oldest known teleosts. Late Jurassic, Solnhofen, Germany.*

Class	Subclass	Superorder	Order	Age
Osteichthyes	Actinopterygii	Chondrostei Holostei Teleostei		Triassic–Recent Devonian–Recent Jurassic–Recent
	Sarcopterygii		Crossopterygii Dipnoi	Devonian–Recent Devonian–Recent

Amphibians

Ichthyostega, the oldest known amphibian, lived during the Late Devonian. Although it was a true amphibian, with tetrapod appendages, this animal possessed several traits that tie it to the Crossopterygii rhipidistians from which it is believed to have evolved.

The skull, about 20 cm. (8 in.) long, was flat and solid, the cranial bones had the same alignment as those observed in Eusthenopteron, with the pineal hole located at the conjunction of the parietal zones. The opercular bones, well developed in the Crossopterygii and absent in terrestrial tetrapods, were also absent in Ichthyostega. The teeth, as in the Crossopterygii, were of a complexly folded, or labyrinthodont, structure.

The skull of the first amphibian was very similar to that of the rhipidistians, but it had certain differences, reflecting the fact that Ichthyostega was a terrestrial tetrapod. For example, the eyes were farther back than those of the Crossopterygii, and the snout was therefore more developed. The skull was not fused to the scapular girdle, as in fish, so Ichthyostega could move its head as it wished.

The postcranial skeleton of this first amphibian was a mixture of evolved and archaic traits. The vertebra were little differentiated in respect to what we saw in the rhipidistians. There was a long tail, but it still had a caudal fin like those of fish, and there were strong bones that supported the appendages, well formed and adapted to permit movement on dry land.

All these traits render Ichthyostega the direct descendant of the Crossopterygii rhipidistians and show that the amphibians originated, during the Devonian, from that group of fish. Ichthyostega is classified in the group of the Ichthyostegalia, held to be the progenitor of all the amphibians.

Beginning with the Mississippian period, the amphibians, profiting from that period's vast, widespread and humid forests, went through a rapid adaptive spreading. Since they had occupied a new ecological niche—thanks to their ability to survive on dry land—they became differentiated into numerous groups that paleontologists unite in the two subclasses of Labyrinthodontia and Lepospondyli.

The Labyrinthodontia, to which Ichthyostegalia belonged, are so called because of the presence of teeth with a complexly folded structure. They were widespread throughout the Carboniferous and the Permian and survived up to the Triassic. The labyrinthodonts include numerous groups of amphibians, some of gigantic size, such as the genus *Pteroplax* of Carboniferous, which was more than four meters (13.2 ft.) long, or like the Permian genera *Eryops* and *Cacops*, nearly 1.5 meters (4.95 ft.) long. Not all the labyrinthodonts reached large sizes, however. Examples have been found of genera of the Permian, such as *Branchiosaurus*, that were barely 20 centimeters (8 in.) long.

In general, however, the labyrinthodonts were large-proportioned animals; the genus *Mastodonsaurus* of the Triassic of Germany had a skull that was itself 1.25 meters (4.125 ft.) long.

Top: *Footprints left by seymouriamorphian amphibian. Permian, France.*
Above: Branchiosaurus *sp., small amphibian of the Permian, Germany.*

Class	Subclass	Age
Amphibia	Labyrinthodontia Lepospondyli	Devonian–Triassic Carboniferous–Permian
	Lissamphibia	Triassic–Recent

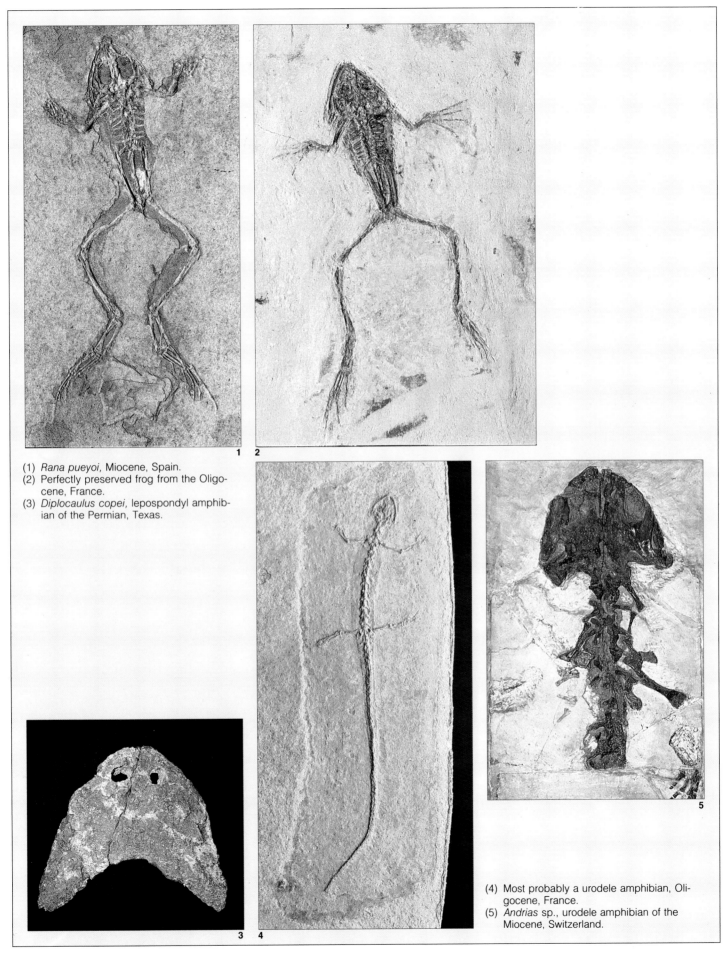

(1) *Rana pueyoi,* Miocene, Spain.
(2) Perfectly preserved frog from the Oligo-cene, France.
(3) *Diplocaulus copei,* lepospondyl amphib-ian of the Permian, Texas.

(4) Most probably a urodele amphibian, Oli-gocene, France.
(5) *Andrias* sp., urodele amphibian of the Miocene, Switzerland.

Seymouria baylorensis, *Permian, Texas.*

They lived usually immersed in water and only rarely came out onto dry land since the poor development of their limbs did not favor movements on the ground.

The most interesting group of the subclass Labyrinthodontia, from the evolutionary point of view, is certainly the order Anthracosauria, which includes certain highly developed forms from which reptiles are believed to have evolved. Among these is the genus *Seymouria*, a tetrapod that was near a meter in length and that has been found in Permian rocks in Texas. This genus presents such a mosaic of amphibian and reptilian traits that its classification has long been the subject of discussion.

Today, Seymouria, together with all the Seymouriamorpha, is classified among the amphibians because of a series of traits, including the structure of its skull. This was flattened and widened in an almost rectangular form and had an auditory notch for the placement of the tympanum in the ear, a trait typical of labyrinthodonts. All the cranial bones of the labyrinthodonts were present, including the intratemporal bones, which are absent in almost reptiles. On the jaw and the mandible were labyrinthine teeth, while on the palate were present, as in many amphibians, palatine teeth. Like the Anthracosauria, the Seymouria had a single occipital condyle, a round protrusion on the skull allowing a nodding movement of the head.

Although the skull was typical of labyrinthodont amphibian, the postcranial skeleton presented indisputable reptilian traits, and the limbs were very similar to those of reptiles, most of all in the number of phalanges.

The Seymouriamorpha cannot be considered the direct progenitors of the reptiles, since reptiles were already present during the period in which they lived. They do, however, prove that it was from a group of Anthracosaurs that the Cotylosaurs—the first and most primitive reptiles—broke away, presumably during the Carboniferous.

Less interesting from the evolutionary point of view is the subclass Lepospondyli. These appeared during the Mississippian, probably derived from Ichthyostegalia. The Lepospondyli were never very abundant and reached only modest sizes. Among the more primitive forms that lived during the Carboniferous was the genus *Dolichosoma*, which had no limbs and a serpentine body. Diplocaulus lived during the Carboniferous and Permian. It had a grotesque form, with a salamanderlike body and an enormously enlarged, triangular head.

The final subclass in which the amphibians are divided is that of the Lissamphibia, which includes all modern-day amphibians—the Anura (frogs and toads) on one side and the Caudata (salamanders and newts) on the other.

Modern-day amphibians do not have a distant origin: Paleontological data show that the Anura first appeared during the Triassic (the first frog was the genus *Triadobatrachus*, found in Madagascar). They probably originated from labyrinthodont amphibians. There is, in fact, a labyrinthodont of the Carboniferous, the genus *Miobatrachus*, which seems to show a tendency toward the Anura, both in the anatomical shape of its cranium and in the form of the vertebra. Even more recent is the origin of the Caudata, whose first representatives date to the Cretaceous.

Reptiles

With the Seymouriamorpha, we saw that reptiles originated from a group of labyrinthodonts known as the anthracosaurs. This evolutionary step was probably taken during the Carboniferous. The passage from amphibians to reptiles was an event of great importance to the history of vertebrates since it meant the complete separation of these animals from the aquatic environment. Although amphibians, in fact, can live outside water, they must periodically return to it to lay their eggs,

they cannot survive excessively dry climates and they are completely aquatic in the larval (tadpole) stage.

With the coming of reptiles, the break with water became complete thanks to the appearance of a new type of egg, the amniotic egg. This does not need to be deposited in water, like the eggs of amphibians, because it contains in itself, enclosed in a porous shell and a system of membranes, both a reserve of nutritive substance and a liquid environment that encloses

Class	Subclass	Order	Suborder	Age
Reptilia	Anapsida	Cotylosauria	Captorhinomorpha Procolophonia	Carboniferous–Permian Permian–Triassic
		Chelonia	Proganochelydia Amphichelydia Cryptodira Pleurodira	Triassic Jurassic–Eocene Jurassic–Recent Cretaceous–Recent
	Lepidosauria	Mesosauria		Permian
		Eosuchia		Permian–Triassic
		Squamata	Lacertilia Ophidia	Triassic–Recent Cretaceous–Recent
		Rhynchocephalia		Triassic–Recent
	Archosauria	Thecodontia		Permian–Triassic
		Crocodilia		Triassic–Recent
		Pterosauria	Rhamphorhinchoidea Pterodactyloidea	Triassic–Cretaceous Jurassic–Cretaceous
		Saurischia	Theropoda —⟨ Coelurosauria Carnosauria Sauropodomorpha —⟨ Prosauropoda Sauropoda	Triassic–Cretaceous Triassic–Cretaceous Triassic Jurassic–Cretaceous
		Ornitischia	Ornithopoda Stegosauria Ankylosauria Ceratopsia	Triassic–Cretaceous Jurassic–Cretaceous Cretaceous Cretaceous
	Euryapsida	Araeoscelidia		Permian–Cretaceous
		Sauropterygia	Nothosauria Plesiosauria	Triassic Triassic–Cretaceous
		Placodontia		Triassic
	Ichthyopterygia			Triassic–Cretaceous
	Synapsida	Pelycosauria	Ophiacodontia Sphenacodontoidea Edaphosauria	Permian Permian Permian
		Therapsida	Phthinosuchia Theriodontia Anomodorintia	Permian Permian–Triassic Permian–Triassic

Below: Labidosaurus homatus, *cotylosaurian reptile of the Permian, Texas.*
Bottom: Stylemis nebrascensis, *Oligocene, United States.*

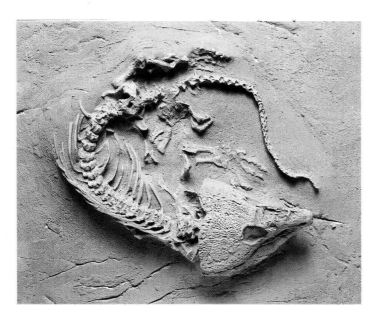

the embryo. The young born from an amniotic egg are similar to the adults and capable of living outside water.

The borderline between amphibians and reptiles was thus drawn by the appearance of the amniotic egg. This event, however, has not been documented by fossils. The oldest known egg, in fact, dates to the Permian, by which time reptiles were already widespread, and it is at least 50 million years younger than the Carboniferous rocks that witness the appearance of reptiles.

The distinction between amphibians and reptiles is not based only on the presence of the amniotic egg but must also take into account osteological differences, since skeletal remains are the only parts of vertebrates preserved in the fossil record. These differences are notable and, with the exception of such transitional organisms as the Seymouriamorpha, are easily recognizable. The cranium of reptiles, for instance, compared to that of amphibians, has a tendency to become narrow and high, to grow thin toward the front end and thicken to the rear,

where in certain types, because of the reduction of certain bones, there are openings that serve both to lighten the structure and to furnish a base for the attachment of muscles. The teeth, replaced in some forms by a horny beak, do not have the complexly folded structure. In the spinal column, the sacral vertebra are joined to each other and to the base of the skull. The scapular girdle, the pelvic girdle and the limbs have the same construction as in the amphibians but are stronger and more functional, thus permitting more rapid movements and greater activity on dry land.

All these traits, and above all the ability to make greater movements on land, made the reptiles masters of the land world beginning with the Permian and most of all during the Mesozoic. During that period of time they were so abundant and so differentiated in groups adapted to all environments that the Mesozoic is often called the Age of Reptiles. The reptiles alive today are few compared to other types of vertebrates and are the only remains of numerous groups that lived before the Cretaceous, many of which had become extinct at the end of that period, 65 million years ago.

The classification of reptiles is based primarily on the presence, absence and conformation of the temporal fenestrations of the skull. The most primitive reptiles, such as the chelonians, had a cranium without openings, which is called an anapsid cranium. In the more evolved reptiles various openings begin to appear. Thus the diapsid cranium appeared, with two temporal openings, characteristic of the lepidosaurs and the archosaurs, the euryapsid cranium, with a single upper temporal opening, and the synapsid, with a single lower opening. On the basis of the openings (and, of course, several other traits), the class of reptiles is subdivided into six subclasses: Anapsida, Lepidosauria, Archosauria, Euryapsida, Ichthyopterygia and Synapsida.

Subclass Anapsida (Testudinata)

Anapsid reptiles are characterized by a cranium without temporal openings. They are thought to be the oldest and most primitive of the reptiles, and the subclass includes the genus *Hylonomus,* which lived during the Carboniferous and is the oldest known reptile.

The subclass is divided into two orders, the Cotylosauria and the Chelonia. The cotylosaurs include the oldest and most primitive reptiles and can be considered the basic type from which all other reptiles originated. The cotylosaurs lived during the Permian and the Triassic; two separate groups are recognized: the suborders Captorhinomorpha and Procolophonia.

The Captorhinomorpha, the most primitive in the absolute sense, include numerous genera, such as, for example, the *Limnoscelis,* which can be considered a typical captorhinomorph. It was nearly two meters (6.6 ft.) long and was shaped like a big lizard. These animals were probably adapted to life in swamps or lakes and, judging by the structure of their limbs, they must not have been very agile out of water.

The Procolophonia were slightly different from the Captorhinomorpha. Some of them, such as the genus *Pareiasaurus* of

Mesosaurus brasiliensis, *Permian, Brazil.*

the Permian of South Africa and Europe, were squat and strong animals.

The chelonians—turtles and tortoises—are the only anapsids still living. Their beginnings are obscure, since the first turtles appeared during the Triassic with the genus *Triassochelys* (or *Proganochelys*), which already had all the traits typical of the group. It had a dorsal carapace, or shell, made of a single plate; but, as in earlier forms, it had some palatine teeth. Today's chelonians do not have any teeth at all, having instead a horny beak.

As has been noted, the origin of the chelonians is unknown, for up to now no organisms have been found that might represent stages in the passage to these animals from some group of cotylosaurs. The only fossil that could possibly belong to the evolutionary line that led to the chelonians is the genus *Eunotosaurus* from the Permian in South Africa. This, at least by what can be judged from what remains in the fossil state, was a rather particular cotylosaur in that its dorsal ribs were so enlarged they touched one another, making it possible that they represent a first, rough version of the turtle's shell.

The evolutionary history of the chelonians is not particularly dramatic. After Triassochelys two other suborders were developed during the Jurassic—the Amphichelydia and the Cryptodira. The first, far more evolved than the Triassic forms, had lost the palatine teeth and had a cranium with a much more modern structure. The second, the cryptodires, is without doubt the most evolved chelonians, the group with the most species still living, characterized by the ability to withdraw their head completely into the shell thanks to vertical movements of the neck. To this group are attributed many fossil genera, including *Testudo*, which appeared during the Tertiary, and *Archelon*, a marine chelonian about two meters (6.6 ft.) long that lived during the Cretaceous.

The members of a third suborder of Chelonians, the Pleurodia, or pleurodires, can withdraw the head into the shell only with horizontal movements of the neck. These appeared during the Cretaceous. They are very rare in the fossil record and today are confined to the warm regions of the southern hemisphere.

Subclass Lepidosauria

The lepidosaurs are reptiles with a diapsid cranium, which means they have two openings at the sides of the skull. They include groups that are completely extinct and most of the reptiles that are still living. This subclass includes the problematic group of the Mesosauria; the order Eosuchia, which constitutes the primitive group held to be the progenitors of the modern lepidosaurs; the order Squamata, which includes the lizards and snakes; and the order Rhynchocephalia, which flourished during the Mesozoic and is today reduced to a single genus, *Sphenodon*, which lives in New Zealand.

Like almost all the major groups of reptiles, the lepidosaurs appeared during the Permian period. The uniformity of the climate and environment of the Carboniferous had facilitated the development of the amphibians and the first reptiles, but during the Permian certain climatic and environmental varia-

tions occurred that broke the preceding uniformity and led to a differentiation in environments, which in turn led to a differentiation of the reptiles into numerous different groups.

The mesosaurs (Mesosauria) are attributed to the lepidosaurs, but a certain amount of doubt is still attached to that classification. These were animals adapted to life in fresh water. They were small, at the most about 30 to 40 cm. (12–16 in.) long, and had anatomical traits that indicate they spent most of their time in water and were capable of fast swimming. With many sharp teeth, the mesosaurs were predators that probably ate small fish, insects and other types of aquatic invertebrates. They have been found in Permian rocks in Brazil and South Africa, a geographical distribution that proves that those two continents were joined at that distant time.

While the mesosaurs were well adapted to swimming, the eosuchians (Eosuchia) were perfect terrestrial animals. The genus *Youngina*, a typical representative of this group, was a kind of lizard with a more primitive head. In modern lizards the

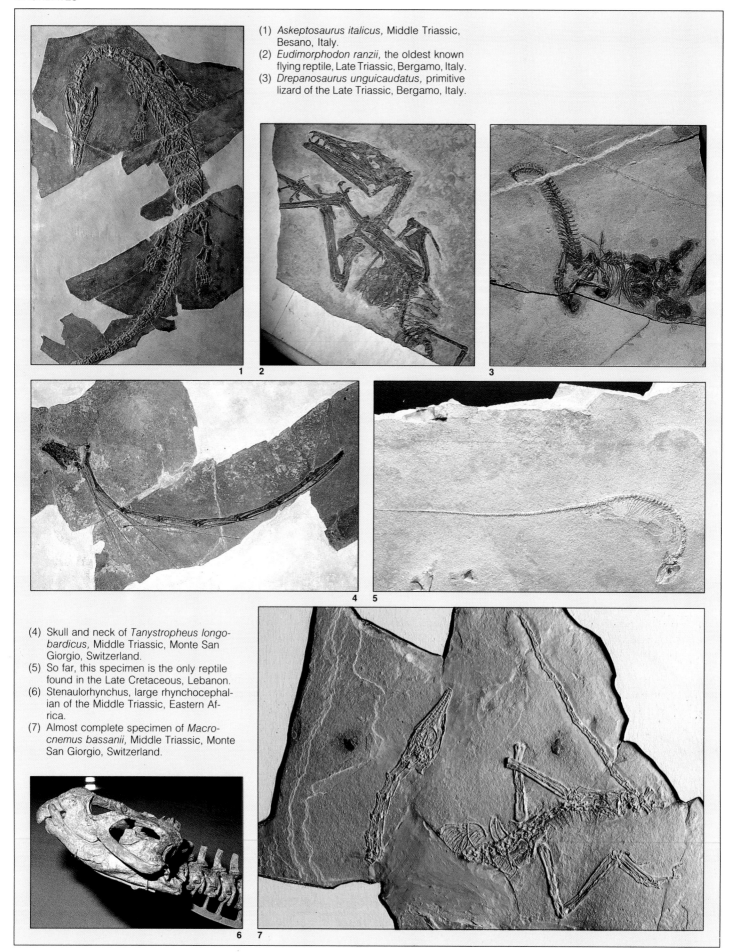

(1) *Askeptosaurus italicus,* Middle Triassic, Besano, Italy.
(2) *Eudimorphodon ranzii,* the oldest known flying reptile, Late Triassic, Bergamo, Italy.
(3) *Drepanosaurus unguicaudatus,* primitive lizard of the Late Triassic, Bergamo, Italy.

(4) Skull and neck of *Tanystropheus longobardicus,* Middle Triassic, Monte San Giorgio, Switzerland.
(5) So far, this specimen is the only reptile found in the Late Cretaceous, Lebanon.
(6) Stenaulorhynchus, large rhynchocephalian of the Middle Triassic, Eastern Africa.
(7) Almost complete specimen of *Macrocnemus bassanii,* Middle Triassic, Monte San Giorgio, Switzerland.

cranium has a complete upper temporal opening, while the lower temporal opening is open toward the bottom; in the eosuchians, both temporal openings are complete. The eosuchians include many genera, some of which have been found in the famous Triassic deposit of Besano, in Italy. This deposit includes the genus *Macrocnemus bassanii*, a small reptile, similar to a lizard, with a pointed head and long rear legs that must have enabled it to run on hard ground. Another eosuchian found in Triassic deposits of Besano is *Askeptosaurus italicus*, a swimming reptile about two meters (6.6 ft.) long that may have been adapted to life in marine waters. Another species from the same formation is the *Tanystropheus longobardicus*, an amphibian eosuchian with an extremely long neck it may have used to catch fish.

From such primitive eosuchians as Youngina evolved, during the Triassic, the Rhynchocephalia and, at the same time, the first lizards. The rhynchocephalians (Rhynchocephalia) were very abundant during the Triassic. During that period many forms reached large sizes, such as the genera *Scaphonyx* and *Stenaulorhynchua*, found in African and South American deposits.

During the Triassic, lizards were less abundant. Some were characterized by strange adaptations: the genera *Kuehneosaurus* and *Icarosaurus*, for example, were adapted to flight, while the genus *Drepanosaurus*, found in Italian deposits at Edenna, was a digger with two strong claws and a long tail that ended with a hook.

One group of lizards, related to the modern-day varanus, lived during the Late Cretaceous and must be mentioned: these are the mosasaurs, animals adapted to life in the sea that were sometimes more than 10 meters (33 ft.) long. The body of these animals shows a special adaptation to swimming, particularly the long tail, which was the principal organ of propulsion, and the reduced, paddlelike limbs, probably used for stabilization. The mosasaurs were not the only reptiles that adapted during the Mesozoic to life in the sea; this adaptation took place in other groups, in the ichthyosaurs and the plesiosaurs, for example, and it led each time to special modifications of the skeleton.

With the Squamata, the ophidians, or snakes, appeared last; the oldest known snake dates to the Cretaceous and is related to today's boas.

Subclass Archosauria

The subclass of the archosaurs includes numerous groups known from fossils and several modern-day representatives. They have craniums with two temporal openings, and the tendency to assume, through the modification of the rear legs, a bipedal posture, as happened in particular in two groups: the flying reptiles, or pterosaurs, and the dinosaurs.

The archosaurs are one of the largest groups of reptiles. They include numerous fossil orders: the primitive Thecodontia; the two groups of dinosaurs Saurischia and Ornithischia; the Pterosauria, or flying reptiles; and the Crocodilia, the crocodiles, the only group of archosaurs still living.

The thecodonts (Thecodontia) appeared during the Late Permian and lived throughout the Triassic period, becoming extinct after giving rise to all the other orders. They are thus the most ancient and most primitive of the archosaurs and include various suborders, each of which was characterized by special forms. The pseudosuchians, for example, of which the characteristic genus is *Euparkeria* of the Triassic of South Africa, were about a meter (3.3 ft.) long and had a strong tendency toward bipedal posture. The rear legs were long and thin, distantly similar to those of flightless birds like ostriches. The rear legs were much more developed than the forelegs, which were instead used to grab prey when hunting.

The cranium, solid but lightened by several openings, was similar to that of the dinosaurs and was armed with numerous sharp teeth, typical of predators, inserted in deep sockets. The skeleton of the trunk was adapted toward development of a bipedal stance: There was a long tail that must have been used to balance the weight of the front part of the body during movements undertaken only on the rear legs, while the rather primitive pelvis is similar to what became the typical pelvis of bipedal dinosaurs, tending toward cylindrical and elongated elements.

Along with these forms, which tended to assume the appearance that was later typical of certain dinosaurs, there were thecodonts with different structures: The aetosaurs, for example, with the genus *Aetosaurus* from the Triassic of Germany, were armored quadrupeds, while the phytosaurs, also quadrupeds, probably inhabited the environment later typical of crocodiles.

The crocodiles themselves evolved from thecodonts during the Triassic period. The first crocodile, grouped in the suborder Protosuchia, were contemporaries of the thecodonts. The genus *Protosuchus*, from the Triassic in Arizona, was an armored reptile about 90 cm. (36 in.) long. With a small cranium, flattened and not yet specialized, and with well developed claws that held the body well raised above the ground, the animal could attain a certain speed.

A more evolved group of crocodiles appeared from these first forms during the Jurassic. This was the suborder Mesosuchia, which survived up until the end of the Cretaceous. These were certainly more advanced than the preceding forms but still did not have, as do the modern forms, a complete secondary palate. Many mesosuchians were marine crocodiles. These had, as in the genus *Mystriosaurus* of the Early Jurassic in Germany, an elongated body covered by strong armor composed of big bony plates aligned in long series along the entire back.

Modern crocodiles, which make up the suborder Eusuchia, appeared at the end of the Mesozoic. They are characterized most of all by the presence of a complete secondary palate and are today divided into three principal groups: the gavial, which lives in rivers of the Indian peninsula; the alligators, typical of the American continents; and the crocodiles, widespread in Africa.

The flying reptiles, too, of the order Pterosauria, are probably evolved from thecodonts. They constitute a unique group of reptiles that, having appeared at the end of the Triassic, lived in a great variety of forms throughout the entire Mesozoic.

Below left: *Footprint of a saurischian dinosaur, Cretaceous, Italy.*
Below right and center: *Footprints of Anchisauripus, a saurischian dinosaur of the Triassic, United States.*
Bottom: *Dinosaur egg, Cretaceous, France.*

The conquest of the air by reptiles appears a perfectly reasonable occurrence when viewed in the light of the history of this group of vertebrates. During the Mesozoic the class of the reptiles reached its maximum expansion, and its members had by then occupied all the major environments. Some were completely terrestrial, some completely marine, many had adapted to life in coastal waters, many others had adapted to life in the high seas, and a great number had become inhabitants of continental bodies of fresh water. It was thus only logical that they attempted in this same period the conquest of the air.

This attempt is not unique in the history of the vertebrates, for the mammals, too, during the Cenozoic era, having reached the height of their expansion, attempted adaptation to flight with the chiropterans (bats). After the pterosaurs, another group of archosaurs attempted flight and were completely successful. These were the saurischians, the order of dinosaurs from which, during the Late Jurassic, birds originated.

Flying reptiles, birds and flying mammals conquered the air in very different ways. In the pterosaurs, the anterior limbs changed, with a lengthening of the radius and the ulna and, most of all, the fourth digit of the "hand," which became very long. This bone supported a membrane that permitted pterosaurs to glide, making use of air currents, and perhaps, as many believe, to effect powered flight. In truth, we do not know whether pterosaurs were capable of active flight, which requires a great expenditure of energy. For them to have done so, they would have had to be warm blooded, which reptiles, unlike birds and mammals, are not. (Cold-blooded animals do not metabolize rapidly enough to allow for the sustained rapid expenditures of energy required for active or powered flight.)

The entire body of the pterosaurs, not just the upper limbs transformed in wings, showed good adaptation for flight. The cranium was lightened by wide holes, the bones were furnished with air cavities and the tail, present in the more primitive forms, disappeared in the more evolved forms. Some of the vertebrae were fused to form a bony plaque that reinforced the scapular girdle, which bore the weight of the strong wings.

In other respects, the pterosaurs were typical reptiles. The wings still had clawed fingers, while the smaller rear feet, awkward when moving on land, allowed the animal to clutch onto a support when roosting, very much like today's bats. The order of the pterosaurs is divided into two suborders: the Rhamphorhynchoidea, which lived from the Late Triassic to the Late Jurassic, and the Pterodactyloidea, which lived from the Late Jurassic to the end of the Cretaceous.

The rhamphorhynchoids, whose most ancient representative is the genus *Eudimorphodon*, found in Triassic deposits at Cene, near Bergamo in northern Italy, have left numerous traces of their existence in deposits of marine origin, a sign that they must have lived in coastal areas where they found sufficient food in the fish of that period, somewhat like today's sea birds. The rhamphorhynchoids are primitive pterosaurs that preserved a long tail and had numerous teeth. Among the best-known genera is *Rhamphorhynchus* of the Late Jurassic, numerous specimens of which have been found in the deposits at

Solnhofen, in Germany. This animal was about 40 cm. (16 in.) long and had a tail that ended in a kind of rudder.

The pterosaurs appeared during the Late Jurassic, just before the extinction of the rhamphorhynchoids. Representatives of both groups have also been found together at Solnhofen, including the genus *Pterodactylus*, of which about 20 different species are known. These were small animals without tails.

During the Late Cretaceous, slightly before becoming extinct, the pterodactyls reached exceptional sizes. The genus *Pteranodon* from the Cretaceous in the United States and Russia had a wingspan of about seven meters (22.1 ft.). Its head was very characteristic, with the rear elongated in the form of a narrow crest that probably served to balance the weight of the long beak. The beak had no teeth and must have had a pouch membrane similar to those of modern sea birds, such as the pelican. Recently, bones of a pterosaur have been found that lead to the conclusion that the animal was even bigger.

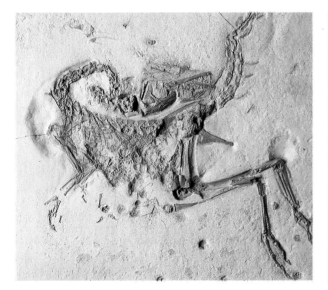

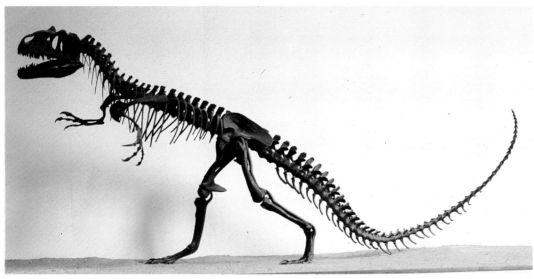

Above left: Compsognathus longipes, *the smallest known dinosaur, Late Jurassic, Solnhofen, Germany.*
Above right: Coelophysis bauri, *ancient saurischian dinosaur, Late Triassic, New Mexico.*
Left: Allosaurus fragilis, *saurischian dinosaur, Late Jurassic, United States.*

Below left: *Skull of* Parasaurolophus walkeri, *a duck-billed dinosaur of the Late Cretaceous, Canada.*
Below right: *Skull of a plateosaurus, a sauropodomorph dinosaur of the Late Triassic, Germany.*
Bottom: *Skull of a psittacosaurus, the progenitor of the ceratopsians.*

The Quetzalcoathlus—as the animal, whose bones were found in Texas, was named—must have had a wingspan of more than 15 meters (50 ft.).

The last two orders of the subclass of archosaurs are the Saurischia and the Ornithischia, groups that include a great number of reptiles, some of enormous dimensions and known under the general name of dinosaurs. This name, which means literally "terrible lizard," was coined by the celebrated English paleontologist Richard Owen during the first half of the last century and was applied to several gigantic reptiles that had been discovered in that period. Under the name "dinosaur" are united members of these two distinct orders of reptiles that lived exclusively during the Mesozoic era.

The first dinosaurs appeared during the Triassic, a little more than 200 million years ago. In rock strata of that period have been found remains of both proterosuchian (saurischian) and ornithischian dinosaurs, an indication that the two groups were already differentiated at that time.

The oldest representatives of the saurischians were found in the Middle Triassic in Europe and Argentina. Their structure allows them to be grouped phylogenetically both with the bipedal pseudosuchian thecodonts, such as Euparkeria, and with the quadruped pseudochuian thecodonts, such as Ticinosuchus of the Middle Triassic. On the basis of these primitive dinosaurs, paleontologists believe that the two groups of bipedal saurischians, the celurosaurs and the carnosaurs, were derived from bipedal thecodonts, while the three groups of quadruped saurischians, the sauropodomorphs, originated from the quadruped thecodonts.

The oldest representatives of the ornithischian dinosaurs were found in South Africa and Argentina. These are two genera whose structure seems to demonstrate that all the ornithischians are derived from a single group of pseudosuchian thecodonts. Among the ornithischians, the ornithopods developed first, and the other groups later evolved from them.

Before turning to the systematics of the dinosaurs, it must be pointed out that the fundamental difference between the two orders is based substantially on the shape of the pelvic girdle. In saurischian (meaning "lizard-hipped") dinosaurs, the pubis of the pelvic girdle points forward, as it does in most reptiles. In ornithischian ("bird-hipped") dinosaurs, the pubis points backward and is parallel to the tail bone. Both the ornithischians and the saurischians include biped and quadruped forms, for in both groups the pelvis was formed in a way to permit a columnar disposition of the back limbs and thus a movement of the body onto the back limbs. This development gave dinosaurs, even the quadruped forms, great agility, one of the reasons for the great success of these animals, which dominated the earth until the Late Cretaceous, a period of more than 130 million years.

The order of the saurischian dinosaurs includes, as we have seen, both biped and quadruped forms, and both carnivorous and plant-eating forms. The order includes the suborder Theropoda, made up of carnivorous bipedal dinosaurs, which is further subdivided into two infraorders. The first of these infraorders is the Coelurosaurs, which includes the oldest known carnivorous dinosaurs, such as, for example, the genus *Coelophysis* of the Triassic of New Mexico. The coelurosaurs were small and agile. Coelophysis was just two meters (6.6 ft.) long, and the Compsognathus of the Late Jurassic of Solnhofen, the size of a chicken, was the smallest known dinosaur.

The second infraorder is that of the Carnosauria. It includes the most fearsome and large carnivorous dinosaurs to exist,

Below: Camptosaurus browni, *ornithischian dinosaur, Late Jurassic, United States.*

including the allosaurus of the Jurassic and the tyrannosaurus of the Cretaceous, which, 15 meters (50 ft.) long, was probably the most fearsome predator that has ever existed on earth. Both the coelurosaurs and the carnosaurs lived at the end of the Cretaceous period.

The second suborder into which the saurischians are subdivided is that of the Sauropodomorpha, including in turn the infraorders Prosauropoda and Sauropoda. The prosauropods were biped or semibiped dinosaurs of large sizes, well represented by the genus *Plateosaurus* of the Triassic of Germany. This animal was about 8 meters (26.4 ft.) long, and its hind limbs and forelimbs were not of the same size. It was not, therefore, a perfect biped, like the carnivorous dinosaurs discussed above, although it must have been able to move on only its rear legs. It had a rather long neck and a skull of very reduced size, two traits typical of members of the second infraorder of the sauropodomorphs, the Sauropoda.

These appeared during the Jurassic and were probably derived from the prosauropods. They were decidedly quadruped and were herbivores with a very long neck and a cranium that was very small with respect to the general size of their bodies. The best known members of this group are the genera *Brontosaurus* and *Diplodocus* of the Late Jurassic in America, which could reach 20 to 25 meters (66–82.5 ft.) in length, and the genus *Brachiosaurus* of the Late Jurassic in Africa, which was even larger.

More complex is the classification of the ornithischian dinosaurs. This group includes four suborders: Ornithopoda, Stegosauria, Ankylosauria and Ceratopsia.

The ornithopods appeared during the Triassic and lived until the end of the Cretaceous. These biped herbivores were stockier than the saurischian biped carnivores, and probably less agile and fast. Among the most famous genera are the *Camptosaurus* of the Jurassic in North America and the *Iguanodon* of the Lower Cretaceous in Europe, which reached, respectively, seven and nine meters in length. The members of the Hadrosauridae family are intriguing. They lived during the Cretaceous and were adapted to life in swamps or at least to areas rich in water. They are commonly called duck-billed dinosaurs because of the strange shape of their beaks.

The stegosaurs appeared during the Early Jurassic and became extinct during the Early Cretaceous. These were very squat quadruped dinosaurs with a small skull and, along the back and tail, bony formations in the form of long spines, as in the genus *Kentrurosaurus*, or plates, as in the genus *Stegosaurus*. The ankylosaurs, too, were stocky and strongly armored. They lived during the Cretaceous.

The last group of ornithischian dinosaurs, the ceratopsians, also lived exclusively during the Cretaceous. Some of the forms of these animals were very odd. The ceratopsians were, in fact, large quadruped dinosaurs (in truth, the first ceratopsian, the protoceratops, was actually rather small), characterized by the presence of a large bony collars, behind the head, and one or more horns. The ceratopsians were the last of the dinosaurs and became extinct at the end of the Cretaceous, 65 million years ago.

The Extinction at the End of the Cretaceous Period. At the end of the Cretaceous dinosaurs became extinct. Although their decline had started six million to 10 million years earlier, the disappearance was sudden and complete enough to make any plausible explanation complicated.

Because it is so difficult to find a cause that might biologically explain the disappearance of these reptiles—at that time so widespread on the earth—many theories have been put forth over the years. Many of them are catastrophic and barely credible: the explosion of a nova, which would have killed off the dinosaurs by radiation; a drop in the amount of oxygen in the air; heat or cold waves; and so on. One recent theory claims that the earth was struck by a large asteroid and that the dust thrown up by the explosion darkened the sky, creating what has been likened to a "nuclear winter."

In reality, the rapid decline leading to extinction of many animals at the end of the Cretaceous was a complex phenomenon. Many groups disappeared—the dinosaurs, flying reptiles, great sea reptiles, ammonites, belemnites, rudists. Other

Below left: *Skull of* Nothosaurus mirabilis, *Triassic, Germany.*
Below right: *Sauropterygian similar to the genus* Lariosaurus *found in Triassic deposits at Besano, Italy.*

Bottom left: *Specimen of young* Pachypleurosaurus edwardsi, *a nothosaur of the Middle Triassic, Monte San Giorgio, Switzerland.*
Bottom right: Ceresiosaurus calcagnii, *large sauropterygian, Middle Triassic, Monte San Giorgio, Switzerland.*

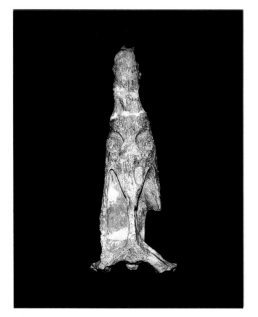

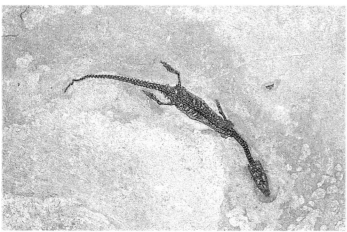

groups were diminished, yet still other groups were not even touched by the phenomenon. Plants, for example, experienced no loss whatsoever. The catastrophic theses do not explain why in the Late Cretaceous flying reptiles became extinct but not birds, why the dinosaurs became extinct but not the crocodiles, why the great sea reptiles became extinct but not the sharks, why the ammonites and belemnites disappeared but not the other cephalopods then present in relative abundance.

The "truth" is that, aside from extinctions, the time of the Late Cretaceous (about 76–66 million years ago) was one of a true biological crisis that led to a drop in the number of taxa (species, genera, families, etc.). It was a crisis that touched, however, only groups with a high taxonomic diversity, those characterized by a high number of different species.

The biological crisis of the Late Cretaceous can be explained without recourse to catastrophic phenomenon by following the biological and geological laws that usually act in nature. With all probability, the extinction of the dinosaurs, as with that of

other groups, was merely the result of changes in environmental stability that occurred at the end of the Cretaceous, associated with the drifting of the continents, the redistribution of the continental masses with respect to the masses of water, and to the variations in the surface of the dry land.

Before the end of the Triassic (about 208 million years ago), the great continent called Pangaea, at that time the single continental landmass in existence on earth, broke into small landmasses, the beginning of the modern continents. These, once separate, experienced a transgression or incursion, of the seas, which covered them under shallow waters that covered about 26 million square kilometers (10,400,000 sq. mi.). It has been calculated that at that time there was 60% less dry land than there is today. In a few million years the land areas had practically disappeared, the earth went from a single enormous continent, characterized by conditions of environmental instability, to an archipelago of island-continents, separated by ecological and geographical barriers, which were characterized by a high environmental stability.

It thus happened that the communities of animals adapted to the unstable environment of Pangaea had to adapt to an environment that required opposite characteristics. In modern stable environments (such as those in the tropics), communities are composed of numerous species, with few individuals, in limited areas of distribution. Just so, the stable, isolated continents of the Jurassic and Cretaceous were a home to numerous species.

Just before the end of the Cretaceous communities of high diversity developed (among the ammonites and the dinosaurs that is particularly evident), communities of few individuals for each of numerous species, which were adapted to life in restricted areas, separated one from another by insurmountable barriers.

At the end of the Cretaceous, 65 million years ago, the epicontinental seas suddenly retreated, and since the continental masses were farther distanced one from another following the drift movement, the archipelago of island-continents was replaced by continental areas isolated by ocean basins and each characterized by a new regime of environmental instability.

The extinction at the end of the Cretaceous period occurred just at this point, that is, when the communities well adapted to the stable environment of the isolated archipelago had to readapt to an unstable environment that necessitated low taxonomic diversity (because the community areas were not only larger but also more homogeneous).

Not all of the animal groups survived this change. In particular, the groups best adapted to a regime of stability, which is to say those rich in species, and most isolated in restricted environments, disappeared. Among these groups were the dinosaurs.

Subclass Euryapsida

During the more than 200 million years between the beginning of the Permian and the end of the Mesozoic, numerous groups of reptiles appeared that were adapted, more or less completely, to life in the water. Some of these reptiles are grouped in the subclass Euryapsida since they had a cranium with a single temporal opening, comparable to the upper temporal opening in the cranium of the diapsids. Many of the animals classified among the euryapsids were thus swimmers, most of all marine, and lived in great abundance during the Mesozoic. These include the orders Sauropterygia and Placodontia, both now extinct.

Included in this subclass is the order Protorosauria, small terrestrial animals with bodies shaped like modern-day lizards but with a cranium with an upper temporal opening. The protorosaurs were not particularly specialized animals. At the beginning of the Triassic period, the protorosaurs led to the sauropterygia.

The sauropterygia appeared during the Triassic. Reptiles well adapted to aquatic life, they survived, undergoing great modifications, up until the end of the Cretaceous period. During the Triassic period, the sauropterygia were represented by the suborder Nothosauria, a group imperfectly adapted to life in water (at least, not as well as their descendants, the plesiosaurs of the Jurassic), and they have left numerous fossil remains in European rocks.

Because of their incomplete adaptation to aquatic life, the nothosaurs are believed to have been organisms that lived in littoral, or shoreline, environments, thus being able to spend much of their time out of the water. Their limbs were poorly adapted to swimming. The phalanges, in fact, although in-

Above: *Skeleton of* Pliosaurus ferox, *pliosaur of the Jurassic, England.*
Left: Plesiosaurus hawkinsi, *Early Jurassic, Lyme Regis, England.*

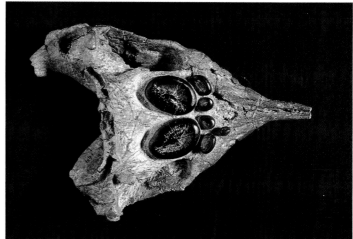

creased in number, were as transformed as they would be in the plesiosaurs. Their body was something like that of a lizard, but they had an elongated cranium, with long teeth, and a long tail that must have served as the principal organ of propulsion when they swam.

The nothosaurs have been found in abundance in Triassic rocks in the Alps. From deposits in Besano, Italy, and Monte San Giorgio, Switzerland, have come numerous specimens of the genus *Pachypleurosaurus,* 30 to 40 cm. (12–16 in.) long, and of Ceresiosaurus, a notosaur that reached three meters (9.9 ft.) in length. In other Triassic rocks in Italy specimens have been found of Lariosaurus, a small notosaur similar to those discovered at Besano.

These forms, still poorly adapted to life in the water, gave origin, presumably toward the end of the Triassic, to the plesiosaurs, members of the suborder Plesiosauria, which reached levels of specialization far more elevated than those reached by the notosaurs.

The plesiosaurs became well adapted to the aquatic life in a way much different from that of the ichthyosaurs, which, as we will see, were the marine reptiles par excellence. Instead of assuming a hydrodynamic, "fishlike" form, with pectoral and pelvic fins and a dorsal and caudal fin, the plesiosaurs developed a flattened and wide body in which swimming was performed by front and rear limbs transformed into swimming flippers thanks to the shortening of the proximal bone and an increase in the number of phalanges, which were flattened. The scapular and pelvic girdles were very well developed and formed large plates for the attachment of strong muscles. Between the two girdles were strong belly ribs.

This structure of the limbs makes one think the plesiosaurs were incapable of fast swimming. This would have constituted a notable defect (which, among other things, would have kept them from becoming as widespread as they did), had these animals not developed an extremely long neck due to a surprising increase in the number of vertebrae. This very long neck, also extremely mobile and with a small head with strong, sharp teeth at its end, was the structure that enabled these animals to live as predators.

The reduction of the limbs and the general structure of the body indicate that the plesiosaurs were not fast-moving animals. The paddle movements of the limbs enabled only a forward motion and prevented them from turning or changing their direction rapidly. The mobility of the long neck made up for this slowness; it could move in all directions and snap out at prey. These traits made the plesiosaurs great predators of fish and cephalopods, remains of which have been found in the fossilized stomachs of several specimens.

These typical plesiosaurs, which had a long neck and small head, are grouped in the suborder Plesiosauria. They originated at the beginning of the Jurassic from primitive forms that had a rigid neck, which are in turned grouped with the notosaurs of the Triassic, with which they lived for a certain period of time. In addition, at the beginning of the Jurassic appeared members of the suborder Pliosauroidea, which were plesiosaurs with a short neck and a much larger skull than the preceding types.

These two groups lived throughout the Late Jurassic and for all the Cretaceous, becoming extinct at the end of that period after giving rise to animals of truly large size. While the Jurassic forms, such as the genus *Plesiosaurus,* reached lengths of three meters (10 ft.), some of the Cretaceous forms were enormous. Among these was Elasmosaurus, which had 76 neck vertebrae and was 13 meters (43 ft.) long, while the short-necked Kronosaurus had a head 3.5 meters (11.55 ft.) long and a total length of more than 12 meters (39.6 ft.).

The final group attributed to the subclass Euryapsida is the order Placodontia. This order includes marine forms with euryapsid craniums that lived only during the Triassic on the borders of the Tethys Ocean and the epicontinental sea that then covered Germany. They were reasonably large organisms (the largest were more than 1.5 meters (4.95 ft.) in length), some covered with armor, others without.

The most outstanding trait of all placodonts is the presence of flattened, peglike teeth adapted to the grinding of the shells of mollusks or brachiopods, which evidently constituted their preferred food. The origin of the placodonts is unknown, and their assignment to the euryapsids is uncertain.

Below left: *Skull of* Stenopterygius hauffianus, *ichthyosaur of the Early Jurassic of Holzmaden, Germany.*
Below right: *Specimen of Stenopterygius that preserved the impression of the profile of the body; Early Jurassic, Holzmaden, Germany.*

Subclass Ichthyopterygia

With the Ichthyopterygia, commonly called icthyosaurs, we arrive at one of the most interesting aspects of the evolution of reptiles. Although, as we have seen, many reptile groups adapted to life in water (mesosaurs, mosasaurs, sauropterygians and placodonts), none of these groups reached an adaptation as perfect as that of the icthyosaurs. These were animals of the open seas, similar in appearance to sharks (justifying their Latin name, which means "fish lizards"), which during the Mesozoic represented, by their way of life and the habitat they inhabited, the equivalent of modern-day dolphins. The perfect adaptation to the life of open seas took place in icthyosaurs through a number of transformations.

In order to swim fast, an indispensable attribute in the open-sea habitat in which the icthyosaurs lived, their bodies assumed a perfect hydrodynamic shape. They developed caudal and dorsal fins, and the fore and hind limbs transformed into pectoral and pelvic fins with the primary function of stabilization. Push during swimming was furnished by the caudal fin, through undulating movements of the body made possible by the modification of the vertebrae of the spinal column, which became similar to those of fish. This caudal fin was hypocercal and thus tended to push downward, a thrust counterbalanced by the action of the limbs. These were transformed in true fins and were joined to somewhat smaller girdles. The bones of the limbs were shorted and, with the exception of the femur and the humerus, all the bones were flattened and had a circular or polygonal shape. The "fingers" formed a flexible whole in the form of a paddle due to the increase in the number of the phalanges and in the number of the fingers themselves. These could vary from a minimum of three to a maximum of eight in the most advanced forms.

The caudal fin and the dorsal fin were without bony supports, which would have been fossilized. For this reason, the first reconstructions of ichthyosaurs were made without them, and they were discovered only when several specimens, complete with the skin, were found in a Jurassic deposit at Holzmaden, Germany.

Even the skull of the ichthyosaurs was modified for a swimming mode of life. It was long and pointed, with numerous small, conical teeth adapted to capturing the fish and cephalopods that constituted the basic diet of these animals. In the stomach of several ichthyosaurs that were completely fossilized have been found the numerous horny hooks of cephalopods.

Around the eyes of ichthyosaurs were rings made of bony plates, called sclerotic rings, which probably served to protect the eyes from the changes of pressure common in life in seas.

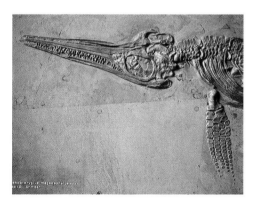

Bottom left: *Embryo of an ichthyosaur, Early Jurassic, Holzmaden, Germany.*
Bottom right: Mixosaurus cornalianus, *primitive ichthyosaur of the Middle Triassic, Besano, Italy.*

Below: *Complete skeleton of a dimetrodon, pelycosaurian reptile of the Late Permian, Texas.*

This ring is present in other marine reptiles, such as, for example, the *Askeptosaurus italicus.* The eyes of ichthyosaurs must have had good vision and were, in fact, large and located in large openings. These openings affected the temporal area of the skull, which was very narrow. On the upper part of the temporal area was a temporal opening, while the nostrils, as in all aquatic forms, were located toward the back, at the beginning of the long snout.

This body structure, so specialized to life in the sea, brought about important physiological changes in the ichthyosaurs. Since they could not leave the water to lay their eggs, the ichthyosaurs became ovoviviparous, thus giving birth to small living ichthyosaurs encased in a membrane (sac), as demonstrated by several female specimens found in deposits at Holzmaden in which the small embryos were preserved.

The ichthyosaurs appeared during the Triassic with forms already so specialized that this group cannot be connected to any preceding group of reptiles. The origins of these animals are not, however, unknown: During the Triassic they were represented by small forms, about one meter (3.3 ft.) long. These were mixosaurs already specialized for aquatic life but probably without the strong caudal fin that was typical of the more evolved forms. Mixosaurs are very abundant in Italian deposits at Besano and at Monte San Giorgio, in Switzerland. Ichthyosaurs more advanced than mixosaurs appeared during the Early Jurassic and are grouped in the families Ichthyosauridae and Stenopterygiidae, to the first of which belong the most classic forms of the genera, the Ichthyosaurus. The two families survived until the end of the Cretaceous period, with forms in sizes that varied from 1.5 meters (4.5 ft.) to five meters (16.5 ft.) in length.

Subclass Synapsida

The subclass of the synapsids appeared at the beginning of the evolutionary history of the reptiles, during the Permian (286–245 million years ago). The members of this group are of fundamental importance in the history of the evolution of vertebrates since they led, presumably during the Triassic, to the first mammals.

While the first synapsids demonstrate characteristics that tie them unquestionably to cotylosaur reptiles, from which they were probably derived, the groups that came after these most primitive forms present a clear tendency toward the acquisition of mammalian traits, and the most advanced forms show such strong mammalian characteristics that it is often difficult to understand where the synapsids end and the mammals begin. They are called mammal-like reptiles.

In general, one can say that during the course of their evolution the synapsids underwent a reduction in the bones of the skull, the development of differentiated teeth, an enlargement of the neurocranium, and the creation of columnar (more directly positioned underneath the body)—all traits typical of the mammals. Thus, the subclass Synapsida includes reptiles with mammalian traits characterized by a skull with one lower temporal hole (synapsid skull). These are divided in two large groups: the pelycosaurs, the most ancient and most primitive, tied by some traits to their cotylosaurian ancestors, and the therapsids, the most advanced forms.

The pelycosaurs appeared during the Early Permian and lived throughout that period, becoming extinct at its end. The oldest are the ophiacodonts, which include the genus *Ophiacodon,* 2.5 meters (8.25 ft.) long, which lived in the lakes and plains of the Permian, and the genus *Varanosaurus,* much smaller and

Below left and center: *Skull of a dicynodont, mammalian reptile of the Late Permian, South Africa.*
Below right: *Skull of a lystrosaurus, Early Triassic, South Africa.*
Bottom: Cotylorhynchus romeri, *a pelycosaur of the Permian, Texas.*

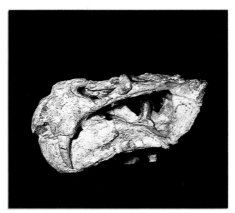

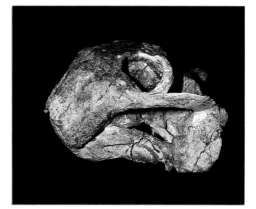

similar to a large lizard. At the end of the Early Permian the ophiacodonts became extinct after forming two groups with distinct forms: the sphenacodonts and the edaphosaurs.

The sphenacodonts were carnivorous reptiles with differentiated teeth and a narrow cranium, with powerful jaw muscles. Undoubtedly the most celebrated of these animals was the genus *Dimetrodon*, a giant lizard 2.5 meters (8.25 ft.) long whose most distinctive trait was the presence of dorsal vertebrae with very elongated spines, which in the living animal supported a large "sail." The use the animal made of this structure is unclear: Some paleontologists hold that it served to increase the animal's body area and thus to shed and to gain heat more quickly. This would have been very useful to a large-size reptile, with very low basal metabolism, that lived in a hot, arid environment, which is indicated by the Permian sediments of Texas, in which they are found in abundance.

The edaphosaurs were large plant-eating reptiles without differentiated teeth but with equal teeth set in a continuous line along the entire arch of the jaw and the mandible. Some of these animals, including the genus *Edaphosaurus*, had the same kind of sail as dimetrodon.

The order of the therapsids developed during the middle Permian. The members of this order populated all the continents and survived until the beginning of the Jurassic. These were the synapsids most evolved toward the mammalian form, so much so that they have been given the name mammal-like reptiles. They developed the traits noted above, morpholic features that became established progressively in the course of evolution and that are fully documented by paleontological data. In particular, paleontology has documented very well the progressive changes of the skull. During the course of evolution, there was a progressive enlarging of the temporal opening, which led at the end to the formation of the "arches" characteristic of mammals. The square jugular bones and the quadrate (an upper jaw bone), well developed in classic reptiles, became smaller. Some forms developed a secondary palate similar to that present in mammals. The dental bone became progressively a single bone of the mandible, with the disappearance of all the others. The teeth became increasingly specialized, with the formation of incisors, canine teeth and molars. Two occipital condyles (at the back of the skull) appeared, and the limbs assumed a columnar disposition (more directly

under the body), thus increasing the height of the body off the ground.

These tendencies appeared in the therapsids along two principal evolutionary lines represented by the suborders of the anomodonts and the theriodonts. The anomodonts include, together with a few other minor groups, the dinocephalians and the dicynodonts. The first were very primitive and had several traits of the pelycosaurs, from which they were probably derived. Their principal characteristics were their large size, still undeveloped dental bone, and the absence of the secondary palate. To this group is attributed the genus *Moschops*, an animal about as large as a rhinoceros, which lived during the Permian. Moschops was a plant-eating animal with a thick skull with undifferentiated teeth.

Lycaenops, Late Permian, South Africa.

The dinocephalians became extinct before the end of the Permian period, but the dicynodonts survived until the Late Triassic. These reptiles were distributed over a very large area. The genus *Lystrosaurus*, for example, ha been found in South Africa, India and the Antarctic, and these findings constitute one of the proofs that favors the concept that all those continents were joined at that time in a single continent (called Gondwana). The dicynodonts were far more specialized than the dinocephalians, were smaller and had a cranium with certain clearly mammalian structures.

The suborder of the theriodonts is certainly the most interesting group of synapsids, at least in terms of the passage from reptile to mammal. The theriodonts are in turn divided into six infraorders—gorgonopsians, cynodonts, tritylodonts, therocephalians, bauriamorphs and ictidosaurs—that reached a high level of specialization. Mammals originated from one or more of these groups, but precisely which group or groups has not yet been determined.

Among the cynodonts—the most widespread of the six groups—the genus *Cynognathus* can be considered a typical representative. It was about the size of a sheep dog, with a very mammalian skull, narrow and elongated, with a temporal opening located behind the eyes, and with a mandible formed almost entirely of the dental bone. The teeth were very differentiated and specialized for a carnivorous diet.

The other five groups represent more or less parallel evolutionary lines to that of the cynodonts. It is probable that among these lines the tritylodonts and the ictidosaurs had an important part in the origin of mammals. These animals lived during the Triassic in Europe, Asia and Africa. The structure of the cranium and the dentition of these animals are such that they would be included among the mammals if their mandible did not have an articulated bone and if their skull did not have a quadrate, a bone that in mammals is relocated to the middle ear, where it is used for the transmission of sound vibrations.

The tritylodonts must have been distantly similar, at least in appearance, to rodents. They had a skull with a sagittal crest running lengthwise down the middle of the skull, zygomatic arches for the attachment of mandible muscles, and incisors and side teeth almost square and multicuspid. They had the same number of phalanges (finger bones) as mammals and, like mammals, had two occipital condyles and a secondary palate.

Modern mammals are distinguished from reptiles by a certain number of traits that cannot be revealed in fossil forms: Mammals have, in fact, a constant body temperature, a high metabolism and a covering of hair, and they give birth to live young and nurse them. With fossil forms, in which only the skeleton is preserved, it is obviously difficult to establish the transition between reptiles and mammals, most of all since the reptiles, as in the case of the mammal-like reptiles, share a large number of skeletal traits with mammals.

From the paleontological point of view, this boundary has been established arbitrarily and is based on the bones that articulate the jawbone with the skull—the articular bone and the quadrate. When these bones are part of the joint of the skull-jawbone, the fossil is reptilian; when part of the skull, the fossil is mammalian. Although paleontology has not yet been able to decipher the origin of the mammals—that is, to determine from which group of mammal-like reptiles the mammals are derived—it is clear nonetheless that reptiles gave rise to the mammals during the Jurassic, more than 200 million years ago.

Birds

Throughout the story of life, several animal groups have tried to conquer the air. Some of these groups have had remarkable success, while the attempts of others have remained at a primitive level. The first animals that succeeded at flight were the insects. This happened 330 or 320 million years ago, during the Carboniferous.

The first flying vertebrates appeared many millions of years after the winged insects. This was the genus *Eudimorphodon*, discussed earlier, found in deposits of the Late Triassic near Bergamo, Italy. Many millions of years after the pterosaurs, the first flying mammals appeared, of the order chiropterans, the first representatives of which date to the beginning of the Tertiary. Both the reptiles and the flying mammals adapted to flight by developing a wing of the same type, a thin membrane extended between the "finger"-bones of the front limbs of the body.

The pterosaurs and chiropterans were good flyers (the second certainly more than the first), but they did not reach the diversity that characterizes another class of vertebrates, the birds. This is precisely due to the fact that the wings of birds are far more functional than those of the flying reptiles and the mammals. The wing membrane of those groups can be easily torn and, once torn, cannot be repaired, causing the animal's death. Bird wings, composed of many individual elements (feathers), can undergo greater trauma without the danger of breaking. Feathers also provide greater aerodynamic efficiency and control, their principal advantage over the membrane or skin wing. Birds are therefore vertebrates adapted to flight in the best way. They are derived from archosaurian reptiles and in a particular way from a group of saurischian bipeds.

Because birds possess many of the traits of their reptilian predecessors they have been called "glorified reptiles." But they are in fact different, not only because of their feathers, but also due to a more evolved physiology. They are warm-blooded animals, which allows them far greater activity than their predecessors, who may, in fact, have been warm-blooded dino-

Impression and counterimpression of a specimen of Archaeopteryx lithographica *from the Late Jurassic from Solnhofen, Germany, now displayed in London.*

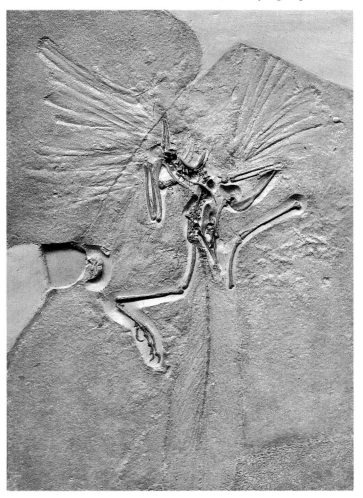

Complete skeleton of Dinornis, a flightless bird of New Zealand, Pleistocene.

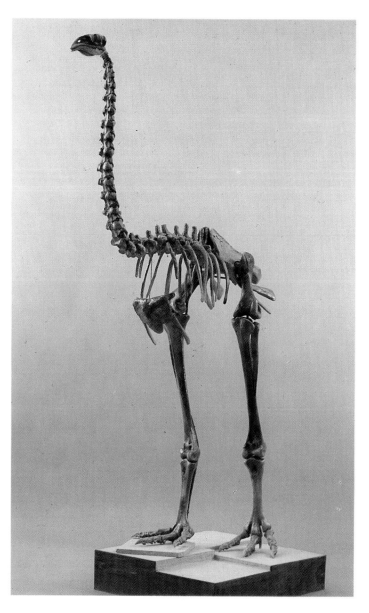

the finding of a bird of the Late Jurassic in the deposits at Solnhofen in Germany. This is the genus *Archaeopteryx*, the oldest known bird. It was assigned to this class of vertebrates because the fine rock of the deposit preserved, in addition to the bones of the skeleton, some impressions of feathers.

Archaeopteryx, about the size of a crow, was a bird, but its skeleton reveals many reptilian traits. The cranium was supported by a long, flexible neck constructed like the neck of a saurischian dinosaur. The cranium had a large orbital opening and anterior of this a notably big opening. The jaw and mandible had a series of sharp teeth similar to those in predatory reptile. Like the reptiles, this animal did not have pneumatic cavities in its bones and had a long tail formed of distinct vertebral segments into which the feathers were inserted, as with a fan.

Further reptilian traits were found in the limbs and the scapular girdle; the sternum was short and not keeled, and the front limbs retained some free clawed fingers.

Archaeopteryx was definitely not a good flyer due to its primitive structure. It was, instead, able to glide from tree to tree and to climb about with its clawed hands. The structure of archaeopteryx, almost a mosaic of avian and reptilian traits, is the sure sign of the derivation of birds from saurischian dinosaurs, and in particular from forms similar to the genus *Compsognathus*, the small dinosaur that, fatefully, was found precisely in the same deposit.

Precisely how the first bird developed from reptiles remains an unsolved mystery. According to some theories, the feathers, present in reptile predators without wings, may have permitted more agile hunting with longer leaps. According to others, feathers would have allowed these reptiles to leap from one tree to another. In either case, it is certain that feathers came first, as a modification of the reptilian scales, and the creation of the wing structure came later.

Whatever the origin of birds may have been, it is certain that the new structure and the new way of life had great success. As early as the Cretaceous, in fact, birds more advanced than archaeopteryx had reached a certain level of diversity and differentiation in their adaptations. The genus *Hesperornis* was adapted to swimming, while the genus *Ichthyornis* must have been an excellent flyer, similar to the modern-day gull.

The differentiation of the birds into the numerous groups known today began in the Late Cretaceous and carried on through the Early Tertiary, after the disappearance of the flying reptiles. During the Tertiary, giant and unusual forms of birds appeared, such as the phororhacos, a bird 1.5 meters (4.95 feet) tall with a very strong beak, found in Miocene deposits in South America. Even more impressive must have been the genus *Diatryma* of the Eocene in Europe, which was two meters (6.6 feet) high.

In conclusion, we must cite certain forms of flightless birds, related to today's flightless birds (ostriches and others), which lived until recently; aepyornis, which lived in Madagascar during the Quaternary, with species up to three meters (9.9 ft.) high; the moa of New Zealand, which numbers several species, including the dinornis, a bird known to the ancient Maori, which reached a height of 2.5 meters (8.25 ft.).

saurs, according to current evidence. Some authorities even believe birds to be the last surviving lineage of dinosaurs, that they should not be placed in a separate class.

The skeleton of a bird retains many aspects of the general structure of that of dinosaurs but has certain innovations fundamental for success as a flying animal. Some bones, such as part of the skull, the cervical vertebrae, the humerus and the femur, are hollow, thus reducing the general weight of the body; the fore legs are altered; the tail has almost disappeared; and the sternum is transformed in a keeled bone that serves as the base for the strong wing muscles. The rear legs are very similar to those of dinosaurs, and as with dinosaurs they have no secondary palate, while there is a temporal opening, sometimes in line with the eyesocket. Birds have no teeth, but a horny beak instead.

The basic proof of the derivation of birds from reptiles was

Mammals

Mammals appeared during the Triassic, more precisely during the Late Triassic, having evolved from one or more groups of synapsid reptiles.

Paleontology has not yet been able to establish the exact origin of mammals. It has been seen that the tendency to reach the mammalian state is present in different groups of therapsids that had a more or less parallel evolution. Available paleontological data are not sufficient to clarify from which of these groups the mammals originated.

Mammals can be differentiated from reptiles, their predecessors, on the basis of certain traits: the presence of a double occiptal condyle; the presence of a double palate; a single external nasal opening; the joining of the cranium and the mandible; the greater size of the cranial cavity; the differentiated dentition; the neck ribs fused with the vertebrae; the lombar vertebrae without ribs; the fused bones in the pelvis; the reduced number of bones in the fingers; and the transformation of the quadrate bone in the cranium and the articulate bone of mandible into elements able to transmit sound vibrations in the middle ear.

Living mammals can be divided into three large groups: monotremes, mammals that lay eggs; marsupials, animals that give birth to young at an immature fetal stage; and placental mammals, in which the young are born at a more advanced stage of development. These three groups do not have the same importance from the taxonomic point of view: The monotremes constitute, in fact, an order in the subclass Prototheria,

while the marsupials and the placental mammals (corresponding to two infraclasses, Metatheria and Eutheria) are grouped in the same subclass, Theria.

Monotremes, marsupials and placental mammals probably correspond to three successive stages in the evolution of mammals, and it is believed that they must have appeared progressively in that order. In reality, the monotremes are almost unknown in the fossil state, and their history cannot thus be reconstructed. They have, however, certain reptilian traits (the beak and the eggs, for example) that lead to the conclusion that they belong to a group strongly tied to the mammal-like reptiles.

The first mammals appeared during the Late Triassic. These were of the order Docodonta. During the Early Jurassic other groups appeared: the orders Triconodonta, Symmetrodonta, Multituberculata and Pantotheria. These groups are not well known, having few and often incomplete fossils.

The docodonts and the triconodonts may represent the most primitive stage of mammals. The docodonts, in fact, are represented by the genus *Morganucodon,* the oldest known mammal, which still has reptilian traits in the articulation between the mandible and the cranium and thus seems to represent an excellent stepping stone between the true mammals and the mammal-like reptiles.

The triconodonts, which appeared in the Early Jurassic, are better known than the docodonts because more fossil remains attributed to them have been found—craniums, teeth and

Above left: *Skull of Merycoidodon, Oligocene, South Dakota.*
Above right: *A perissodactyl of the extinct family of the Palaeotheriidae,* Plagiolophus annectens, *Eocene, France.*

Class	Subclass	Order	Age
Mammalia	Prototheria	Monotremata	Quaternary–Recent
	Allotheria	Docodonta Triconodonta Multituberculata Symmetrodonta Pantotheria	Triassic–Jurassic Triassic (?)–Cretaceous (?) Jurassic–Eocene Jurassic–Cretaceous Jurassic–Cretaceous
	Metatheria	Marsupialia	Cretaceous–Recent
	Eutheria	25 placental orders	Cretaceous–Recent

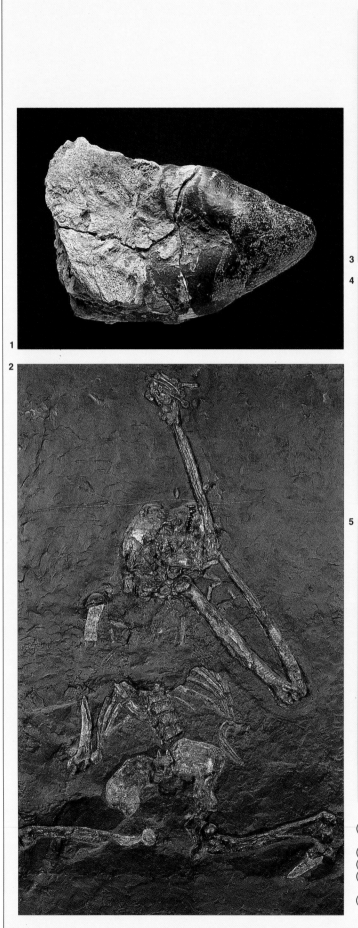

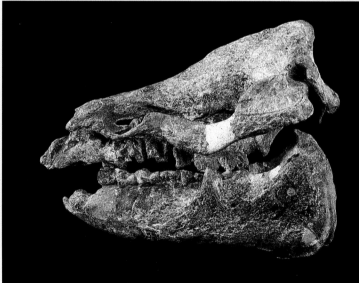

(1) Tooth of a primitive swine, *Archaeotherium* sp.; Oligocene, South Dakota.
(2) *Oreopithecus bamboli,* an ancient primae of the Miocene, Italy.
(3) Skull of Miohippus, the small horse of the Oligocene, South Dakota.
(4) Skull of the oldest known horse, Hyracotherium or Eohippus; Early Eocene, United States.
(5) Skull of the oldest known proboscidean, the Moeritherium; Eocene and Oligocene, Egypt.

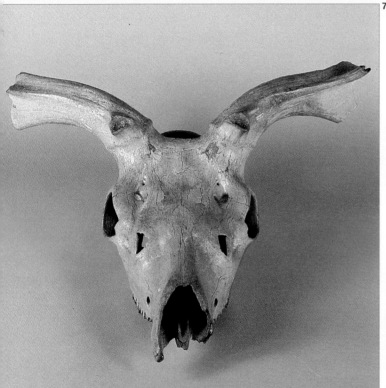

(6) Skull of a cave bear, *Ursus spelaeus;* Quaternary from the Alpine foothills of Lombardy.
(7) Skull of Megaloceros, the large elk widespread in Europe during the Quaternary.
(8) Skull of Poebrotherium, a primitive camel; Oligocene, South Dakota.
(9) *Hyaenodon* sp., ancient predatory carnivore; Oligocene, South Dakota.
(10) Mandible of *Brontotherium gigas,* Oligocene, South Dakota.
(11) Ancient tapir, *Lophiodon* sp., Late Eocene, France.

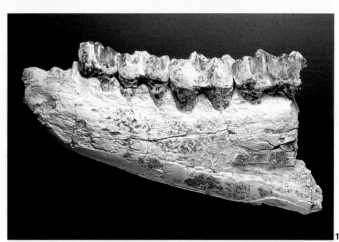

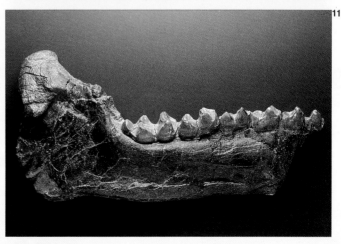

fragments of the postcranial skeleton. The triconodonts were about the size of a cat and had a cranium with an elongated jaw with highly specialized teeth, formed of four incisors, a canine, four premolars and five molars. The molars had three conical cuspids.

The multituberculates, which appeared at the beginning of the Jurassic period, were also highly specialized mammals. These were reasonably small animals, probably herbivores, with a very specialized dentition, with molars characterized by rows of cuspids aligned longitudinally. In the front were two long incisors, which seem to have made these animals resemble modern-day rodents, and they probably exhibited similar behavior.

Another group, the symmetrodonts, were predatory mammals. Their name comes from the fact that each of their molars was composed of three cuspids aligned to form a symmetrical triangle. These appeared during the Early Jurassic and became extinct before the end of the Mesozoic.

The pantotheres, finally, are the group most interesting from the evolutionary point of view. Both the marsupials and the placental mammals are derived from them. The pantotheres had very specialized teeth, with triangular upper molars with a principal cuspid accompanied by true cuspids on the side. These cuspids left many spaces in which were subsequently inserted smaller triangular molars. The whole of the dentition, with the upper molars with their tops turned toward the inside of the mouth and with the lower molars with their tops turned outward, formed a complicated cutting system. This system is present also in the first Mesozoic representatives of the marsupials and placental mammals, which, based mainly on this characteristic, are believed to be derived from pantotheres.

During the Mesozoic, the mammals, like the birds, did not really thrive and were always relegated to second place, in terms of diversity, compared with the archosauran reptiles, which at that time dominated most environments.

The various orders that we have cited underwent very different evolutionary histories. The docodonts disappeared entirely before the end of the Jurassic, together with the symmetrodonts. The triconodonts disappeared during the Early Cretaceous, and the multituberculates barely survived the interval between the Mesozoic and the Tertiary. Apparently, none of these groups left descendants; only the pantotheres gave origin, as we have seen, to the marsupials and the placental mammals, which began their evolution on two divergent lines.

The docodonts, triconodonts, multituberculates, symmetrodonts and pantotheres constitute the first phase of the three-phase, adaptive radiation (many types in a short period of geologic time) of the mammals, which took place in the interval between the Triassic and the Jurassic. The second phase occurred during the Cretaceous, when the first marsupials and placental mammals, derived from the pantotheres, appeared.

The third, largest and best-documented phase of the adaptive radiation of the mammals took place at the beginning of the Cenozoic (about 66 million years ago). During this phase the marsupials and placental mammals underwent enormous development. In particular, the placental mammals adapted to a wide variety of ecological niches, returning to the water with the Cetacea, invading the sky with the chiropterans and differentiating into 25 different orders, as many as all the groups of mammals, fossil and alive, known today.

The marsupials constitute today a somewhat restricted group of mammals, located in part in the Americas and in part in Australia, where they are the only endemic mammals in existence. To understand this strange distribution of marsupials it is necessary to go back in time and glance at the geographical situation that existed in mid-Jurassic times, before the first phase of mammalian radiation, when Australia and Antarctica to-

Complete skeleton of Arsinoitherium, a strange mammal that lived in Egypt during the Oligocene.

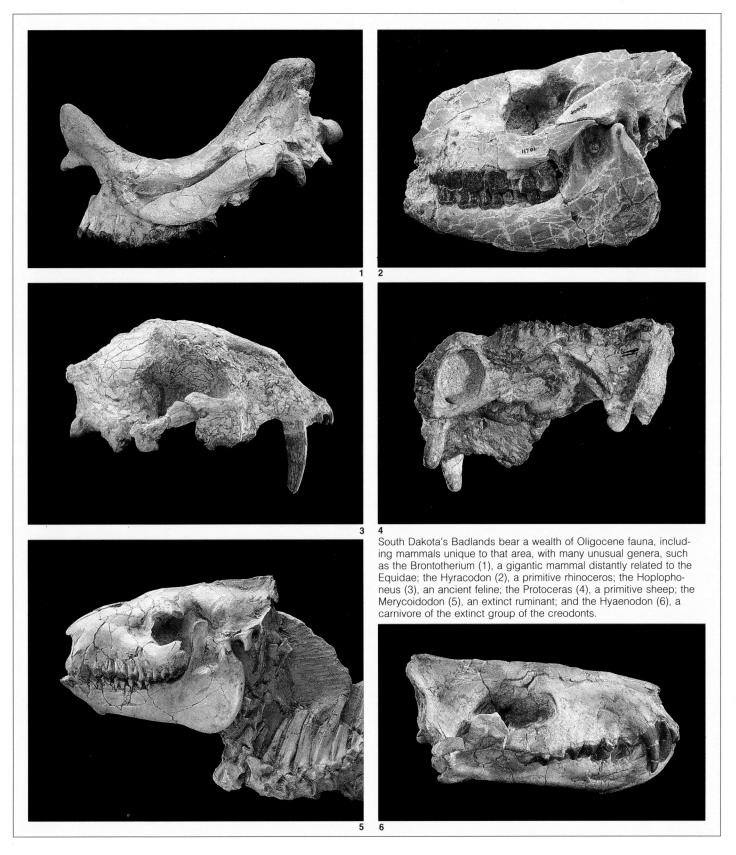

South Dakota's Badlands bear a wealth of Oligocene fauna, including mammals unique to that area, with many unusual genera, such
as the Brontotherium (1), a gigantic mammal distantly related to the
Equidae; the Hyracodon (2), a primitive rhinoceros; the Hoplopho-
neus (3), an ancient feline; the Protoceras (4), a primitive sheep; the
Merycoidodon (5), an extinct ruminant; and the Hyaenodon (6), a
carnivore of the extinct group of the creodonts.

Complete skeleton of Uintatherium, a strange member of the extinct order of the amblypods; Eocene, North America.

gether separated from the other continents and drifted southward with climates unfavorable for most of the still nascent mammals. In mid to late Cretaceous Australia began to drift northward. Its native marsupials later evolved along lines parallel to the placentals that were flourishing on the other continents but had failed to arise during Australia's meanderings in southern latitudes.

At the end of the Cretaceous the placental mammals were soon to begin their full radiation which eventually drove the less evolved marsupials into increasingly smaller areas, leading to their disappearance. This placental radiation took place during the Tertiary (66.2 million years ago), long after Australia had separated from the other continents. In Australia the marsupials survived as the only mammals because the continent had been isolated from placental mammals during their time of greatest adaptation. In South America, the marsupials were less fortunate. The placental mammals drove back the marsupials, which are today much more reduced than in Australia. During the Cretaceous and during the first period of the Cenozoic era, the marsupials were reasonably widespread in most parts of the world, with some species of large size. Most of these forms were swept away by the rapid evolution of placental mammals during the Cenozoic era.

During the 65 million years that run from the Paleocene to today, many different orders appeared among the placental mammals. Many still exist, but many have become extinct, some without leaving any descendants. The placental mammalian fauna of the Mesozoic was therefore much different from our own age. During those distant times many odd and giant animals existed side by side with the mammals that were the progenitors of the mammals that today inhabit our planet.

The modern-day mammals are thus the product of a history that lasted at least 100 million years. This fauna, well-known to us, took its form at the end of the current Quaternary Period, after the great glaciations that signaled the extinction of many Tertiary mammals.

The fauna that today inhabit the earth are thus the product of a long evolution, an evolution that began many millions of years ago with the development of the first single-celled organisms. This evolution has led, over the course of time, to a continuous flow of new flora and fauna—and the prospect of always new and different worlds.

These are the worlds paleontologists try to reconstruct through the study of fossil remains.

ADDITIONAL READING

AGER, D.V., *Principles of Paleoecology*. San Francisco: Freeman, 1971.

BABIN, CLAUDE, *Elements of Palaeontology*. New York: John Wiley, 1980.

BEERBOWER, JAMES R., *Search for the Past*, 2nd ed. Englewood Cliffs, N.J.: Prentice-Hall, 1968.

BLACK, F.M., *The Elements of Palaeontology*, 2nd ed. Cambridge: Cambridge University Press, 1989.

BOARDMAN, RICHARD S., ALAN H. CHEETHAM and ALBERT J. ROWELL, *Fossil Invertebrates*. Palo Alto: Blackwell Scientific Publications, 1987.

BROUWER, A., *General Palaeontology*. Chicago: University of Chicago Press, 1968.

CARROLL, ROBERT L., *Vertebrate Paleontology and Evolution*. New York: W. H. Freeman, 1968.

CLARKSON, E.N.K., *Invertebrate Palaeontology and Evolution*. London: George Allen & Unwin, 1979.

COLBERT, EDWIN H., *Dinosaurs: An Illustrated History*. New York: Hammond, 1983.

———, *Evolution of the Vertebrates*, 3rd ed. New York: John Wiley, 1980.

———, *The Great Dinosaur Hunters and Their Discoveries*. New York: Dover, 1984.

DONOVAN, D.T., *Stratigraphy*. Chicago: Rand McNally, 1966.

EICHER, D.L., *Geologic Time*, 2nd ed. Englewood Cliffs, N.J.: Prentice Hall, 1976.

ELDREDGE, NILES, *Life Pulse: Episodes from the Story of the Fossil Record*. New York: Facts on File, 1987.

KUMMEL B. and D. RAUP, *Handbook of Paleontological Techniques*. San Francisco: Freeman, 1965.

LAMBERT, DAVID and THE DIAGRAM GROUP, *A Field Guide to Prehistoric Life*. New York: Facts on File, 1985.

LANE, N. GARY, *Life of the Past*, 2nd ed. Columbus: Chas. E. Merrill, 1986.

MOODY, RICHARD, *Fossils*. New York: Macmillan, 1986.

MOORE, R.C., ed., *Treatise on Invertebrate Paleontology*. Boulder: Geological Society of America, 1971.

RAUP, DAVID M. and STEVEN M. STANLEY. *Principles of Palaeontology*. San Francisco: W. H. Freeman, 1978.

ROMER, A.S., *Vertebrate Paleontology*, 3rd ed. Chicago: University of Chicago Press, 1966.

RUDWICK, MARTIN, *The Meaning of Fossils: Episodes in the History of Paleontology*, 2nd ed. Chicago: University of Chicago Press, 1985.

SCIENTIFIC AMERICAN, EDITORS OF, *The Fossil Record and Evolution* (Readings from Scientific American Series). San Francisco: W.H. Freeman, 1982.

SHROCK, R.R. and W.M. TWENHOFEL, *Principles of Invertebrate Paleontology*. New York: McGraw Hill, 1953.

SIMPSON, GEORGE, G., *Fossils and the History of Life*. New York: W.H. Freeman, 1984.

STERN, COLIN W. and ROBERT L. CARROLL, *Paleontology: The Record of Life*. New York: John Wiley & Sons, 1989.

SWINTON, W.E., *The Dinosaurs*. New York: John Wiley, 1970.

TASCH, PAUL, *Paleobiology of the Invertebrates*, 2nd ed. New York: John Wiley, 1980.

THOMPSON, IDA, *The Audubon Society Field Guide to North American Fossils*. New York: Knopf, 1982.

ZEUNER, F.E., *Dating the Past*. New York: Hafner Press, 1970.

GLOSSARY

The names of only the largest orders and classes of plants and animals are included here. For more information on individual species, the reader should consult the index and accompanying text.

acanthodians an extinct class of spiny sharks, the first vertebrates to have jaws and appendages

aculeus a sharp apparatus at the end of the abdomen of some insects; used to sting or bore a hole for eggs

adductor muscles paired muscles that close the shell of the bivalve mollusks and other animals

agglutinate a sedimentary deposit in which volcanic fragments are held together by glassy material

agnatha jawless fish, including the lampreys and some extinct species; the oldest and most primitive of known vertebrates

allochthonous fossils that have been transported from the region where they originated to the region where they have been discovered

ambulacrum in echinoderms, the radial area along which run the arteries, nerves, and internal water tubes

angiosperms flowering plants, which reproduce sexually

annelid a worm-like invertebrate characterized by a segmented body with a distinct head and appendages. Since they lack hard parts, their fossil evidence is often only in the form of trails and impressions.

apterous without wings

arenaceous sediment or sedimentary rock composed wholly or partly of small sandy fragments; organisms occupying sandy habitats

arthropod a large group of invertebrates, including trilobites, crustaceans, and insects, characterized by segmented bodies, jointed appendages, and an exoskeleton or carapace of chitin

asconoid pertaining to the ascon sponges

autochthonous fossils that originated in the region where they are found

benthic of organisms that live on or in the sea bed or attached to bottom objects; compare to pelagic

biconvex having two surfaces that are convex (curving outward)

bivalve marine and freshwater mollusks having a shell composed of two hinged valves; including oysters, mussels, clams and other species

brachiopod marine invertebrates that live attached to a firm substratum in shallow waters. With bivalve shells, they have an appearance similar to mollusks. More plentiful in Paleozoic times, they now constitute a small phylum, including the lamp shells.

Bryozoan a marine invertebrate, characterized by a branching or fanlike structure, that grows in colonies. The skeleton may be chitinous or calcareous, but only the latter are found in fossil form.

budding a type of asexual reproduction among primitive animals, like sponges and coelenterates, in which an out-growth, or bud, forms, eventually breaking away to form a new organism; also called gemmation

calcareous a substance containing calcium carbonate

calcification replacement of the original hard parts of an organism by calcium carbonate; common among corals, brachiopods, echinoderms, and mollusks. The siliceous skeletons of some animals, including sponges and radiolarians, may also be calcified.

calyx in the echinoderms, the spherical or elongated body of the organism, covered with hexagonal, pentagonal, or irregularly shaped plates, housing the vital organs, mouth, and anal openings

carbonization the process of fossilization found most often in plants. During decomposition of the organic matter under water or sediment, hydrogen, oxygen, and nitrogen are exhausted, leaving a carbon residue that may retain many of the features of the original organism. This process resulted in the formation of the great coal deposits during the Carboniferous period, beginning at least 340 million years ago.

cardinal pertaining to the hinge of a bivalve shell

carapace in some arthropods (crustaceans, spiders, crabs, etc.), a hard protective covering shielding the soft parts of the organism

caudal pertaining to the tail region, as in caudal vertebrae or caudal fin

centrum the center of a vertebra, cylindrical in shape, attached to a cartilaginous disc

cephalon pertaining to the head, including the brain, sense organs, and feeding apparatus

chela large pinching claw on the appendage of crustaceans, scorpions, and other invertebrates

chitin a nitrogenous material. The outer covering of arthropods, the cuticle, is impregnated with chitin, which makes the exoskeleton more rigid, yielding a tough yet light and flexible, waterproof skeleton; also found in the hard parts of several other groups of animals.

chondrite a branch-shaped fossilized impression in sediment made by burrowing worms

chronospecies a paleontological species

chronostratigraphic subdivision subdivision of the layers of rock within a strata, reflecting changes over time

cilium a whip-like extension of certain mollusks and other invertebrates, which creates a current of water toward the body, filters out food particles and transports them to the mouth; pl. cilia

class in systematics, the category of plants and animals between phylum and order; several orders comprise a class

clastic pertaining to sediment or rock composed mainly of fragments (clasts) derived from a pre-existing, larger rock mass

coccolithophorids microscopic algae formed of calcareous disks, called coccoliths, which can produce calcareous sedimentary deposits

coelenterate more developed than the porifera, these multicelled organisms (including the corals) appeared during the middle Archean and are widely distributed

cohesion attraction between molecules of the same substance, which, in rocks, resists stress

columella the central axis of a bivalve shell, or a central axis or column in gastropods and other animals

condyle the curved surface at the end of a bone that forms a joint with another bone, allowing movement

conglomerate coarse-grained sedimentary rock, cemented with calcium carbonate, silica, or other material, in a matrix of sand or silt

conodonts fossilized mouth parts of primitive organisms, often of calcium phosphate

coprolite fossilized excrement

coralline of or pertaining to coral

correlation the determination of geological age by comparing fossils from different times and regions

cosmoid scales spiny scales on the skin of fish, covered with an enamel-like substance

costa a rib or other linear part or border

cranium the skull of vertebrates

cryptogram nonflowering plant, such as algae and ferns, which reproduces by spores

decapods an order of the most developed Crustacea, including prawns, shrimps, lobsters, and crayfish, with five pairs of legs

dendrite a branching pattern of deposited minerals, often mistaken for fossilized ferns or leaves

dentition the arrangement of teeth

diagenesis the sum of all changes—physical, chemical, and biological—to which a sediment is subjected after it is deposited but before the effects of weathering or new physical or chemical conditions occur

diapsid a subclass of reptiles, like crocodiles, snakes, and lizards (including dinosaurs and pterosaurs), with two temporal openings

diatomaceous of sedimentary deposits comprised of diatoms

diatoms deposits of chalky, lightweight, friable rock composed of the accumulation of tiny organisms with a small shell of siliceous materials; fossil algae that appeared during the Jurassic, around 180 million years ago

dichotomous characterized by a division into two similar halves

discoidal disc-shaped

distillation a process of fossilization during which the more volatile elements of an organism (liquids and gases) are distilled, leaving a thin film of carbon on the sediment

dolomite see dolomitization

dolomitization the process by which limestone becomes dolomite by the substitution of magnesium for the original calcite; common in organisms whose original hard parts were composed of calcite or aragonite, such as corals, brachiopods, and echinoderms

dorsal the upper part of an organism; compare to ventral

echinoderms a phylum of marine invertebrates (including starfish, sea urchins and sea cucumbers), some of which first appeared in the Early Cambrian

ecosystem all of the living and nonliving components of a particular area that interact with each other

endemic a population of species unique to a

particular geographic area

endocranium the inner surfaces of the cranium, or skull

endopodite the inner branch of a two-branched appendage found in crustaceans

eolian pertaining to or caused by wind

eon on the gelogic time scale, the longest unit of time, comprised of several eras

epiplanktonic organisms that float or drift in the ocean to a depth of about 100 fathoms

epoch an interval of geologic time longer than an eon and shorter than a period

equivalve having valves of equal size and shape

era on the geologic time scale, the unit of time below eon; comprised of several periods

eukaryote an organism sufficiently developed so that the genetic material (DNA) is enclosed by membranes, forming a nucleus; compare to prokaryote

evaporite minerals and sediment deposited from a saline solution, usually seawater, as it evaporates

evolute to evolve or develop

exoskeleton the hard outer covering of the body of certain animals, such as the thick cuticle of insects and crustaceans or the shell of mollusks; protecting the internal organs and supporting the body

expodite the outer branch of a two-branched appendage found in crustaceans

external mold impression of the exterior of an organism's shell left on sediment when the shell and other organic material have dissolved

facies fossil a representative fossil from a particular environment, which enables paleontologists to deduce the characteristics of that environment; also called index fossil and guide fossil

family in systematics, the category of plants and animals between order and genus; several genera comprise a family

fenestration the openings or breaks in the wall of a membrane

filament a narrow threadlike structure; in algae, a line of similar cells joined by their end walls

fluvial of or pertaining to rivers and streams

foramen a natural opening in an animal organ or other structure, especially in a bone or cartilage

foraminifer the most common marine protozoa, either benthic or free-swimming, found in fossil form

fucoide similar to chondrites; fossilized branching tubular impressions left by burrowing marine worms

fusulina the most ancient of the large foraminifers, appearing during the Carboniferous about 345 million years ago and becoming extinct 115 million years later

ganoid scales hard ridged scales on the skin of a fish, with the outer layer consisting of ganoin, a calcareous substance

gastropod a large class of mollusks, including slugs, snails, and others, characterized by a well-developed head with tentacles and eyes, a single shell (often coiled), and a large flat foot. None of the gastropods are attached to the substrate; some forms are air-breathing and adapted to terrestrial habitats.

gemmation a type of asexual reproduction, involving the production of a group of cells, a gemma, that develops into a new individual, before or after separation from the parent; also called budding

genus in systematics, the category of plants and animals between family and species; several species comprise a genus

glaciation the covering of the Earth's surface by glaciers, sheets of flowing ice. In the Earth's history, periods of glaciation (ice ages) have alternated with warmer intervals (interglacials).

gnathostoma all the vertebrates that possess jaws, including fish, amphibians, reptiles, birds and mammals

graptolites invertebrate organisms that form small colonies, rhabdosomes, enclosed in chitinous exoskeletons

gymnosperm a class of vascular plants and trees with seeds encased in cones rather than in fruit; including ginkgo, fir, pine, and spruce

hard parts those parts of an organism, such as the shell, skeleton, bones and teeth, that resist decay. Usually made of silica, chitin, calcium carbonate, or keratin, they make up the majority of fossilized remains.

helicoid having a spiral shape

helminthoida a fossilized impression left by marine worms; consisting of many equidistant furrows, sometimes arranged concentrically

heterocercal having a tail fin in which the end of the vertebral column is extended and turned upward

hexapod a superclass of arthropods, the insects

histology the study of tissues and cells at microscopic level

hyoid arch an arch in the mouth behind the jaws; supports the tongue

igneous rock that comprises the Earth's crust, formed of hardened magma

impregnation see permineralization

incohesive sediment lacking adhesiveness

incrustation a process of fossilization occurring with more recent fossils, as calcium-rich water flows over organic remains and covers them with a thin mineral film. When the organic material dissolves it leaves a negative imprint on this mineral layer.

index fossil a representative fossil that allows paleontologists to identify those strata in which it is found; also called facies fossil and guide fossil

intercalated layered material or sediment

interglacial period the warmer periods of time between glaciations (ice ages)

internal mold the impression of the inside of an organism's shell. An internal mold results when a shell becomes filled with sediment and then dissolves, leaving the impression.

labyrinth the system of cavities and canals in the inner ear of vertebrates

labyrinthodont a member of an extinct subclass of amphibians resembling crocodiles

lacustrine pertaining to lakes, as in a lacustrine environment

lamella layer of photosynthetic membrane; a thin layer

lamina the thinnest layer in the sedimentary

deposits that differs from other layers in composition; a structure is laminar if it is arranged in alternating thin layers of differing composition

lenticel a pore in the stem of a plant that allows oxygen, carbon dioxide, and other gases to pass between the internal tissus and the atmosphere

leuconoid a type of sponge

limiting factors characteristics such as temperature and depth and salinity of water that determine an organism's environment

lithostratigraphic subdivision the division of the sediment in a particular area into layers according to the composition of the rock

lophophore in the bryozoans, the crown of tentacles surrounding the central opening, or mouth·

macrofossil a fossil large enough to be examined with the naked eye; compare to microfossil

macrophyll a leaf with a branched system of veins, such as ferns, gymnosperms, and angiosperms; compare to microphyll

magma molten rock generated within the Earth's crust

mandible the feeding mouthparts of arthropods, the upper and lower jaws of birds (the beak), or the lower jaw of vertebrates

mantle the layer of rocks between the Earth's crust and outer core; parts are semi-molton and flow in sluggish currents

margin in plate tectonics, the seam where two plates collide; the plates may slide past each other, or one may slide over another

marl a type of friable rock, containing micrite, clay, and other minerals

matrix the background material in which a fossil is embedded, or the fine-grained igneous rock in which larger grains are suspended

medusa a free-swimming organism, like a jellyfish, in which the body is shaped like a bell or inverted saucer with a fringe of tentacles hanging downward from the rim

metasomatism the process of mineralization in which existing minerals are replaced by new minerals, molecule by molecule, changing the chemical composition of the fossil while its appearance remains intact

metazoa multicellular animals, more advanced than the protozoa and the sponges, in which specialized cells are grouped together to form tissues with a particular function and with a coordinating nervous system

microfossil fossil remains so small that a microscope is necessary to observe them; compare to macrofossil

microphyll a leaf with a single vein; compare to macrophyll

mollusks a very large phylum of invertebrates, characterized by an internal or external shell surrounding a soft body; appearing during the Early Cambrian, mollusks are known to paleontologists almost exclusively by their shells

mummification a rare process of fossilization in which the organism is completely preserved. It occurs only when the fossil is isolated from water and minerals (usually in sand) that would act on it in other ways.

nektonic organisms that are free-swimming

neritic a shallow sea region

notocord the flexible supporting rod of the chordate, similar to the vertebral column in vertebrates

nummulite a large foraminifer with disc-shaped, multichambered cells; abundant in the Mediterranean seas in the Eocene and Oligocene, contributing to widespread nummulite limestone found in the region

ocellus a simple eye in arthropods and some other vertebrates in which light-sensitive cells detect the direction and intensity of light but can not form an image

onychophora a small invertebrate phylum with both annelid and arthropod features, including a soft cuticle, segmented legs, and cilia

operculum the bony plate covering the gill chambers of a bony fish; the horny disc that closes the aperture of the shell of some gastropod mollusks

order in systematics, the category of plants and animals between class and family; several families comprise an order

oscillation a rippling effect, a fluctuation

osculum the opening in sponges through which water passes from the internal canals

oside made of glycoside, a sugar-like compound

osseous pertaining to or made of bones

osteichthyes the most evolved class of fish, characterized by an internal skeleton and covering of scales; appeared in the Devonian and are the most abundant vertebrates found today

osteological the study of the bony structure and organization of an organism

ostium a mouthlike opening or pore

oviparity of invertebrates (fish, birds, reptiles and other animals) that lay eggs or spawn eggs to develop outside of the female

ovoviviparous of invertebrates (fish and reptiles and other animals) in which eggs are produced and retained in the body of the female during development

palatine pertaining to the roof of the mouth, or palate

paleobotany the study of fossil plants

paleoclimatology the study of the climates for the most distant periods of the Earth's history

paleoecology the study of the complex of fossils in a particular environment

paleogeography the study of the geographic characteristics during the various geological ages

paleomagnetism the study of changes in the Earth's geomagnetic field

pantopod having seven pairs of legs

parietal pertaining to the posterior region of the head or skull

patella the small bone over the knee joint in some birds and reptiles and in most mammals

pelagic of organisms, such as plankton, that live in the upper ocean rather than on the seabed; compare to benthic

period a division of geologic time longer than an epoch and included in an era

peristoma the funnel around the mouth of some protozoans in which food is collected before it is ingested

permineralization the process of fossilization by which mineral substances replace the tissues of an organism over time, rendering it more resistant to change and decomposition; also called impregnation

petaloid having petals or petal-shaped

phalange finger bone

photosynthesis the synthesis of organic compounds as the source of energy by plants using light energy absorbed by chlorophyll

phylum in systematics, one of the major groups in which the animal kingdom is classified; several classes of animals comprise a phylum

pineal eye a third eye, thought to have existed in fossil vertebrates, which could detect light but not resolve images

placoderm a extinct class of chordates, fish with armorlike plates and articulated jaws

plankton organisms that are free-floating or drifting

polyp the tubular-shaped body of hydrozoans and coelenterates; polyps may form branching colonies or may break off, in the process of budding, to form new organisms

porifera the sponges, multicelled primitive animals

postmortem transport movement of fossil remains from the area in which the organism lived to the location where they are discovered

plano-convex having two opposite surfaces, one of which is a straight plane and the other convex, or curving outward

pleura the membrane that surrounds the lungs and lines the walls of the thorax in mammals, cushioning the lungs against damage

pneumatofore the root of certain aquatic plants covered with pores, through which gases can diffuse to and from internal tissues

prokaryote a primitive organism, like bacteria, in which the genetic material (DNA) is not enclosed by membranes to form a nucleus; compare to eukaryote

protoplasm the living components of a cell, made up of the cytoplasm and the nucleus

protozoa a large phylum of single-cell organisms, usually microscopic; the most primitive invertebrates

pseudopod a temporary fingerlike projection or lobe on the body of a protozoan, like the amoeba, formed by the flowing action of the cytoplasm

pterosaur an extinct order of flying reptiles, with leathery wings

pterous having wings or winglike parts

pygidium the caudal or tail area of trilobites and certain vertebrates

quadruped having four feet

radial symmetry a pattern of symmetry in which similar parts of an organism are arranged about an axis or central point, as in a starfish

radiolarians a group of simple planktonic marine protozoans, which first appeared in the Cambrian 570 million years ago

radiometry a method of dating fossil remains by testing radioactive material

radula a ribbon-like strip on the tongue of most mollusks; covered with tiny horny teeth that act like a file to scrape away the surface of the vegetation on which it feeds

rhabdosome a graptolite colony, enclosed in a chitinous exoskeleton

rostrum the anterior beak, snout, or other projection of an organism

rugose of corals, having a wrinkled or rippled appearance

sclerite a hard, chitinous or calcareous plate or spicule

scolecodonts the fossilized chitinous-siliceous mouthparts of primitive organisms

sediment the debris, organic or inorganic, that is transported and deposited by wind, water, or ice. It may form loose sediment, like sand or mud, or become consolidated to form sedimentary rock

sedimentary gaps see unconformity

sedimentation the process by which sediment is formed, transported, and deposited

septum the wall or membrane separating two cavities; pl. septa

sessile of organisms, like sponges, that live attached to the sea bottom

sicula the conical chitinous skeleton formed by a colony of graptolites

siliceous referring to sand, rock, or other substance containing abundant silica (silicon dioxide)

silicification the fossilization process in which the hard parts of an organism are replaced by silica (quartz, chalcedony, or opal)

siphon a pair of posterior tubes common in many mollusks. One tube conducts water to the mouth and gills, the other carries away waste water.

soft parts those parts of an animal, such as internal organs or tissues, that decompose rapidly after death and are rarely preserved in the fossil state

species in systematics, the lowest classification, below genus; all members of a species share similar characteristics and are able to breed amongst themselves

spermatophyte a vascular, seedbearing plant, like the angiosperms or gymnosperms

spicule in the sponges and other invertebrates, a small calcareous or siliceous point or spike that provides support

spire in gastropods, the upper whorls of the spiral shell

spongocoel the internal cavity of a sponge

sporangium the part of a plant in which asexual spores are formed

stabile sediment resistant to chemical change or to decomposition

stellate star-shaped

stigmaria a root system of some trees consisting of horizontally spreading main trunk roots without a tap root; the rootlets extend directly from the side of the trunk roots and extend radially

stratification a pattern of layering in sedimentary rock, lava flows, or water, or materials of different composition or density

strobila the part of an animal in which asexual reproduction occurs by division into a number of separate individuals

stromatolite sedimentary formation in the shape of cushions or columns produced by lime-secreting blue-green algae

sublittoral a shoreline environment, from the point exposed at low tide to the edge of the continental shelf

sulcus furrow or groove

suture in the mollusks, suture lines are visible where the internal septa are joined to the inside of the shell

systematics the science of biological classification that establishes a hierarchy of groups of plants and animals according to family, class, order, species, etc.; also called taxonomy

taxon the name applied to a single group of plants or animals

taxonomy the study of the classification of plants and animals. See systematics

tectonics in geology, the story of the larger features of the Earth (rock formations and plates) and the forces and movements that produce them

test the hard covering or shell of many invertebrates

tetrapod an animal having four legs

thanatocoenosis a group of fossils present in a given locality and certain stratum of rock

thecodont the most ancient and most primitive order of reptiles, now extinct, which gave rise to all the other orders, including dinosaurs, crocodiles, and birds

thoracic pertaining to the thorax, the region of an animal located between the neck and abdomen

torsion in the gastropods and other invertebrates, the twisting of the body, causing a rotation

trabeculae a suspended cell or line or cells across an internal cavity

transpiration the process by which water vapor is expelled by plants

trilobite an extinct marine arthropod, characterized by a body divided into three lobes, each bearing a pair of jointed appendages, and a chitinous exoskeleton

tympanum a thin membrane that separates the outer and middle ear of the vertebrates

ulna one of the two long bones of the lower forelimb in tetrapods

umbilicus the point at which the umbilicus is attached; when severed, a scar remains

unconformity a lack of continuity in the stratigraphic record, caused by a weathering or erosion of a surface before new layers are deposited

univalve marine and freshwater mollusks having a single shell

valve one of the two articulated parts (shells) of a bivalve mollusk or other organism

vergilian in the geographic time scale, relating to the Pennsylvanian

ventral the lower or under part of an organism; compare to dorsal

vomer a skull bone in most vertebrates

zooid an individual organism in a colony of certain types of bryozoans, with a saclike body and a mouth surrounded by tentacles. Zooids form tubular zooecia, which are covered by a horny chitinous or calcareous skeleton.

zoophytes lower invertebrates with a plant-like appearance, including bryozoans, coral, sponges, etc.

INDEX